THe
MIRTH of
NATIONS

THE
MIRTH of
NATIONS

Christie Davies

Routledge
Taylor & Francis Group

LONDON AND NEW YORK

First published 2002 by Transaction Publishers

Published 2017 by Routledge
2 Park Square, Milton Park, Abingdon, Oxon OX14 4RN
711 Third Avenue, New York, NY 10017, USA

Routledge is an imprint of the Taylor & Francis Group, an informa business

Library of Congress Catalog Number: 2001027884

Library of Congress Cataloging-in-Publication Data

Davies, Christie.
    The mirth of nations / Christie Davies.
        p. cm.
    Includes bibliographical references and index.
    ISBN 978-0-7658-0096-1 (cloth) ; 978-1-4128-1457-7 (paper)
    1. Ethnic wit and humor.   I. Title.

PN6149.E83 D395 2002
818'.60208—dc21
2001027884

ISBN 13: 978-1-4128-1457-7 (pbk)
ISBN 13: 978-0-7658-0096-1 (hbk)

For Jan
and in memory of my father Christy Davies

Contents

Acknowledgments

This book was written with the help of research grants which enabled me to work in several different countries where I was, in turn, greatly assisted by local scholars. I wish to acknowledge funding from the Canadian Department of Foreign Affairs and Trade to work on materials in M.U.N.F.L.A., the Memorial University of Newfoundland Folklore Archive, in the Université de Moncton, the Université Laval and the Musée de L'Humeur in Montréal; in each institution the librarians and archivists were exceptionally supportive and helpful. I also owe a special debt to Peter Narváez, Paul Smith, and Gerald Thomas of the University of Newfoundland for their advice and support. I also record here the assistance given to me by the Reading University Research Board to visit Australia, and my thanks to the staff of the State Library of New South Wales in Sydney and also to Jessica Milner-Davis and Gerard Matte for their advice and encouragement. I must also acknowledge the assistance of the Arts and Humanities Research Board UK whose grant enabled me to work in California and Utah on the folklore archives at the University of California at Berkeley and at Brigham Young University and in the Fife Folklore archive at Utah State University and the Schmulowitz library in San Francisco public library. Alan Dundes was outstanding in the liberality with which he granted me access to the collections and in the interest he took in my research, and Anthea Grimes and her colleagues helped me to derive the maximum benefit from the Schmulowitz collection. I was lucky to be working in California at the same time as two distinguished European humor scholars, Anna Litovkina and Willibald Ruch, with whom I could discuss work in progress.

Many of the ideas incorporated in the different chapters were in each case first explored with audiences in the territories of the national, ethnic or regional group concerned, including Australia, Scotland and Newfoundland. In addition, I was able, with the assistance of the British Council, to lecture at the Jagiellonian University of

Kraków in Poland and on a later occasion at Opole University as well. Wladyslaw Chlopicki of the Jagiellonian University of Kraków has given me a great deal of help and advice over many years and Dorota Brzozowska and Stanislaw Gajda of Opole University have also been most supportive.

In Israel, thanks to Avner Ziv, I was able to take part in a symposium on Jewish humor at Tel Aviv University and thanks to Ernest Krausz in a symposium on Jewish identity at Bar Ilan University. It was at the latter that I first met Irving Louis Horowitz and Mary Curtis, both of whom encouraged me to write this book. I must further thank them and their colleagues at Transaction, notably Anne Schneider, for their kindness as well as hard work in seeing this book through to publication.

Early versions of the ideas expressed here about Jewish humor were first explored with audiences at the Jewish Cultural Foundation in Kraków, the Spiro Institute, Manchester University, the Institute of Jewish Studies at University College London and the School of Oriental and African Studies of the University of London, and I must express my appreciation to those who invited me and to the audiences who provided critical but helpful comments. Even though I have been studying Jewish humor for nearly twenty years, writing about it has required consultation with those of greater experience as well as knowledge. I must thank Emil Draitser, Elliott Oring, Victor Raskin, Rabbi Barry Schechter, Roy Wolfe, and Anat Zajdman for their patient willingness to answer questions, their wise advice and, indeed, their welcome friendship over many years. None of them is, of course, responsible for any errors I may have made in this field.

The Scottish materials I have used are based on a number of foraging visits to Scotland. I must also thank my audiences at University College Dublin and at the Social History Society conference at Glasgow University and for their helpful comments on my lectures on Scottish humor. In particular, I must thank Stephen Mennell and his colleagues for inviting me to Dublin to lecture and the British Council for funding my visit. I also owe a debt to the Japanese Society for Laughter and Humor Studies and to Hiroshi Inoue for helping to make possible my two visits to Osaka. I must add that my work in Japan would have been quite impossible without the help of Goh Abe, a valued collaborator for many years past.

It is appropriate also to note here the value and importance of ISHS, the International Society for Humor Studies, to humor scholars and, in particular, Victor Raskin, Don and Alleen Nilsen, and Larry Mintz, who have over many years worked hard to provide humor scholars with a forum, a place to meet, and one in which to exchange ideas.

Many of the ideas expressed in this book were first explored at conferences organized under the aegis of ISHS. An earlier version of chapter 5 was published in the journal, *Humor, the International Journal of Humor Research*, the world's leading humor research journal, and the helpful comments I subsequently received led me to revise considerably my perception of the relationship between jokers and those joked about.

The manuscript was word-processed by Helen Davis. I am grateful to her for her speed, accuracy and good nature. These qualities were especially needed in the final stages of checking the manuscript, and at this point I also relied on the erudition of John Davies, Jon Doust, Brian Kemp, Ronald Knowles, and David Martin. Any errors that remain are my own.

My final acknowledgements are, as in my previous books, to my cousin David Williams of Oakland, California, for his hospitality and to Janetta Davies for all manner of continuing help, support, and encouragement. Let me also remember here my father Christy Davies who first encouraged me to take humor seriously and whose memory continues to inspire my work.

1

Introduction

The Mirth of Nations is a book analyzing the jokes told by or about particular peoples, viewed in a comparative and historical context, and examining the social circumstances of the particular time when the jokes emerged and flourished. Particular emphasis is given to the jokes of those people with a well-deserved reputation for self-consciously telling jokes about themselves, notably the Jews and the Scots but also other nations and regions with a distinctive humor of their own making, such as the Australians and the Newfoundlanders. Each of these is looked at in detail, but with an eye to making comparisons and this has determined the order in which the chapters about each group are presented. Finally, in the light of what has been learned from the study of these self-mocking, joke-telling peoples we will look in detail at a case of a people who have been the subject of an enormous number of jokes in the main invented and circulated by outsiders–the Polish Americans. Whereas the Jews and the Scots and to a substantial extent the Australians and the Newfoundlanders can claim to *own* the jokes that are told about them, Polish Americans, although able to laugh at jokes at their expense (Kusielewicz 1969), have had no real ownership stake in them. There was and is no distinctively Polish-American humor in the sense that there is a distinctive Jewish, Scottish, Australian, and Newfoundland humor.

The particular cases that have been considered in detail were chosen in order to be able to make meaningful comparisons between substantial aggregates of jokes and other humorous items, particularly when these were available and accessible in the form of extensive archive material collected from contemporary joke tellers over many years. Both Jewish jokes and American jokes about Poles have been the subject of many previous studies, some of them insightful,

1

logically consistent, and based on extensive empirical research and others somewhat lacking in these attributes. However, most of the earlier studies lacked a proper comparative dimension. Their authors failed to ask questions such as "What *other* peoples besides the Jews have shown a marked capacity for self-mocking humor?" or "What peoples other than Polish-Americans have been the butts of stupidity jokes on such a large scale?"

In order fully to understand the self-mocking Jewish sense of humor it was necessary to locate a people with a similar tradition and the Scots of the late nineteenth and early twentieth centuries are the closest case. At that time Scottish ministers of religion and intellectuals produced for Scottish publishers several large collections of self-mocking jokes and anecdotes about the canny (crafty, stingy, calculating, money conscious), argumentative, Sabbatarian Scots, interwoven with moral comment and observations about Scotland's national character and traditions. They were the precursors of the many excellent selections of and commentaries on Jewish jokes and humor produced by rabbis and Jewish academics particularly in the latter part of the twentieth century (Blue 1985 and 1986; Raskin 1993 and 1993A; Rosten 1970 and 1983; Telushkin 1992). These books are not only sources of insight into the self-mocking humor of the Scots, an important phenomenon in its own right, but they also enable us to examine Jewish humor in a new way using the comparative method. There are important parallels and also differences between the social backgrounds to these two similar sets of jokes and it is here that we must search for an explanation for them. A broader-reaching explanation that will cover both is superior to mere commentaries on either one of them, for it is better founded, more easily tested, more elegant and parsimonious, and more likely to be fruitful and to produce explanations of an even greater range of phenomena.

There is not, for instance, and indeed never has been a hostile ideology of anti-Caledonianism comparable to anti-Semitism nor have the Scots been persecuted in the course of the last two centuries. Hostility and persecution are *not* then necessary pre-conditions for the development of a self-mocking humor. In one respect Scottish jokes and humor are even more distinctly self-mocking than their Jewish equivalents for the self-mockery of the Scots is not supplemented by such an extensive derisive humor about outsiders as that found in Jewish sources. Rather the source of both Jewish self-mockery and Jewish pre-eminence in joking generally are best sought in the factors the Jews have in common with their runners-up, the Scots, notably intelligence, education, a love of speculative argument for its own sake and a marked capacity for self-reflection about their own identity. However, in order to see this point it is necessary to examine the less familiar Scottish evidence first and only then to proceed and look anew at Jewish humor.

There is, however, no Scottish equivalent of the uniquely Jewish jokes about Jewish women. Because they are unique there is nothing similar with which to compare these jokes and so following a method successfully employed by the author in earlier research involving different themes (Davies 1990 and 1998) they are compared here with their exact opposite, with Australian jokes about Australian men. In general it is very difficult to compare jokes about the sexes and about sexuality between different societies for though there are very many jokes on these subjects we cannot easily tie them to a particular social location. In consequence such extensive studies of sex jokes as do exist tend to be wildly speculative, oddly opinionated, and rooted in a variety of inconsistent yet dogmatic theories and lead nowhere (see, for example, Legman 1968 and 1975). Jewish jokes about women and Australian jokes about men provide us with a rare opportunity to make reasoned contrasts and comparisons and thus to infer connections and perhaps even causal links.

The author has analyzed ethnic jokes about stupidity elsewhere (Davies 1990 and 1998) by examining stupidity jokes in many languages from a very large number of countries in order to extract the factors common to them all, but a quite *different* comparative approach is adopted here based on the detailed study of a linked set of particular cases. First, detailed analyses of Canadian jokes about Newfoundlanders and of Newfoundlanders' jokes about themselves are presented and only then are the more controversial studies of American jokes about Poles looked at. The Canadian jokes about Newfoundlanders which make them out to be stupid and dirty were and are essentially the *same* as American jokes about Poles but the social background to them is different. The Newfoundlanders in Canada are not by origin an alien immigrant group, but similar in ancestry to other old-stock English-speaking Canadians; the Newfoundlanders are not numerous and no one has even suggested that they might pose a threat to other Canadians. Yet the ethnic stupidity jokes told in the two countries did not and do not differ significantly from each other. This completely undermines accepted explanations of the origin and *timing* of the very large and long-lasting cycle of stupidity jokes about Polish Americans in the United States, a group that was numerous, ethnically distinct, and allegedly threatening to and resented by others (Bier 1988). In order for this point to be fully understood it is necessary for the Newfoundland jokes to be analyzed in advance of the jokes about Poles. Once this has been done, it is then possible to ask other awkward comparative questions about the history and origins of Polish jokes in America which further undermine the conventional analysis of ethnic jokes in terms of hostility, aggression, and conflict.

The Newfoundlanders have always spoken their own distinctive, indigenous brand of English, which is quite unlike that of the rest of North America (Storey, Kirwin, Widdowson 1990), and have long had a well-established local tradition of self-mocking stupidity joking all their own, which deserves a chapter in its own right. When the new-style short blunt stupidity jokes about Poles were invented in America and adapted by the Canadians to apply to Newfoundland, the Newfoundlanders were able to merge them with their older tradition of joking and thus to establish ownership of the jokes in a way that would have been difficult for Polish Americans to do. This helps to explain the peculiarities of the Newfoundland case but it also suggests further questions to ask about the American jokes concerning the Poles.

The existence of the older indigenous Newfoundland tradition of wit, humor and joking has led to the collection and recording of those traditional jokes and anecdotes, complete with the joke tellers' comments on their own jokes, in the Memorial University of Newfoundland's Folklore Archive, one of the world's great repositories of local folklore of all kinds. The collectors of the items in the archive were mainly interested in obtaining traditional materials including humorous items but they *also* collected modern Canadian jokes about Newfoundlanders as told and interpreted by the Newfoundlanders themselves. It is thus possible to study Newfoundland self-mockery in depth.

The method that is used throughout this study is to compare differences and similarities in the aggregate patterns of jokes between different nations and to try to match these with the social circumstances of those about whom the jokes are told and their relationship to the joke tellers. In the case of the self-mocking jokes those who invent and circulate the jokes will, of course, also be more or less the butts of their own jokes. I say more or less because all groups and nations are internally differentiated by geographical location or origin, by occupation and social class, by generation and sex, and by the nature and degree of their religious beliefs and observances. Self-mocking jokes often refer far more strongly to another section of one's nation than to one's own and from the point of the view of the immediate teller and listener *can* always be perceived or represented as about someone else.

In order to establish connections of this kind it is necessary to obtain two quite separate kinds of data. First, it is necessary to assemble the texts of the jokes themselves, which in this study have been recorded directly by the author from those then in oral circulation, obtained from folklore archives in a number of different locations in America and Canada, and taken from the compilations and collections of others which are both particularly important for the study of jokes from earlier times and for the most recent of jokes which are often best found on the Internet. Second, it is necessary to seek *independent* evidence concerning the relevant social and historical circumstances in the society where the jokes were told at the time when they were told. As will be demonstrated in the chapters that follow, what has often been done in previous studies is to infer the social background to a particular joke, set of jokes or joke cycle from the texts of the jokes on the basis of some unsubstantiated theory about human nature or taken for granted ideological assumptions and then to use it to explain and account for the existence of the very same jokes on the basis of these inferences. One of the purposes of this study is to expose and explode circular arguments of this kind and instead to obtain evidence about the social background to particular kinds of joke by consulting local empirical studies carried out by specialists such as historians or anthropologists for quite other reasons. Then an attempt can be made to match the two sets of data by making systematic comparisons between societies or over time.

In order to be able to gauge which of the independently observed social circumstances are relevant to an explanation of why the jokes exist it is also necessary to ask the question, "Why have certain jokes that could exist or could have existed never been invented or circulated?" (Davies 1998A: 295). Why, for example, were there no American ethnic jokes about Poles in the late nineteenth and early twentieth centuries when Polish immigration was at its peak and the Poles were seen as serious competitors for jobs and housing and even for control over the Roman Catholic Church? Why are there no American jokes about Japanese-Americans or, indeed, the Japanese? Why are there no jokes about drunken Jews or dirty Irishmen or Costa Rican American Princesses? Why were there no jokes about William Jefferson Clinton's oral utterances and pious ejaculations *about politics* and so many about those of Leonid Brezhnev? Why are there so few purely political jokes in a democracy? It is only possible to understand the jokes that do exist by studying those that could exist but do not, a crucial methodological point that the author has discussed in detail elsewhere (Davies 1998A).

The purpose of the exercise is to establish a direct relationship between two sets of social facts, an aggregate pattern of jokes on the one hand and an aspect of a nation's or, better still a common aspect of many nations' social structure or cultural traditions on the other. What must be avoided is illicit movements between levels of explanation such that the existence of a particular pattern of jokes is explained in terms of the motives, intentions, feelings, anxieties or attitudes of a particular set of individuals. Explanations of this kind are inherently problematic.[1] In the first place we can *not* infer any of these attributes from the text of a joke and often that text is all the information we have. Attitudes, motives, intentions and feelings will differ from one individual to another and even from one joke-telling session to another, for they are the ephemeral qualities of particular situations. Any joke can be used in a very large number of different ways even without altering the text by changing the manner in which it is presented and the tone with which it is told. We cannot know these things without being present at the time and even then it is difficult to be sure. Even if we did have a large and varied number of such observations it would be very difficult to aggregate them and even if we could do so it is doubtful if we could use information of this kind to explain why a set of jokes exists in one culture but not another. Speculation about the psychological needs and instincts of individuals is not at all helpful in explaining the existence of particular *aggregate* patterns of jokes nor can appeals to supposedly constant aspects of human nature be used to explain differences in these patterns. Observations of how jokes are used in the functioning of small groups to promote cohesion and morale, although valuable in themselves (Coser 1959; Obrdlik 1942), are likewise of little use for this purpose and to employ the language of functions appropriate to such groups at the level of entire nations as this author erroneously did in an earlier study (Davies 1982) is simply mistaken. The needs of particular sets of individuals or the functioning of small groups might well be better met or assisted by patterns of jokes that could but do not exist rather than by those that are actually in circulation. It is not valid to try to explain the particular patterns of jokes found in or discovered to be absent from the real world in terms of the supposed pay-offs that jokes have either for individuals or for the face-to-face groups within which the jokes are told.

The main evidence from individuals that will be used in this study consists of the comments made by those from whom jokes have been collected by the author or by folklorists or by those who have compiled collections of tales about their own group. Such evidence, however, will mainly be used negatively to refute theories that rely on the imputing of particular feelings and perceptions to individual joke tellers by showing that such empirical evidence as does exist is contrary to what is being suggested and also to stress the sheer ambiguity and complexity of humor itself and the enormous variety of ways in which individuals use and react to jokes. Evidence collected from the individuals who are the original sources of the jokes to be found in archives as to the meaning of the jokes themselves is often mainly valuable for its destructive impact, for the way in which it contradicts and even renders foolish expectations that the collectors have brought to the situation, expectations rooted in their taken-for-granted implicit theories of humor. If a theory of humor depends upon assumptions about or makes predictions concerning the ways in which individuals relate to their jokes, then it is legitimate to use evidence gathered from individuals to refute it, even though for reasons indicated earlier the mere providing of examples of individuals acting in ways that conform to such a theory is insufficient evidence for believing that it is true. Where examples of individual joke-telling are cited in support of the author's own generalizations they are there only as illustrations of theories linking two sets of aggregates, as a way of showing how these are manifested in particular cases. They are not the basis on which the theory rests, but this does *not* mean that the theories are protected from falsification; they could be overturned by another scholar producing new aggregate data incompatible with them. It is difficult to argue this point in advance of the presentation of the detailed empirical arguments of the chapters that follow, but it can be demonstrated by reference to the author's earlier research findings, a brief outline of which is, in any case, necessary for the understanding of the work that follows.

In his earlier research (Davies 1990, 1990A, 1991, 1998) the author suggested that the largest body of national, ethnic and regional jokes to be found in countries throughout the world involved two opposed qualities: the jokes about stupid and canny (crafty, calculating and stingy) groups, respectively. The almost universal popularity of these jokes is illustrated in table 1.1.

It may be suggested that the dominance of these jokes in modern societies rather than jokes about other human qualities is related to the nature of modern societies with their emphasis on success and failure in a world that becomes ever more technically sophisticated and the subject of greater economic calculativeness. Canny and stupid jokes are the natural jokes of advanced capitalist societies or of societies in the process of becoming so. The canny jokes only emerged after the Industrial Revolution and the stupidity jokes, though much older, multiplied remarkably in the modern period and became more bluntly decisive–they are now jokes about mere fools, not wise fools. It is possible to suggest psychological reasons and mechanisms for the popularity of these jokes, but the theory advanced here does not in any way depend on them; it merely says that opposed pairs of jokes will exist in a society that are centered around a dominant moral axis of that society such as a stress on individual achievement through merit. If the society were to change, so would the jokes, but so long as competition and mobility through merit remain central to a society then the theory predicts that jokes of this kind will be popular, though they need not always take an ethnic form as may be seen from the huge waves of jokes about stupid blonde girls and canny lawyers.

In the case of the ethnic jokes listed in table 1.1, a further question arises, namely given that jokes about stupidity and canniness

Table 1.1
The Stupid and the Canny

Country where both "stupid" and "canny" jokes are told	Identity of "stupid" group in jokes	Identity of "canny" group in jokes
United States	Poles (and others locally, e.g., Italians, Portuguese)	Jews, Scots, New England Yankees, Iowans
Canada (East)	Newfies (Newfoundlanders)	Jews, Scots, Nova Scotians
Canada (West)	Ukrainians	Jews, Scots
Mexico	Yucateocos from Yucatan, Gallegos from Galicia in Spain	Regiomontanos, the citizens of Monterrey
Colombia	Pastusos from Pasto in Nariño	Paisas from Antioquia
England	Irish	Scots, Jews
Wales	Irish	Cardis from Cardiganshire, Scots, Jews
Scotland	Irish	Aberdonians, Jews
Ireland	Kerrymen	Scots, Jews
France	Belgians, French Swiss	Auvergnats from the Auvergne, Scots, Jews
Netherlands	Belgians, Limburghers	Scots, Jews
Germany	Ostfrieslanders, Saxons	Swabians, Scots, Jews
Italy	Southern Italians	Milanese, Genovese, Florentines, Scots, Jews
Switzerland	Fribourgers/Freiburgers	Jews, Genevans, Bâlois from Bâle/Basel
Spain	Gallegos from Galicia Leperos, the people of Lepe in Andalucia	Catalans
Finland	Karelians	Laihians from Laihia
Bulgaria	Šopi, the peasants from the rural area outside Sofia	Gabrovonians from Gabrovo, Armenians
Greece	Pontians (Black Sea Greeks)	Armenians
India	Sardarjis (Sikhs)	Gujaratis, Sindis
Pakistan	Sardarjis (Sikhs)	Hindus, especially Gujaratis
Iran	Rashtis from Rasht	Armenians, Isfahanis from Isfahan
Nigeria	Hausas	Ibos
South Africa	Afrikaners (van der Merwe)	Jews, Scots
Australia	Irish, Tasmanians	Jews, Scots
New Zealand	Irish, Maoris (in the North Island), West Coasters (in the South Island)	Jews, Scots, Dutch

get pinned onto a variety of groups, what determines which groups become the butts of the jokes? After all the jokes could be told about quite other groups of people but are not.

In the case of the stupidity jokes what is common to all the butts of the jokes is that they live on the geographical, economic or linguistic edge of the society or culture where the jokes are told. They are not distant, alien or incomprehensible foreigners but peoples who can be portrayed as, in each case, a comic imitation of the joke tellers themselves. The butts of the jokes tend either to live in small communities or rural areas on the periphery of a nation or to be immigrants concentrated in blue-collar, hard-hatted occupations such as working on building sites or both. Thus, while there is no evidence that any of the peoples who are the butts of stupidity jokes really are stupid (indeed sometimes there is proof that they are not (Helmreich 1982: 168) they do occupy stupid locations. In modern societies with very high rates of social and geographical mobility able people tend to seek social promotion by moving up from blue-collar occupations into the middle class and to seek greater opportunities by moving from the edge of a society or culture to the main commercial and intellectual centers, in either case leaving behind a residue of relatively stupid people (Helmreich 1982: 168; Lynn 1979 and 1979A; Saunders 1996: 30-3). The jokes are thus once again congruent with a central feature of modern capitalist societies, namely their very high absolute rates of mobility both social (Saunders 1996: 10-18) and geographical.

What is also clear from an inspection of column two in table 1.1 is that the examples given contradict theories of humor that would suggest that the jokes are an expression of actual hostility, aggression or conflict. In some cases there are conflicts between the joke tellers and the butts of their jokes and in others there are not, but the content of the jokes is exactly the same regardless of whether or not there is conflict and hostility; it is an irrelevance. This point will be explored in detail in the chapters that follow in relation to North America. What might be noted in passing is that many of the countries in column one where the stupidity jokes are told have been involved in conflicts with other more alien neighbors that have not given rise to jokes about their enemies' stupidity. To take a case not so far listed, the Syrians have suffered annexation by Turkey, waged war against Israel and Iraq, "protected" and dominated Lebanon, and been on bad terms with Jordan, but their stupidity jokes are about the familiar unresented Homsiots, the citizens of Homs (and adjoining Hama), on their own periphery. If, as the distinguished sociologist of religion and of smoking Peter Berger states, these "morally reprehensible" stupidity jokes merely display a universal capacity for "ethnocentric malice" (Berger 1997: 52) then why did the Syrians not choose more wisely and economically and pin them on a neighbor who in their eyes deserved to be the recipient of their malice? Conflict and hostility are neither a necessary nor a sufficient condition for the generation of jokes about stupidity.

The model could and would be falsified if major instances of ethnic or regional stupidity joking were to be discovered operating in a converse direction so that those living in the commercial and intellectual centers of a society became the butts of stupidity jokes. In practice when new instances of stupidity jokes not listed in the original table have been found (Davies 1998: 168-9), such as those told in Romania about the people of Altena or in the Faroes about the people of Klaksvik, they fit the model. The model also explains the stupidity jokes told about the politicians, apparatchiks and militia in the former socialist countries of Eastern and Central Europe who enjoyed monopoly power rather than occupying positions obtained by open competition. This latter case should also make it clear that what is being advanced here is *not* a power relations model, for each of these groups exercised considerable power, but a power based on the use of force rather than obtained from the market place or the examination hall. It is the *kind* of power that is exercised that is crucial to an understanding of who becomes the butt of stupidity jokes, not the mere fact of who is relatively powerful and who is powerless by comparison. Indeed, the distinction between kinds of power, which the jokes make obvious, undermines the very coherence of all power relations theories (e.g., see Sargent 1979). It makes no sense to lump different kinds of power together in this way; to do so is a trick that obscures and does not illuminate.

By contrast, those groups whose cultural traditions have enabled them to succeed in the market place or the examination hall, notably the Jews and the Scots, are the butt of jokes about their being canny. It is not entirely surprising that they should also often prove to be the chief inventors and purveyors of jokes about themselves. They have the ability to invent them and the means of circulating them, and the jokes, though self-mocking, also imply success. It is an important point to be explored in depth in the chapters that follow.

There are, of course, other pairs of jokes about winners and losers (Gruner 1997) in other fields of human activity although there is an ambiguity about winning, for success is achieved only at a cost. To win through postponing gratification, controlling one's immediate impulses and conforming to rules and expectations also involves the losses inherent in self-denial. Many other pairs of jokes exist that parallel the contrast between the stupid and the canny as shown in table 1.2. It is this broader contrast that underpins the analysis of jokes about Jewish women and Australian men in chapter 4.

Table 1.2 is an attempt to classify the most common forms of ethnic joke in a way that is congruent with a weak version of the superiority theory of humor (Gruner 1997; Hobbes 1840 [1650]; Koestler 1964). The weak version employed here is purely descriptive for it merely tells us what we can see by observation, namely

Table 1.2
Opposed Sets of Ethnic Jokes

Human activity underlying the joke	Comically defective attributes displayed in opposed sets of ethnic jokes	
	Activity is not taken seriously enough	Activity is taken too seriously with too much emphasis on long-term goals at the expenses of present pleasure
	Butts of jokes are inept, heedless, reckless	Butts of jokes are too calculative
	Consequence is crass failure	Consequence is joyless failure
Work and other similar purposive activities	Stupidity	Canniness
Sex, family, female roles	Reckless and stupid promiscuity	Calculated and begrudging sexlessness
Consumption of alcohol	Drunkenness	Bigoted teetotalism
War	Cowardice	Militarism

that in laughing at ethnic jokes we are laughing at comically defective attributes ascribed to others.[2] The jokes play with superiority and disparagement. Whether they coincide with a real sense of superiority or real expressions of disparagement is an empirical question. Sometimes they do and sometimes they do not, but it makes no difference to the content of the jokes whether or not this is the case. Even if there is a corresponding reality in which the joke tellers actually do feel superior it does not follow that their disparagement of the others is based on hostility for we do not necessarily dislike or even despise those whom we disesteem.

It should also be remembered that the jokes are texts not descriptions of patterns of interaction between known individuals and are not comparable to a witty put down or a practical joke, which require a real victim and his or her (at least potential) discomfiture. It is illicit to slide between these two phenomena relying on their superficial similarities as the stronger version of the superiority theory would have us do. Jokes are forms of play, but contrary to Charles Gruner (1997: 3-25) they are not games in the usual sense. Games are acted out safer versions of reality. Football, chess, bridge, the Olympic Games (Davies 2000) and the assembling of armies of toy soldiers are little wars. There are winners and losers and only a few get prizes. Petty gambling is an imitation of economic life in a competitive society. They are all games of skill and chance. The forms of communication used (Raskin 1985) are, as in real wars and real economic life, a mixture of the bona fide and of lying, cheating and deceit in order to obtain advantage. These games closely mimic the real world and, indeed, there is an overlap between them. Even spectators have their own side and a serious involvement in the outcome.

Jokes also play with superiority but they are not games to decide superiority, for their outcomes are already known in principle if not in detail. The teller and the listener play with the idea that the members of some other group are inferior and yet they may also have some sense of affiliation with that group as in the case of self-mocking jokes. The sudden but momentary sense of glory from a joke has little in common with the exultation felt by a winning team and its supporters or by the winner of a lottery. The parallels are clear but the differences are very great indeed. Jokes and games both involve playing with aggression, with superiority, and with risk but there the similarity ends. The language of jokes is closer to, though different from, that of the stage (another kind of play) than to that of games; it involves the creation of illusion, a form of temporary deception by agreement that does not usually involve a seeking of advantage. Jokes play with deception. You can cheat at cards or at cricket (as when New Zealanders jokingly claim that "Australians have an underarm problem"), but what would it mean to cheat in a joke? You can laugh all the way to the bank by betting money on a race you have fixed but if you fix a joke, *quid rides*? Analogies based on similarities of language and use of metaphor tend to be misleading for the similarities pointed up may be less important than the differences that are then ignored. There is less in language than meets the ear.

Propositions about humor being based on playing with superiority or risk or aggression or the forbidden are descriptions based on common sense observations and nothing more. They have the merit of pointing out certain unities between otherwise diverse genres of jokes such as ethnic jokes, disaster jokes and political jokes. To try to go behind these propositions and to search for (or more accurately to speculate about) anxieties or instincts or evolutionary imperatives or unconscious drives is to move from that which we can describe with clarity into a murky region about which it is not possible to speak clearly. It is better to be silent on these subjects and to work only with what is visible. There is nothing worse than a fog of "profundity," for even though the "profound" may think they know where they are they have no idea where they are going.

Contrary to what Gruner (1997:10) suggests the weak version of the superiority theory of humor is true but not very useful. It is true only because it employs a notion of what constitutes superiority that is vague but in consequence the theory has little predictive power. When it is useful, it is useful in the same way that script theory (Raskin 1985) or notions of appropriate incongruity (Beattie 1778; Oring 1992) are useful, namely in helping to explain how jokes work but it is not useful as an explanation of the social and historical setting of jokes. It is of no use, for example, in explaining why jokes involve some kinds of superiority rather than others or why they get pinned on one group rather than another, precisely the kinds of questions where one might have expected it to prove helpful. The question of why the types of jokes listed in table 1.2 get pinned on particular groups can, as we shall see, be answered only by looking at aggregates of jokes comparatively and in their social and historical context. Yet there *is* a simple pattern to the table. What is being suggested is that in most societies people have a socially acquired sense of how deviations in either direction from a reasonable if not necessarily a happy or golden mean tend to lead to comic disaster. Joke tellers are social not ideological creatures and laugh at groups whom they can portray as expressing an exaggerated version of their own failings rather that groups whom they regard as completely strange and alien. Their most important jokes mocking these extremes naturally refer to the activities that have most impact on their lives, namely work, war, sexuality, and the recreational depressant alcohol. These are the themes of ethnic jokes.

In chapter 4, a further more general version of this model will be presented when the jokes told by Jews about Jewish women will be contrasted with the jokes told by Australians about Australian men. These jokes and comic images are popular far beyond their group of origin because they again play with two extremes that everyone can understand, namely restraint and control versus rumbustious excess, the contrasting discontents of civilization and anarchy, respectively. They are part of the general pattern, but it also has to be explained in comparative social and historical terms why the jokes are pinned on these particular national and ethnic groups. Here again we will be seeking to provide accounts that are elegant and parsimonious, accounts that explain many things using few variables and making few assumptions.

Notes

1.   To those who object that all jokes are told by individuals it is necessary to reply that even though all suicides are committed by individuals it is unhelpful to try and predict or explain the relative suicide *rates* of different societies or groups by examining the motives or mental states of individuals (Durkheim 1970 [1898]). Despite his being one of Durkheim's more severe critics (Davies and Neal 2000) the author agrees that Durkheim's view that relative suicide rates are social facts to be explained in terms of other social facts is correct. Those of Durkheim's critics who start from the individual and his or her intentions and motives are never able to do more than speculate about purpose and cause and construct clumsy fragmented models that contain too much description and provide no explanations (e.g., see Baechler 1979). It is a dead end! While it is true that the suicide of individuals is linked to discontent and depression there is no evidence that the incidence of depression or of general dissatisfaction with life is greater in societies with high suicide rates than in societies where there are few suicides. Durkheim's model is flawed but his insight that the aggregate patterns of even this the most private and individual of acts need a social explanation is valid. The same is true of jokes.

2.   It might be possible for the supporters of Hobbes' (1840 [1650]) view of humor to construct an Adlerian release theory of humor showing how the jokers benefit from their brief escape from the psychological forces that normally maintain them to a greater or lesser extent in a state of inferiority, but it would be pointless in the same sense that Freudian release theory or notions of mental economy are *pointless*. Such theories sound profound but they are merely intuitive ex-post accounts of why a joke was found funny rooted in competing forms of psychoanalysis that we have other good reasons for mistrusting and disbelieving. We have, for one thing, no way of choosing between competing schools or deciding which of them is true and they can not all be true because they make contradictory predictions. In the case of Freudian psychoanalysis it is worth noting that it has a poor track record in its main activity of curing people (Eysenck 1985: 69-80), that experimental research has disproved many of its findings (Eysenck 1985: 149-170) and that historians have accused Freud of seriously falsifying or misinterpreting his data. The authority of psychoanalysis as a system cannot, therefore, be invoked in support of Freudian perceptions of humor (Freud 1960 [1905]). Freud might be right in some respects about humor; that is an empirical question. What is quite unjustified is to evoke his wider theories about human psychological functioning in support of his views on humor since these wider theories have been found wanting. The most that can be said is that Freud had the inspired, intuitive mind of a gifted creative writer and that Freud's work has at times led later scholars to produce uniquely insightful work such as Alan Dundes' studies of German (1984) and Hindu (1997A) folklore including humor. General propositions about humor based on Freudian theory, however, have to be tested using evidence *independent* of that theory. When this is done they tend to collapse.

2

The Self-Mocking Scottish Sense of Humor

Jokes about the Scots have a truly international popularity for the crafty, stingy, calculating canny Scotsman is the butt of jokes and humor not only in Scotland's neighbors England, Wales and Ireland or in countries like Canada, New Zealand, Australia and the United States where many Scots have settled and prospered but even in countries such as Bulgaria, the Czech Republic, France, Italy, Germany, Sweden, Finland, Hungary, Slovakia, Croatia and Greece (Bramieri 1980: 292, 314; Climent-Galant 1979; Davies 1990; Guillois and Guillois 1979B; Horecký 1985: 191-6) that have had relatively little historical contact with the Scottish people. However, the Scots have also long been noted for inventing, telling and compiling collections of humorous anecdotes about the foibles of their own people; indeed historically the Scots were the main inventors and circulators of such jokes.

The Scottish writer on Scots humor, A. H. Charteris, then Professor of International Law at the University of Sydney in Australia, noted in 1932 during the golden age of the Scottish joke that:

> A curious and interesting phenomenon is the creation of simplified national types by a people, or for a people, as a vehicle for humorous comment abroad. The Scots excel in its manipulation, as do the Jews...what two races are more notorious for telling jokes against themselves. (Charteris 1932:14)

The Scots and the Jews have indeed shown a remarkable zeal in creating and circulating comic tales about their own people, many of which seem to mock traits and characteristics such as canniness which others may see as not entirely desirable. The propensity of the Scots and the Jews to invent and tell jokes of this kind is fatal for the unproven but widely accepted theory that ethnic jokes are an expression of conflict, hostility and aggression. If this were the case,

17

then the phenomenon of the members of a group revelling in jokes about their own people would be an inexplicable paradox. Accordingly it is necessary to protect the theory by putting forward the equally undemonstrable assumption that the inventors and tellers of such "self-derogatory" jokes are hostile to their own people and to themselves. The jokers are held to be either disloyal or masochistically self-hating or both. The thesis as applied to Jewish jokes is unconvincing as we shall see in chapter 3. It is even more obviously false in the case of the Scots who have not been the victims of systematic persecution, nor the focus of a hostile and defamatory ideology. There may well be many individuals who for idiosyncratic reasons dislike the Scots (see Ginger 1974. Comment on Anecdote 30), but there is no anti-Caledonianism corresponding to anti-Semitism. There are no evil, malign and absurd accusations suggesting that the Scots conspire to cause international wars and to dominate the entire world or to indulge in ritual child murder. No one has been motivated to invent a set of mendacious protocols of the learned elders of the kirks of Scotland. Scottish self-mockery is not in any sense a product or a reflection of other peoples' rejection of or antipathy towards the Scots. Scots living abroad, of whom there are many, need not fear attack nor does it ever cross the minds of those of partly Scottish ancestry (including the author) that their ancestry would ever be held against them.

Indeed, it is striking how jokes about the Scots have flourished most, when there has been least hostility between the Scots and their neighbours. If we go back in time to the era of intermittent border warfare and mutual antipathy between the English and the Scots before James VI of Scotland became James I of England in 1603, we find no jokes about the Scots and humorous references to them were rare (Bartley 1954). The main butt of English jokes in the Tudor period were their nearer, more familiar and unthreatening neighbors the Welsh (Davies 1985, 1999A) and the Scots were not at that time interested in telling or purveying jokes about themselves. In the seventeenth and early eighteenth centuries when dynastic and religious disputes involving both England and Scotland led to military incursions from each country deep into the heartland of the other, there were still very few jokes about the Scots. Most of the English jokes were jibes about the dire poverty of Scotland, which forced its inhabitants to dine on oatmeal and offal (Charteris 1932:

22; Davies 1990: 287-8) and led them to emigrate to England. It was only in the late eighteenth and early nineteenth centuries that jokes about canny calculating Scotsmen emerged to compete with the by now well-established tales of Irish bulls and blunders (Bartley 1954:233-5). However, by the early nineteenth century an appreciation of the achievements of Scots such as Robert Adam, Henry Bell, Joseph Black, James Boswell, David Hume, Colin Maclaurin, Adam Smith, Tobias Smollett and James Watt had made Scottish intellectual and practical pre-eminence respected in England. The wearing of the newly invented kilt, albeit with pink tights, by the Hanoverian King George IV on his visit to Edinburgh in 1822 was an indication of how far the once wild, dangerous and Jacobite Highlanders had been incorporated into a popular English sentimental myth. Thus the comic image of the canny Scotsman became increasingly popular in England at the point where the Scots, who had once been perceived as threatening and inferior, were coming to be seen as respected equals, though also as lacking in any sense of humor.

The Reverend Sydney Smith, after spending five years in Edinburgh at the very beginning of the nineteenth century, "discussing metaphysics and medicine in that garret of the earth—that knuckle-end of England, that land of the ingenious Calvin, oatcakes and sulphur," went so far as to declare that "it requires a surgical operation to get a joke well into a Scotch understanding" (Smith 1839: vol. I, 1-20). He later added that the best instrument for this purpose was a corkscrew. Even that champion of Scottish humor Professor A. H. Charteris (1932:13) has conceded:

> Who has not met the literal Scot of intellectual cast of mind, who will wrestle with your joke until it yields its secret, because the integrity of the instrument of his understanding is engaged and during the combat his mind will creak as an attentive listener may perceive. His prototype is Lord Balmuth—at the turn of the eighteenth century who took one of Harry Erskine's jokes to avizandum, and hours later greeted him with the joyful shout "I hae ye noo, Harry, I hae ye noo!" (Charteris 1932: 13)

Charles Lamb, likewise, declared that the Scots were too inclined to take figurative language in a literal way to be able to appreciate a joke, after an incident in Scotland when he was invited to a party to meet one of the sons of the poet Robert Burns who had died some years before. When "Lamb arrived at the party, Burns junior had not yet made his appearance and Lamb in his lack-a-daisical kind of manner said, 'I wish it had been the father instead of the son' (who was due to come); upon which four Scotsmen present with one voice exclaimed, 'That's impossible, for *he's dead.*'" (Ramsay 1874: 244). Lamb saw this as one more proof of Scottish humorlessness, but, such is the ambiguity of humor that it may well be Lamb himself who lacked the sense of humor needed to see that the Scots had responded with deadpan humor to his rather feeble jest.

English jokes about the humorless Scot, rooted in an image of the Scots as a joyless people characterized by reserve, reticence and hard self-control, forever wresting with serious problems both material and metaphysical, survived throughout the nineteenth century:

> *Professor McPhairrson.* "No, Mrs. Brown, it's not that we Scots are dull; but you English see a joke in *anything*! Why, the other day I was in a room with four Englishmen, one of whom told a story, and, would you believe it, I was the only man that didn't laugh!" (*Mr. Punch's Scottish Humor* 1908: 55)

This image of the Scots in general and of Scottish intellectuals and ministers in particular was forcefully refuted in the period between 1850 and 1950, the golden age of the Scottish joke book, when distinguished Scotsmen vied with one another in the production of collections of Scottish jokes and humorous anecdotes. The supposedly humorless Scots now became the people of the joke. In a manner, so far as I know unique to Scotland, these collectors and compilers of jokes and anecdotes put their clerical and aristocratic titles and academic degrees even on the very covers of their books, which in this way made a claim to high seriousness and respectability as well as being a source of mirth.

Charles Rogers LL.D. (1867), Dean E. B. Ramsay LL.D. (1874 [1858]), Charles Mackay LL.D. (1882), John Kerr LL.D. (1903 and 1904), the Very Rev. John Gillespie LL.D. (1904), the Rev. David Macrae (1896 and 1904), Sir Archibald Geikie (1904), Charles Jerdan LL.B., D.D. (1920), Lord Aberdeen, the Marquess of Aberdeen and Temair (1929), Sir James Taggart (1927), and Professor A. H. Charteris M.A. LL.B. (1932) are among the great and the good who have published such collections. It is particularly noteworthy how many clergymen (Ramsay, Rogers, Gillespie, Macrae, Jerdan), LL.Ds and LL.Bs. (seven) are to be found in this far from exhaustive list. These works and others equally erudite compiled by lay and undoctored authors, such as Robert Ford (1891) T. B. Johnstone (1897) and John Aitken (n.d.), are particularly valuable and interesting for our present purposes because they combine jokes and humorous anecdotes with memoirs, scholarly comment and reflections on the state of Scottish society.

Many of the scripts of the jokes and anecdotes in these collections could be read as based on and even expressions of a derogatory stereotype of the canny, thrifty, shrewd, grasping, pawky, dram-drinking, fanatically Calvinist and Sabbatarian Scot and, thus, to parade national faults, but that is *not* how they are presented and used by the authors and compilers. The "faults" of the jokes are but the obverse of what are seen as national virtues and the ambiguity of humor is such that the jokes *both mock and celebrate* Scottishness and the distinguishing traits of the Scottish people. Were the Scots seriously and solemnly to proclaim their virtues, abilities and achievements with the frequency with which jokes are told, they would appear offensively proud and immodest and the lack of variety and surprise in such proclamations would make them boring, irritating and tedious. There is a limit to "Here's tae us wha's like us" (Here's to us, who else can match us). By contrast, humorous self-mockery is acceptable because the speakers can express pride while appearing modest (Mulkay 1987) (such is the ambiguity of humor) and retain the interest and attention of their audience by amusing them.

The largest single theme in the "self-inflicted" Scots jokes is not surprisingly that of the canny Scot, jokes about whom are now to be found throughout the world as we can see from some modern examples:

Why, McTavish, said the psychiatrist, you seem to have lost your stutter.
Yes, said McTavish, I've been telephoning America a lot recently. (MacHale 1988: 41)

While shopping in Scotland an Englishman bought an article, placed a five pound note on the counter and went out without his change. The shopkeeper tried frantically to attract his attention by knocking on the window with a sponge. (MacHale 1988: 73)

Daddy, who is that man running up and down the carriage with his mouth open?
Don't worry son, that's a Scotsman getting a free smoke. (MacHale 1988: 68)

Do you know the best Scottish joke?
No? Give me a hundred francs and I will tell it to you. (Climent-Galant 1979: 54)

The older indigenous Scottish jokes are based on the *same canny script* but are told in a variety of rich and distinctive Scots dialects, exhibit local quirks and idiosyncracies and are often fastened to or fostered on a particular place and even person. A characteristic example has been recorded by the Very Rev. John Gillespie, a minister of the national church, the established Presbyterian Church of Scotland:

> When I was assistant in Dalry, Ayrshire, the wife of a farmer in the parish whom I knew died and was buried in the churchyard of Kilwinning where he was the owner of a farm. The grave-digger who officiated at the interment was Robin Alison, who had not a few idiosyncracies of character, including a blunt abrupt manner and way of speaking. It used to be said of Robin that he never was so far from Kilwinning as not to be within hearing of the bell when it was rung. After the grave had been filled up, the chief mourner said "Robin what's yer chairge?" "Three and saxpence," shortly replied the official. Taking out of his pocket a long silk purse with a knot tied in it, the newly made widower—who, there is reason to believe, had the too well-deserved reputation of being very penurious—took a 2s 6d piece out of it and said, "There's half a crown, Robin; if yer as well paid for every ane ye'll mak' siller at it."
>
> "Ah'll no hae't," replied the grave digger.
>
> "Tak't Robin, tak't, it's sure money."
>
> "Ah'll no hae't," was the characteristically brief rejoiner.
>
> The farmer at that point put the 2s 6d back into the purse saying, "Ah weel! then, ye maun just want." Without dallying a moment Robin, who had still the spade in his hand, energetically put it into the grave, saying with emphasis, "Very weel, then, up she comes!"
>
> The sequel does not need to be told. This incident was told to me as above by one of the best narrators of Scotch stories I ever knew—the late Mr. M'Rorie, Inspector of Poor, Kilwinning. (Gillespie 1904: 74-5)

It is quite possible that this story though polished and embellished is based on an actual event, for the same anecdote is told by Robert Ford (1891: 97) and by John Kerr (1903: 183-4). The three versions are sufficiently alike, for they are all told about the sexton of Kilwinning, and Kerr also calls him Robbie though this may be a generic Robert not a specific Robin just as Ford uses a generic John, both John and Robert being common Scottish Christian names, the plot is essentially the same in each version and all three end with the same punch-line "up she comes" to make one suppose that some such incident really did occur. They are also sufficiently different (Kerr makes the disputed fee four shillings and sixpence and Ford makes it five shillings) to indicate that none of them copied the tale from the work of one of the others but that they followed independent oral sources (Dundes 1999). At the same time, these so-called foaf tales ascribed to a *f*riend *o*f *a f*riend or f.o.a.f., who here would be the friend of Dr. Gillespie's friend Mr. M'Rorie, are often simply modern legends, plausible and appealing but unverifiable tales. What is far more important is that this story of the direct and unabashed pursuit of one's pecuniary dues, regardless of good taste or sensitivity is seen as distinctively Scots and humorous by all three Scots authors. If Robin Alison does not get his pound of flesh, he will gravely disinter two hundred pounds of someone else's.

The same blunt Scots disregard for social conventions that preclude an over-direct demand for payment appears in a further anecdote recorded by Charles Jerdan (1920: 222-3), a minister of the United Presbyterian Church of Scotland, about his revered and respected colleague, the Rev. Alexander Banks of Braehead in Lanarkshire:

> Mr. Banks used to tell a good story about himself which referred to the beginning of his ministry. Early in 1849, when he had completed his first year at Braehead, his modest stipend of £70 had not been fully paid. On the next Lord's Day, accordingly, being the anniversary of his induction, when the hour of public worship arrived, instead of proceeding to the pulpit, he seated himself quietly in the manse pew, and made no sign of preparing to conduct the service. At length one of the office-bearers went to him and enquired if some one was coming to perform that duty. "Not that I know of," replied the minister. Then the elder asked if he was not going to the pulpit himself. Mr. Banks answered, "No, I am not"; and when the question was put, "Why?" he replied that he declined to conduct the service until the congregation paid him the balance of his last year's stipend. And the good man kept his seat in the pew until the money was brought to him!

Given that Mr. Banks lived plainly in this moorland community, which he went on to serve for sixty years, and that he still had to supplement his meagre stipend by also being a working farmer and an unauthorized medical practitioner his determination is understandable. Nonetheless, the anecdote is told as a "*Scottish* clerical story." For Welsh Protestants whose total personal annual contributions to their church or chapel were recorded and published and a source of status competition, there was a further layer of humor about the canny Scots as is recorded by the Very Rev. John Gillespie (1904:141-2):

> On my way home from Edinburgh on one occasion I had as a fellow-traveller a little Welshman who was very talkative, and was specially emphatic on Scotch characteristics—insisting particularly on love of whisky and a disposition to starve the Kirk as being national traits. He repeated the following real or imaginary narrative in an illustration of his contention:—On a Saturday night a Scotchman said to his boy, Bob, "there's half a crown; gang roun' to Sandy McNab's public house and bring in a bottle o' whusky." As the lad was in the act of leaving the house on his errand his father called after him: "Bob, look here—there's a penny bring back twa bawbees for't; ye see, if ma heid and your mother's heid are no ower sair (heads are not too sore) the morn after drinking the

whusky, we'll maybe gang to the Kirk, and if we dae gang we'll each need a bawbee for the collection." "That's the Scotch style," triumphantly added the Welshman: "two-and-six for whisky, and a halfpenny each for the church." I suppose I should have challenged him to a duel on the spot, but I didn't. (Gillespie 1904:141-2)

Here again we see the ambiguity of humor and the way it plays with aggression rather than expressing it. We can see from Gillespie's reference to duelling that he wishes to make it clear that the Welshman's tale is a humorous piece of chaff and banter from a member of a small people closely related to and well disposed towards the Scots and not a concealed insult based on animosity. A Welshman harboring a real grudge would not choose a Scotsman on a train from the Scottish capital as the person on whom to unleash his spite. Accordingly, Gillespie sets aside the kind of crude reductionism that would reduce an entertaining tale to a tendentious statement conveying malice to both Gillespie and his fellow countrymen. Besides, there are many indigenous Scots jokes about the allegedly exiguous extent of Scottish contributions to church collections (Ford 1891: 44-5; Jerdan 1920: 225-6; Ramsay 1874: 297, 232, 336).

There are, of course, many other contexts in which the Scots of the jokes avoid expenditure in ways that are either comical in themselves or for which a comical justification is provided:

A man who had remained unmarried till he was well up in years at last took unto himself a wife. When asked why, after being so long a bachelor, he had thought of marriage, he replied that he had a great objection to waste of any kind; that though he had done his best to make his servant prepare no more food than he could consume, there was always some left over; that this remainder was given to the pig and he thought he might as well keep a wife as a pig. (Kerr 1904:102-3)

It used to be related that some of his friends observed in a standing carriage the Rev. Dr. Ritchie, of Potterow U.P. (United Presbyterian) Church, Edinburgh—who was alleged to be very economical in his expenditure—and on his being bantered on travelling in this way, rejoined, "Where would you expect to find me but among the congregation of the upright?" (Gillespie 1904:133)

Caution and stinginess are only one side of what it means to be a canny Scot, as we can see from a sermon preached by the Scottish clergyman Dr. Rankin in his own church at Muthill about the betrayal of Jesus when he said that Judas Iscariot made as keen a bargain with the chief priests "as if he had been a Scotchman" (Jerdan 1920: 262-3). Canniness also includes cunning, craftiness, shrewdness and even a willingness to indulge in sharp practice. These qualities are also to be found in the classic Scottish anecdotes about their own people, but it is striking that the published jokes about these much more controversial traits are far less likely to be pinned upon particular named individuals as may be seen from the following examples:

> I think about as cool a Scottish "aside" as I know, was that of the old dealer who, when exhorting his son to practice honesty in his dealings on the grounds of its being the "best policy," quietly added, "I hae tried baith" (I've tried both) (Ramsay 1874: 27-28).

> Two workmen met in the morning after a night of heavy drinking. They were very thirsty, but could not muster more than the price of one glass of whisky. While about to share it a friend came in on the same errand. They offered him the glass, which he took and finished. He felt he could not do less than offer them each a glass in return. He then went away. One said to other, "Now, wasna that weel managed?" "It was so," he replied, "but, man it was an awfu' risk." (Kerr 1903: 311-2)

> A North Country laird...was known to be very close-fisted....This laird when riding to a town in Aberdeenshire overtook a lady of his acquaintance, also riding. On arriving at the bar (of the toll gate) the lady found that she had not taken her purse with her. The laird insisted on paying for her. She objected, knowing that he would grudge the small expenditure. He refused to listen to the objection and paid the toll. When they came to the parting of the way she thanked him, adding that his kindness was quite unnecessary as she could have paid for herself the next time she passed that way. "Oh," said the laird, "it doen't matter much; it was an ill shilling I gied the wife." (Kerr 1904:100-101).

Though willing to record this last joke as an authentically Scots humorous anecdote, Dr. John Kerr (1904: 101) felt obliged to distance himself from it and added: "The above is an instance of absolute dishonesty and much worse than meanness." The same point may be made in relation to the case of two adjacent jokes in the Very Rev. John Gillespie's (1904: 138-40) collection:

> Three representatives of the divisions of the United Kingdom—an Englishman, an Irishman and a Scotsman—were going in company along Regent Street when a young lady attendant in a glove-shop looked out of the door as they were passing. All of them were impressed by her surpassing beauty, of an unusual type. They were equally anxious to have a more leisurely opportunity of seeing this high and rare type of beauty. They stopped and entered into consultation as to the way in which they could most easily and successfully accomplish their object. Said the Englishman, "We'll manage it quite easily by going into the shop, getting the young lady to attend to us, and buying a pair of gloves from her." "Yes," chimed in the Irishman, "and as delicately as possible finding out her size, we'll present the gloves to the young lady." "Tuts!" said the Scotsman, "what's the use o' wasting siller (silver), we'll speir the price and no buy them!"

A story to the same effect as the foregoing is told of three representatives of the respective nationalities who were travelling by train to a railway terminus. The English-man left his compartment and walked at once out of the station although it is sometimes alleged he would be more likely to go to the refreshment room! The Irishman, after going from his compartment for a few paces, returned and examined it, in order to ascertain if he had left any of his property behind him. The Scotchman, up to a certain point, did exactly like the son of St. Patrick, but it is more than insinuated that while searching the compart-ment with ever greater care than the Irishman, his object was to see if he could pick up anything belonging to any other person! (Gillespie 1904: 138-40)

The good minister immediately adds after the *latter* joke: "Of course this is a base calumny against the Scottish character which we can afford to repeat seeing no one will believe it" (see also Gei-ger 1923: 207-8 and Telushkin 1992, where the same point is made in relation to a similar Jewish joke). The Rev. Gillespie is quite right in saying that no one will believe it for, other things equal, the more absurd a calumny is, the more obvious it is that it is meant to be and should be taken as a mere joke and not an open or covert serious accusation. For the Scots at least the more base the more baseless. Nonetheless, although Gillespie regards both jokes "as in keeping with [the] highly exaggerated representations of the close-fistedness of Scotchmen." (Gillespie 1904:138), it is *only* in the case of the latter joke that he explicitly tries to quell any anxiety Scots may have that he is providing English or American readers with a true account of Scots reality. Also he distances himself from the joke by his use of the phrase "more than insinuated." In neither joke are the Scottish details of the anecdote stressed (other than through the use of Scottish dialect words that may be unfamiliar to a non-Scot), nor are the individuals identified and both jokes are cast in a familiar three part form. Such jokes are on the verge of going cosmopolitan if indeed they are not adaptations of international jokes, and it is interesting that the Rev. Gillespie writing in 1904 should have slid them into his book on *The Humours of Scottish Life,* which mainly contains highly local and located material. The main point, how-ever, is to note the increased care that Scots writers take over the *presentation* of jokes about canny Scots when canniness takes the form of dishonesty. Jewish compilers of books of jokes and anec-dotes about their own people are even more emphatic that Jewish jokes about their own people involving dishonesty are just jokes (Geiger 1923), for they have a further problem to contend with in the form of an anti-Semitic ideology which claims that all Jews re-ally are dishonest. But a joke's a joke for a' that.

In general, this problem doesn't arise with most "canny" jokes because in a modern capitalist economy it is a virtue to be canny in the sense of being clever, shrewd, enterprising, striving, hard-headed, prudent, far-sighted, economical and thrifty, even if an excess of these qualities is seen as ludicrous. It is precisely for this reason that it is easier for those who are the subjects of canny jokes, such as the Scots and the Jews, to take the lead in inventing and telling jokes about their own people, than it is for those who are the butt of ethnic jokes about being, say, cowardly, stupid or unsure of their father's identity. Such peoples can and do tell ethnic jokes about their own folk being cowardly, stupid or bastards, but they are not famous or prominent for their mastery of joke-telling in the way that the Scots and the Jews are. Perhaps, too, it helps to have a modicum of canny qualities even when it is jokes that are being invented, published, retold and retailed.

Behind the canny jokes lurks a pride in the achievements, culture and character of the canny Scot. T. B. Johnstone (1897) has assembled alongside a smattering of jokes about the canny Scot, a series of fulsome encomiums (or as the Scots would say, encomia) about "Scotland and things Scottish" from the same class of men as the compilers of the joke books we have discussed. Johnstone records the Rev. A. Rattray M.A. as writing in the *Scottish Annual* for 1859:

> Scotland occupies a foremost place in the rank of nations. No natural advantages, no mere accidental superiority have given her this honourable pre-eminence. She has won it by her intelligence—she has deserved it by her moral worth—heroic struggles unsurpassed in the annals of mankind" (Quoted in Johnstone 1897: 49).

> Likewise Dr. W. M. Taylor in his *History of the Scottish Pulpit* in 1897 wrote of "the distinctive features of the Scottish peoples" as including "a persistence amounting almost to dogged stubbornness, which keeps the Scotsman steadily at a thing until he has gained his end. This quality of *dourness*—to give it the vernacular name—makes the true Caledonian everywhere pertinacious.... Happily with this indomitable firmness there is combined a very large measure of caution, or what is commonly ridiculed as canniness. He leaps with intensity, but he looks before he leaps.... The high average of intelligence in the nation, consequent upon its excellent system of education, enables him to see with clearness where the right lies, and so his persistence which might otherwise have been fraught with mischief, has been mainly an immense power for good." (Quoted in Johnstone 1897: 50)

Lest fellow Scots be thought biased, Johnstone quotes the then prime minister, the Englishman Lord Salisbury's, tribute to "the supreme superiority in respect of all mundane affairs, which is shown by those who are born north of the Tweed" (Johnstone 1897: 51), the English historian Froude's declaration that "the Jews and the Athenians excepted, no people so few in number had scored so deep a mark in the world's history as the Scots had done" (Johnstone 1897: 52), and the view of M. P. Villars that the Scots are "indefatigable workers, perservering to the pitch of obstinacy, shrewd, thrifty and industrious men of business...gifted with solid qualities, which in the present age, ensure to those who possess them, victory in the struggle of life" (Johnstone 1897: 53). Johnstone cites many more examples of praise and self-praise but fortunately interspersed with comic interludes, without which Johnstone's work would be so smug as to generate a dislike of the author and the people he seeks to promote. Humorous self-mockery is the best form of self-promotion.

The problem with declarations of national virtue, character and achievement or collections of the praises sung by others is that, however true and justified they may be, they are apt to produce impatience, derision and resentment in outsiders and even desertions from the ranks of one's auxiliaries. Gwen Raverat wrote of the Scottish governesses of her Edwardian Cambridge childhood that :

> And they whahaed about Bruce and Wallace and rubbed in spiders and tartans and porridge and the insufferable and universal superiority of the Scotch (No, I will NOT say Scots) to such an extent, that we could only get into corners and thank our stars that we had not one drop of Scotch blood in our veins. And it was many years before any of us was able to look with unprejudiced eyes at anything Scotch again. (Raverat 1960: 62)

When a Scotsman says "I'm proud to be Scots," or when Scottish publishers bring out annotated lists of great Scots, many of whom are nonentities, their actions are immodest and self-defeating. The use of the words proud or pride and the compilation of questionable lists not only show a lack of self confidence but may well lead others to suspect that the Scots are covering up an actual inferiority. When the Scots joke about themselves by contrast it is an endearing trait and can be used as a way of conveying superiority without irritating outsiders. The same point may be made in regard to Scottish jokes about their religion and identity as a people.

Historically, religion has been crucial to the maintenance of a distinctive Scottish identity for Scotland is a nation without a state. When the Act of Union joined Scotland to England and Wales in 1707, politically speaking, Scotland became North Britain, a part of a political federation, ruled from London. The Act of Union, however, also guaranteed the integrity and independence of many distinctive Scottish institutions notably education, the legal system and above all the Church of Scotland, and these have been both the bearers of Scottish identity and the subject of a great deal of Scottish humor. The Reformation in Scotland had a very different history from that of Anglican Episcopal England. In Scotland the Reformation took a distinctively Presbyterian and Calvinist form, which was expressed in theology, modes of Church government and everyday moral behavior. The religious struggles of the sixteenth and seventeenth centuries ended in victory for the Presbyterians, who subsequently sent missionaries into the remoter Highland areas to consolidate their position, and these last converts became, in many ways, the fiercest of adherents (Carswell 1927: 63-4; Macinnes 1951: 7, 10-78, 110, 146, 153; Reid 1960: 143, 152-5), leaving only small pockets of Roman Catholics and Episcopalians in the Islands and in the North-East. Subsequently, there was a substantial influx of Roman Catholic immigrants from Ireland into the main cities and industrial areas, but this only served to reinforce the view that to be Scots was to be Protestant and Presbyterian.

Many Scottish jokes refer to those Scots who adhered to the *stricter* forms of Presbyterianism. During the eighteenth and the first half of the nineteenth centuries a series of groups left the established Church of Scotland to form new and independent sects and denominations. This was in addition to the Old Cameronians, later known as the Reformed Presbyterians, who had refused to join the established Church in the first place. The Seceders (the Associate Synod) left in 1740 and subsequently split into Burghers and Anti-Burghers, both of whom later divided into Auld Licht (old light) and New Licht factions. The Relief Synod likewise seceded in 1761 and as a result of these several splits, together with some partial reunions, there were by the early nineteenth century no fewer than seven independent dissenting Presbyterian Churches outside the Church of Scotland. Then in 1843 came *the* Disruption with four hundred and seventy ministers, a third of the total, and a fifth of the congregations leaving the established Church of Scotland to found the Free Church (Carswell 1927: 212; Reid 1960: 124-149; Smout 1986: 186). The key issues that provoked the splits were in most cases connected with matters of church government such as who had the right to appoint the minister in a parish or the extent to which the civil authorities could intervene in the Church of Scotland's internal affairs. However, those who left tended to be drawn from the Evangelical rather than the Moderate party within the Church of Scotland and the new denominations they founded were more rigorously Calvinist and more rigidly Sabbatarian than the old Kirk they had left. The old Welsh and Jewish joke about the two chapels or synagogues on a desert island applies equally well to the Scots who share a common religious tradition of argumentative democracy:

> A Welshman was shipwrecked at sea and marooned on a desert island. When a passing vessel picked him up five years later the crew were amazed to find his little island covered in fine buildings that he had built himself. With pride the Welsh Robinson Crusoe took the captain round the island and pointed out to him his house, workshop, electricity generator and two chapels. "But what do you need the second chapel for?" asked the captain. "Oh, that's the one I don't go to," he replied. (Davies 1978: 25). For the Jewish version, see Novak and Waldoks 1981: 116; Telushkin 1992: 20, and also a commentary Telushkin 1992: 20-1)

It is important to note that none of the Scottish dissenters abandoned the Scottish Presbyterian tradition. Jokes about the odd behavior or even beliefs of the most thorough dissenters are still jokes *within the family* about issues that all the parties agree are salient and to be understood in a particular way, even when they are a source of heated disagreement. The jokes of a moderate Scottish Presbyterian about the "wee frees" of the remoter Highlands and Islands are, thus, quite different from, say, Scottish jokes about Roman Catholics, Christian Scientists or Mormons, who are outside the Presbyterian tradition and whose own beliefs, traditions and forms of Church government are too unfamiliar to be easily the subject of a detailed and distinctive Scottish humor.

During the latter part of the nineteenth and early twentieth centuries at the time when the first ministerial joke books were published, there was a reaction against strict Calvinism (Hamilton 1990: 158-189; Kerr 1904: 155; Mackenzie 1941: 185, Ramsay 1874: 56), a slow undermining of dogma and a series of reunions of the Presbyterian churches, leaving only tiny obdurate remnants outside (Reid 1960: 160-73; Sjölinder 1964: 379; Smout 1986: 189). In 1900 the United Presbyterians joined with the Free Church to form the United Free Church which, in turn, reunited with the national Church of Scotland in 1929 to form a body which now contained 43 percent of the Scottish population (Mackenzie 1941: 180-1 and 324-5). By contrast the adherents of the dissenting Presbyterian churches numbered less than 1 percent (Mackenzie 1941: 326).

The scholarly editors of the joke books studied here were all religious moderates and their compilations were made and published at a time when the fierceness of dogma and intensity of schism of an earlier generation were fading away. Dr. Gillespie was the Church of Scotland minister for Mouswald in Dumfriesshire, Dr. Jerdan a minister of the United Presbyterian Church in Greenock, David Macrae an Independent minister who had left the Presbyterians after a dispute over his orthodoxy on the subject of Hell, and Edward Ramsay the Episcopal Dean of Edinburgh, known for his friendly ecumenical attitude to the Presbyterians (*Dictionary of National Biography* 1897: Vol. XLIX: 115-6; *Fasti* 1928: Vol. 2: 220; Innes 1874; Lamb 1930: 159). Sir Archibald Geikie, the noted geologist, and John Kerr, who was for forty years an Inspector of Schools for Scotland, both held moderate opinions that they expressed through their books; their work had led them to travel extensively including the most remote parts of Scotland and to appreciate the full span of the Scots diversity in religious belief and behavior within a common tradition. They did not themselves belong to the stricter congregations, religious factions and denominations, who are the main butt of their jokes, nor did they perceive these ultra strict minorities as being at the center of Scottish society. They saw the stricter Presbyterians of the jokes not as typical Scots but as a kind of *ideal-typical* Scots' who had taken sound Scottish principles and virtues to an eccentric and anachronistic extreme. The joke books in many cases proved very popular and went into several editions. It is impossible to discover precisely how and why the jokes cited below were perceived by different categories of Scots at the time or among whom they originally circulated. We can, however, say from the comments made by the editors themselves that *for the compilers* jokes that mock an excess of Scottish religious zeal are *both* an indirect way of celebrating and drawing attention to shared, valued and distinctive Scottish convictions *and* a means of distancing themselves from those who held these convictions in a fanatical and unsophisticated way.

Predestination was the central doctrine of the Scottish Calvinists. They argued that since God was omnipotent and omniscient He knew in advance which individuals He had chosen to belong to the elect who would be saved and which were the reprobates who would be damned. No practice of good works in a person's lifetime could alter a judgment whose result was already known to God. God's will and justice were beyond human understanding and no one could know whether or not they would be saved, although those whose faith was strong might come to have an inner certainty that they belonged to the elect. According to Max Weber's *The Protestant Ethic and the Spirit of Capitalism* (1930), there is a significant link between the anxieties induced by this doctrine and the tireless pursuit of work, savings and profit pursued by canny Calvinists such as the Scots. The empirical evidence from Scotland shows that the Scots behaved in this way from the time of their Reformation (Marshall 1980: 263, 272; Smout 1972: 80-91), long before the Union with England and Wales made capitalist development possible (Whatley 2000). There is then a clear affinity between jokes about the canny Scot and Scottish jokes about predestination (Davies 1992A,1998: 43-62).

The moral posture adopted by those who were convinced that they belonged to the elect had already long before the golden age of the joke books been satirized by Robert Burns during the period of eighteenth-century laxity that preceded the religious revivals at the end of the century, notably in his poem *Holy Willie's Prayer*:

> O thou, that in the heavens does dwell!
> wha, as it pleases best thysel'
> Sends ane to heaven and ten to hell
> A' for thy glory;
> And no for any gude or ill
> They've done before thee...
> (Robert Burns in Morgan 1970: 73-6)

The Scottish version of justification by faith was still alive and well in the late nineteenth century and Kerr has a humorous anecdote to this effect:

> Nor in view of the rigidity with which the dogma of justification by faith is generally held will it be a matter for surprise that a man on his deathbed being asked if he thought he was prepared for the change, replied, "Oh yes for I have hated gude warks a' ma days." (Kerr 1903: 337-8: Kerr 1904: 158)

What is particularly striking about the pious Scottish Calvinists of the nineteenth century is their willingness to wrestle doggedly with these unanswerable questions, which could of course give rise to humor as in the anecdotes below from Ramsay (1874: 29-30):

A party travelling on a railway got into deep discussion on theological questions. Like Milton's spirits in Pandemonium, they had

> "Reason'd high
> Of providence, fore-knowledge, will, and fate—
> Fix'd fate, free-will, fore-knowledge absolute;
> And found no end, in wand'ring mazes lost."

A plain Scotsman present seemed much interested in these matters, and having expressed himself as not satisfied with the explanation which elicited in the course of discussion on a particular point regarding predestination, one of the party said to him that he had observed a minister, whom they all knew, in the adjoining compartment, and that when the train stopped at the next station for a few minutes, he could go and ask *his* opinion. The good man accordingly availed himself of the opportunity to get hold of the minister, and lay their difficulty before him. He returned in time to resume his old place, and when they had started again, the gentleman who had advised him, finding him not much disposed to volunteer communication, asked him if he had seen the minister. "O ay," he said, he had seen him. "And did you propose the question to him?" "O ay." "And what did he say?" "Oh, he just said he didna ken, and what was mair he didna *care*!"

One can only presume that the disappointed Scottish traveller would have preferred the kind of incomprehensible discourse that figured in another humorous anecdote said to have been told by the Rev. Andrew Thomson:

A clergyman in the country had a stranger preaching for him one day, and meeting his beadle, he said to him. "Well, Saunders, how did you like the sermon today?" "I watna, sir; it was rather ower plain and simple for me. I like thae sermons best that jumbles the joodgment and confoonds the sense. Od, sir, I never saw ane that coud come up to yoursell at that." (Ramsay 1874: 334-5; see also Johnston 1912: 252)

Some may perhaps sympathize with the definition of "metaphysics" given by the Scottish blacksmith: "Weel, Geordie, ye see it's just like this. When the pairty that listens disna ken what the pairty that speaks means, and when the pairty that speaks disna ken what he means himsel', that's metapheesics." (Johnstone 1897: 252)

A love of intellectual dispute, a far more highly educated population than most countries (Johnstone 1897: 199-200) and a religious tradition with a strong element of argumentative democracy naturally also produced jokes about rivalry and secession similar to the Welsh and Jewish joke cited earlier:

A friend of mine used to tell a story of an honest builder's views of church differences, which was very amusing, and quaintly professional. An English gentleman, who had arrived in a Scottish country town, was walking about to examine the various objects which presented themselves, and observed two rather handsome places of worship in course of erection nearly opposite to each other. He addressed a person, who happened to be the contractor for the chapels, and asked, "What was the difference between these two places of worship which were springing up so close to each other?"—meaning, of course, the difference of the theological tenets of the two congregations. The contractor, who thought only of architectural differences, innocently replied, "There may be a difference of sax feet in length, but there's no aboon a few inches in the breadth." "Would that all our religious differences could be brought within so narrow a compass!" The variety of church in a certain county of Scotland once called forth a sly remark upon our national tendencies to religious division and theological disputation. An English gentleman sitting on the box, and observing the great number of places of worship in the aforesaid borough, remarked to the coachman that there must be a great deal of religious feeling in a town which produced so many houses of God. "Na," said the man quietly, "it's no religion, it's *curstness*," i.e., crabbedness, insinuating that acerbity of temper, as well as zeal, was occasionally the cause of congregations being multiplied. (Ramsay 1874: 62-63; see also Johnston 1912: 340)

Ramsay's early tale of curstness of temper was still sufficiently apposite to appear in Johnston's (1912: 340) anthology of types of national humor, but by now the, at first equally controversial, process of reunion of the Presbyterian churches had begun and produced its own jokes in which the few remaining diehard secessionists are contrasted with the majority now willing to compromise and co-operate:

One night, at the breaking up of some social festivity in a remote Highland district, on an occasion in which some of the guests belonged to the United Free Church and others to the "legal" Free Church [those who rejected reunion], one of the latter, when he came out to the fresh air, betrayed signs of having partaken a little too freely, and required to be supported on his homeward journey by brethren who are now in the same communion with the United Presbyterians. He accepted somewhat grudgingly the assistance which was given him, and was heard muttering to himself, "I do not like to be helped along the road by men who are *not sound in the faith*." (Jerdan 1920: 220)

However, as popular interest in and enthusiasm for theological questions waned in Scotland during the twentieth century, as secularization made ecumenical mergers not only possible but necessary, so did the humorous treatment of predestination. The classic joke on the subject provides a mocking of the entire question and this outrageous opinion is conveyed through that stock figure, known for his uninhibited and irresponsible honesty, the drunk:

Always ready in a tight corner and quick to meet an emergency, a faithful member of a Glasgow kirk much addicted to too frequent liquid refreshment, met one of the elders of his congregation as he, the tippler, came out of a public-house one Saturday night. Unsteady, but wary, he bade the elder "a fine night!" But the elder fixed him with a meaning glare in his eye. Not a bit abashed, the unsteady one invited the other to gaze at that "bonnie mune" shining in the clear frosty night. Still that steady, boring gaze. Then, the embarrassed one links his arm in the elder's and confidentially says: "Now, Elder, tell me, between man to man, what dae ye really think aboot predestination?"

"We'll talk about predestination, Sandy, when you are in a more fitting condition."
"Na, Na Elder, when aw'm sober a dinna care a damn aboot predestination!" (Ferguson 1933: 26)

In theory, belief in predestination could lead to a settled fatalism and a withdrawal from a world whose future is already mapped out. In practice, as Max Weber (1930) was able to show, the members of the Calvinist churches developed a Protestant ethic of work, thrift and ceaseless activity, which is the basis of many jokes about canny Calvinists, not just the Scots but also the Dutch, the New England Yankees, the Swabians, the Swiss and, by extension, the Unitarian Cardis of West Wales (Davies 1992A, 1998: 43-62). A theme that is tied even more directly to predestination refers to the way in which the Scotsman's apparent submission to providence coexists with determined struggle on his own behalf. The point is explicitly rammed home by the comments of the learned compilers of the joke books who are deliberately using these humorous tales to illustrate their own general perceptions of Scottish life and character.

> Both in the Highlands and the Lowlands there are not wanting instances in which the relation of individual effort to Providence is not, as with Jonah, one of passive acquiescence, but is tacitly regarded as a kind of limited liability, as when Donald in crossing a ferry on a very stormy night was nearly drowned, and only after severe struggle contrived to scramble ashore. On reaching him his wife said to him, "Ah, Donald, Providence has been very good to you."

> "Yes, Mary," he replied, "but I was pretty clever too myself." (Kerr 1903: 282-3)
> ...the Scottish matter-of-fact view of things (may be) brought to bear upon a religious question without meaning to be profane or irreverent. Dr. Macleod was on a Highland loch when a storm came on which threatened serious consequences. The doctor, a large powerful man, was accompanied by a clerical friend of diminutive size and small appearance, who began to speak seriously to the boatman of their danger, and proposed that all present should join in prayer. "Na, na," said the chief boatman; "let the *little* ane gang to pray, but first the big ane maun (must) tak an oar." (Ramsay 1874: 21)

These last two humorous anecdotes again both contain a form of indirect boasting about Scottish virtues, about the ability of ordinary Scots to seek immediate practical solutions in the face of danger, rather than to acquiesce passively in their fate. In the jokes God helps those who help themselves. The individual Highlanders at the center of the jokes express themselves in a comic way and are indeed comic but they are also admirable and can be identified with the Scots and with Scottish virtues in general.

The keeping of the Sabbath has long been a central part of the teaching of the Presbyterian churches in Scotland and a distinct feature of Scottish national identity. It was upheld by the national Church of Scotland, and those Presbyterians who seceded from the establishment tended to be even stricter in their observation. The antithesis of this to be avoided with horror was not England, where the same regard for the Lord's Day existed though to a lesser degree, but the "Continental Sunday" during which the French, the Italians and the Germans were supposed to wallow in heedless dissipation. The peripheral peoples of Britain, the Scots, the Welsh and the people of Ulster could thus both mark out their separate identity by being stricter upholders of the Sabbath then the English and yet also proclaim that they were, therefore, the most Protestant, the most virtuous and the most British people in the entire United Kingdom (Davies 1992). The stricter churches or factions of churches within Scotland bore the same relation to Scotland as Scotland did to Britain and could claim that they were the most Sabbatarian, the most Calvinist and the most Scottish of Scots. At the same time, the more cultivated, cosmopolitan and well-travelled among the educated Scots realized that this degree of Sabbath observance could be seen as narrow in all senses of the word. Donald Carswell's account of John Stuart Blackie's loss of his vocation to become a Scottish Presbyterian minister while studying at the University of Berlin in 1829 makes this point vividly:

> Even his Sabbatarianism, which hitherto he had continued to wear with a dour defiance, was well-nigh stripped from him by a casual remark of Neander's that the Scottish notion of Sunday observance was "etwas jüdisch, nicht wahr?" (somewhat Jewish, don't you think?) This occurred in the course of a civil conversation at one of the Professor's Sunday evening receptions which Blackie, after some consideration, considered he might lawfully attend. Seldom has so trite a remark excited so much commotion in the hearer. It was the decisive moment of his life. For the first time, as he himself records, he realized that Scottish theology and Christianity were not convertible terms, and the discovery gave him a sudden distaste for the ministry. (Carswell 1927:136)

In the late nineteenth century the Scottish Sabbath was still a formidably rigorous institution such that:

> All secular amusements other than eating and sleeping, which were freely indulged in, were not merely forbidden; they were unthinkable....The writing of letters was winked at in liberal families, always provided that they were not business letters and were posted after dark. To read a novel was scandalous, while to open a newspaper (except for the purpose of referring to church notices) was the abomination of desolation. For the purpose of going to or from church, but not otherwise, it was lawful for the laity (though not expedient) to ride in a Sunday tramcar. For a minister, however, who must testify to the Church's disapproval of Sunday tramways, a cab was a religious necessity. (Carswell 1927: 134-5)

Today such attitudes and social practices have vanished except for a few ultra-strict communities, sects and congregations, notably in the Hebrides. Even in the latter part of the nineteenth century they were being undermined. Sunday trams (streetcars) and trains ran, despite, at times, considerable local opposition (Carswell 1927: 135, 203-4; Crowl 1986: 355) and they not merely involved highly visible Sunday working for their operatives but enabled bored or dissident individuals to escape the Sunday surveillance of their neighbors. In time, ease of travel and the joy of anonymity were to undermine social controls even further in the surveillance-free and in consequence shameless society of the late twentieth and early twenty-first centuries (Davies 1994, 1994 A). Even at the time those liberal Scottish Presbyterians who wrote and posted letters secretively clearly no longer inwardly believed in the sacredness of Sunday nor that God was watching them. If they thought He was, they either didn't care or else assumed that God didn't. Thus, both economic pressures and the slow fading of orthodox belief and practice were undermining the keeping of the Sabbath and those who fought against such changes came to be seen as anachronistic and even ludicrous. The liberal compilers of the joke books and memoirs, were anxious that such trends might go too far and destroy the Scottish Sabbath (which did in time come to pass), but saw the then slight degree of relaxation as a civilizing improvement on past rigor (Geikie 1904: 139-141). The jokes and comic anecdotes about excessive Sabbatarianism distanced the compilers from the ultra-rigorous but at the same time stated the secure Scottishness of and their own insight into and sympathy for the special character of Sunday. The jokes are still jokes between Scotsmen, between Protestants and between keepers of the Sabbath. For the compilers and editors they are in no sense a direct or fundamental attack on Scottish tradition but rather (a) an indirect statement and celebration of the tradition, and (b) a way of defining one's own moderate version of the tradition as the central one and the butts of the jokes as eccentric relations on the periphery. All these points can be illustrated both from the jokes and from the contexts and comments *explicitly* provided by the compilers.

The Scottish jokes and comic anecdotes about the Sabbath tend to have three characteristics. The first is that the excessively Sabbatarian are shown as neglecting other and possibly more central Christian values and virtues in their zeal for the Sabbath. The jokes do not mock the Sabbatarian principle per se but rather the excessive zeal of those who subordinate other principles to it or who follow the letter of the law rather than the spirit which giveth life. The second is that the butts of the jokes are men and women of low social standing and the jokes about them often portray them as seeking to admonish someone of more exalted social position, culture and understanding to whom they would normally defer. The third is the extreme Sabbatarians' laughable extension of Sabbath observance to cover babies, animals and machines, as if it were a law of nature rather than a social rule, albeit one of Divine origin.

Edward Ramsay is quite explicit in stressing the first point when introducing an anecdote that has since become a more modern anonymous joke:

> There sometimes appears to have been in our countrymen an undue preponderance of zeal for Sabbath observance as compared with the importance attached to *other* religious duties and especially as compared with the virtue of sobriety. The following dialogue between Mr. Macnee of Glasgow, the celebrated artist, and an old Highland acquaintance whom he had met with unexpectedly, will illustrate the contrast between the severity of judgment passed upon treating the Sabbath with levity and the lighter censure attached to indulgence in whisky. Mr. Macnee begins, "Donald, what brought you here?"
> "Ou, weel, sir, it was a baad place yon; they were baad folk—but they're a God-fearin' set o'folk here!"
> "Well, Donald," said Mr. M., "I'm glad to hear it."
> "Ou ay, sir, 'deed are they; an' I'll gie ye an instance o't. Last Sabbath, just as the kirk was skailin', (coming out) there was a child frae Dumfries comin' along the road whustlin', an' lookin' *as happy* as if it was ta middle o' ta week; weel, sir, oor laads is a God-fearin' set o' laads, an' they were just comin' oot o' the kirk—'od they yokit (set) upon him, an' a'most killed him!"
> Mr. M., to whom their zeal seemed scarcely sufficiently well directed to merit his approbation, then asked Donald whether it had been drunkenness that induced the depravity of his former neighbours?
> "Weel, weel, sir," said Donald, with some hesitation, "*may*-be; I'll no say but it micht."
> "Depend upon it," said Mr. M., "it's a bad thing whisky." "Weel, weel, sir," replied Donald, "I'll no say but it *may*"; adding in a very decided tone—'speeciallie *baad* whusky!" (Ramsay 1874: 73-4)

It should be noted that Macnee is a named individual and a "celebrated artist" from the city who speaks standard English whereas Donald is only known to the reader by a generic first name used for Highlanders in Scottish jokes (much as the Irish might be represented in a joke as Pat and Mike or other groups as Taffy, Rastus, or Cousin Jack) and speaks in a local dialect. Macnee is clearly the person of higher social standing in the joke. These same points are equally well represented in two tales recorded by John Kerr; the first is humorous, the second is supposed to convey a moral rather than to amuse:

> Another instance of the same narrowness of view is furnished in the experience of a young English lady who, when she was a visitor at a countryhouse in Ross-shire, was reprimanded by an old gamekeeper for a perfectly harmless expression of surprise, which he thought was swearing. On the following Sunday, when she was out walking, she lost sight for a moment of her pet dog and gave a whistle to bring it to heel. This same gamekeeper heard her, and with sternly reproving tone and deprecatory shake of the head said, "Ach, my leddy! sweerin's bad and bad enough, but whustlin' on the Sabbath! Ow!! Ow!!!"
>
> A less ludicrous, but in its moral or rather immoral aspect more objectionable, instance than the foregoing is that of a Sutherland crofter who, in his deathbed, while bewailing his short-comings, confessed to having stolen a sheep two years before—a theft which had not been proved against any one. The minister to whom he made the confession hoped he had prayed for forgiveness.
>
> Yes," said the man; "but that's not the biggest sin I have committed."
>
> "What else have you done?" asked the minister.
>
> "Well, sir," he replied, "there was one Sabbath I did not go to church for I was not well, and I was very thirsty, for it was a very warm day, and I went out to the well and brought in a canful of water, and I cannot get that sin out of my head."
>
> It speaks equally for the irrational state of Sabbatarian feeling, whether we suppose that the man's contrition for carrying in the water was genuine, or that he thought the confession of it would raise him in the minister's estimation. Under either suppositon morality fares badly. (Kerr 1903: 318-9)

It is odd, yet significant, that Kerr should have linked two such disparate tales together in this way and also that he feels it necessary to spell out the significance of the second story to ensure that the didactic point he wishes to make is not blurred even by such little humor as the second tale may possess.

Once again the Sabbatarians of the jokes are humble folk, a game-keeper and a crofter, respectively, who are from the remote highland counties of Rosshire and Sutherland in the far north of Scotland; the gamekeeper is shown admonishing a person of higher status namely a lady visiting a country-house who is not Scots but English and presumably ignorant of local mores. The second tale told by Kerr may well have its roots in actual events.

Sir Archibald Geikie, the noted Scottish geologist, had also had direct experience of the rigid Sabbatarianism of the Northern High-lands, where some of Scotland's most determined Presbyterians lived on top of some of Scotland's most interesting rock formations. He and his fellow geologists often needed to work on a Sunday to take full advantage of those few fine days in summer when exploring remote mountains was possible. The local people disapproved and would not assist him in any way on the Sabbath though they were quite willing to charge him rent or to hire vehicles to him provided he drove himself (Geikie 1904: 128-131). Geikie in a long anecdote about Queen Victoria, also manages to cite what has become one of the classic gags about the Scots' obsession with the Sabbath:

> An incident which illustrates the strictness of Sabbath observance in the North High-lands has been told me by a friend. During one of her tours in the Highlands Queen Victoria visited Ross-shire. When spending a Sunday at Loch Maree, the Royal party, tempted by the beauty of the day, made an expedition by boat to one of the islands of the loch. This "worldly acting" upon the Lord's day caused a great scandal in the neighbourhood, and eventually the Free Church Presbytery took up the matter and addressed a letter to the Queen "dealing with" her for her conduct. Our good Queen was naturally much disquieted that she had unwittingly offended any section of her faithful subjects, and consulted one of her chaplains, a distinguished minister of the Church of Scotland, who was then at Balmoral, as to what she ought to do. He counselled her not to take any notice of the letter, and allayed her anxiety by recounting to her the following incident illustrative of the attitude of mind of the Highlanders towards all departures, however trivial, from their notions of strict Sabbath observance. The story greatly amused the Queen and at her request it had to be repeated to other members of the royal household.
> A Highland minister, after the services of the Sunday were over, was noticed saunter-ing by himself in meditative mood along the hillside above the manse. Next day he was waited on by one of the ruling elders, who came to point out the sin of which he had been guilty, and the evil effect which his lapse from right ways could not fail to have in the parish. The clergyman took the rebuke in good part, but tried to show the remon-strant that the action of which he complained was innocent and lawful, and he was about to cite the famous example of a Sabbath walk, with the plucking of the ears of corn, as set forth in the Gospels, when he was interrupted with the remark: "Ou ay, sir, I ken weel what you mean to say; but, for my pairt, I hae nefer thocht the better o' them for breakin' the Sawbbath." (Geikie 1904: 136-8)

The first part of the tale is set once again in remote Rosshire and involves a Free Church Presbytery, self-confident in its own position as the leaders of a spiritual elite having the democratic temerity to rebuke Queen Victoria for her conduct. She is then reassured by a chaplain from the National Church of Scotland that these remote folk are a bit strange. Queen Victoria was amused and perhaps re-lieved. Once again, of course, the elder is made to speak in dialect. The minister's comments are not quoted but reported in standard English, a technique that avoids giving him a particular kind of voice. It is worth noting, too, that Geikie's version of the minister and elder joke has been very much toned down from the version in circulation earlier, given by Ramsay:

An Edinburgh minister was officiating for a few weeks for a friend, in a country district where Calvinistic orthodoxy and Sabbath observance were of the strictest. On the first Sunday, the Minister, after service, took his stick in his hand and set off to enjoy a stroll. On the outskirts of the village, he happened to pass the house of one of the elders. The old man, who had observed him, came out, and asked if he was going anywhere on a work of mercy.

"No," said the minister, "I am just enjoying a meditative walk amidst the beauties of Nature."

"I was suspectin' as muckle (much)," said the elder. "But you that's a minister o' the Gospel should ken that this is no' a day for ony sic thing."

"You forget," said the minister, "that our Lord Himself walked in the fields with His disciples on the Sabbath Day."

"Weel," said the elder, doggedly, "I ken that. But I dinna think the mair o' *Him* ayther, for it." (Ramsay 1874: 50)

Many of the jokes and anecdotes relate the strange (in the eyes of the outsiders and indeed of the Scottish liberals) lengths to which the determined Scottish Sabbatarian would extend his or her concern so that it covered even interactions with babies and pets and the actions of animals and automata. Once again the contrast between the Sabbatarians who have humble occupations and broad speech and the elevated status of those who recorded the tales and passed them onto collectors such as Dean Ramsay and Sir Archibald Geikie is very striking:

A story is told of a young clergyman on the mainland who had not been long placed in his charge when rumours began to circulate about his orthodoxy. Some of his friends hearing these reports set themselves to enquire into the grounds for them. But they could only elicit vague hints and suggestions. At last they came upon an old woman who declared roundly that the minister was "no soun" (not orthodox).

"Not sound! what makes you think that?" "Weel then," she answered, "I maun (must) tell ye. I was seein' him wi' my ain een, standin' at his window on the Lord's Day, dandlin' his bairn." (Geikie 1904: 136)

There was one lady who carried her sanctimonious scruples so far that she always rose a little earlier than usual on Sunday morning, and took care, as her first duty, to carry a merry-hearted and loud-throated canary down to the cellar that its carol might not disturb the quiet and solemnity of the day." (Geikie 1904: 127)

A manifestation of even still greater strictness on the subject of Sabbath desecration, I have received from a relative of the family in which it occurred. About fifty years ago the Hon. Mrs. Stewart lived in Heriot Row, who had a cook, Jeannie by name, a paragon of excellence. One Sunday morning when her daughter (afterwards Lady Elton) went into the kitchen, she was surprised to find a new jack (recently ordered and which was constructed on the principle of going constantly without winding up) wholly paralysed and useless. Miss Stewart naturally inquired what accident had happened to the new jack, as it had stopped. The mystery was soon solved by Jeannie indignantly exclaiming that "she was nae gaeing to hae the fule thing clocking and rinning about in *her* kitchen a' blessed Sabbath day." (Ramsay 1874: 72-3)

Lady Macneil supplies an excellent pendant to Miss Stewart's story about the jack going on the Sunday. Her henwife had got some Dorking fowls, and on Lady M. asking if they were laying many eggs, she replied with great earnestness, "Indeed my leddy, they lay every day, no' excepting the blessed Sabbath." (Ramsay 1874: 74)

These old-fashioned anecdotes and jokes about canny, Calvinist, Sabbatarian Scots rooted in particular places associated with particular persons and events and sandwiched between memoirs, moral admonitions and assorted pieces of serious folklore were soon supplemented by commercial joke books, a large proportion of which were published in Scotland. The joke books were and are mass-produced paperbacks published for profit and entertainment alone and the jokes are shorter, crisper, more efficient and written in a compromise between standard English and the various Scottish dialects that enabled them to become best-sellers outside Scotland as well as within. The Scots had become the people of the joke book.

Perhaps the most successful of these were the tartan-covered series published by Valentine of Dundee in the late 1920s: including the Marquess of Aberdeen and Temair's *Jokes Cracked by Lord Aberdeen* (1929), John Joy Bell's *Hoots*(1929), Allan Junior's *Canny Tales Fae Aberdeen* (1925) and *Aberdeen Again* (1929) , Sir Harry Lauder's *My Best Scotch Stories* (1929), Graham Moffat's *The Pawky Scot* (1928) and Sir James Taggart's *Stories Told by Sir James Taggart* (1927), together with James Ferguson's (1933) often reprinted collection *The Table in a Roar* most of which is Scots. The appearance of these best-selling Scottish joke books irritated the purist Professor A. H. Charteris (1932: 18-19), who rated them well below the kinds of traditional Scottish anecdotes cited earlier and felt that the Lord Provost (mayor) of Aberdeen, Sir James Taggart and the Marquess of Aberdeen had lost caste by taking part in the 'Tartan Covered Treacheries.' Charteris (1932: 33) seems particularly to have disliked "the trick of surprise ending...in all these mass-production tales." Yet it was this very mechanism, the recognition that jokes consist essentially of a sudden switching between scripts by means of a punch-line (Raskin 1985) that enabled the Scots to transform locally rooted anecdotes into internationally known jokes.

Even so, at that time, the jokes still remained distinctively Scottish, as can be seen from one example that Charteris (1932: 33) does concede is successful.

The scene is Deeside, the time the Aberdonian Spring Holiday (roughly, Easter Monday), the wind is sharp from ENE. —whiles with hail. Stamping about in order to keep warm, a wee laddie falls into the famous river. Among the trippers intense interest, but no effort at rescue, so cold is the day. A strong, silent Englishman, stripping off muffler, over-coat and jacket, plunges in and brings the drookit bairn to land, and himself resumes his welcome garments. An active, wee "thristle" of a mannie worms his way through the crowd, taps him on the shoulder and demands:
"Are 'ee the chielie 'at savit my laddie's life, mister?"
The Englishman breaks silence with a shivering "Yes!" whereat the other:
"*Whaur's his bunnet then* (Where's his cap then)?" (Charteris 1932: 33-4)

Numerous other variants, both Scottish and Jewish (Raskin 1992: 101-8 and 1993: 89-97), of this canny tale also exist but the version given is distinctively Scottish and does contain a good deal of local detail which, though pleasing to the exiled Charteris in Sydney, does not contribute directly to the narrative. The Scots were still in control of their jokes; it was still the golden age of the Scottish joke before the international canny script took over. By contrast the 1978 version of the above joke reads:

Are you the man that dived into the Clyde to pull my wee boy out of the water?
Aye.
Well, where's his cap? (Hodes 1978: 58)

Even though this version appears in a compilation of Scottish jokes by the Scottish journalist Max Hodes (1978) there is little that is Scottish about it other than the canny script and the feeble markers "aye" and "wee." Scottish jokes circulate all over the world today even in Czech, French, Italian, Slovak and Swedish but how Scottish are they? Nonetheless, the Scots of the twenty-first century maintain their own websites full of distinctively Scottish jokes (http://electricscotland.com/kin-Mcgillivray/folio2.html).

The trajectory of the Scottish joke is curiously similar to that of the jokes of the Jews. Until the late nineteenth century neither people enjoyed a reputation for being particularly humorous and, indeed, had to fend off accusations of lacking a sense of humor. Then quite independently they both became peoples of the joke and known for the production of collections of jokes and anecdotes about themselves on a scale unknown among other peoples. Some of the books were learned productions by distinguished scholars and professional men interspersed with comments about ethnic and religious identity, social change and moral values. Others were pure entertainment. It has been in either case a remarkable efflorescence of self-directed humor and of humor directed towards a collective self.

In support of the comparison let me quote the hypothesis put forward by Elliott Oring (1992: 116) concerning the nature and history of Jewish jokes:

> *Jewish humor is a relatively modern invention. The conceptualization of a humor that was in some ways characteristic of and distinctive to the Jewish people begins only in Europe during the nineteenth century.* In support of this hypothesis, I would merely point out that as late as 1893 Hermann Adler, the Chief Rabbi of London, still found it necessary to defend the Jews against the charge that they were a humorless people. Today the great collections of Jewish jokes that are instinctively cited to evidence the existence of a Jewish humor are invariably compilations of the twentieth century....This is not to deny that humor was present in biblical, talmudic and medieval Jewish society but only to suggest that it held no special place and was not bound up with any national, religious or ethnic identity. (emphasis in original)

The Scots may have got there a little earlier (and in a less modern style) than the Jews, but in essence the patterns are similar.

We are now faced with having to explain why the Scots (and indeed the Jews) became the people of the joke and acquired an international reputation for self-mocking jokes when other peoples *did not*. What is it that is special about the Scots? What qualities do the Scots share with the Jews that would account for the pre-eminence of these two peoples in the history of joking? The question "why" is, of course, a macro-question that can *only* be tackled at a macro-level by making broad cultural and historical *comparisons* and the answers can *not* be derived easily and directly from the texts or even from the jokers own perceptions. However, we can get some hints as to where to look for answers by asking the easier question, "how," which *is* rooted in the texts and the comments of the jokers.

The learned compilers of the moralizing joke books had many motives including the laudable ones of entertaining the public both in Scotland and elsewhere (the publishers tend to be Scottish and based in Scotland, but with broad markets and with offices also in London and, indeed, in English-speaking countries outside Great Britain), making money and enhancing their own reputations and popularity. But they also clearly and explicitly wanted to memorialize and celebrate Scotland and its people. At a time of rapid social and economic change they wanted to record in writing Scotland's folklore, peculiarities and distinctiveness before it was erased by modernity, secularization and the ever-increasing degree of contact and commerce with its larger neighbor England to whom Scotland was linked by language and a railway and telephone system that seemed to have annihilated distance.

Many late nineteenth-century folklore collectors had similar motives and feelings (Rockwell 1981), a mixture of nostalgia and romantic nationalism and a fear that distinctive traditions and folkways would disappear altogether. The Scots were only different in that a *very high proportion* of their recorded materials consisted of jokes and humorous anecdotes, no doubt partly because these were very *widely available* among this by now truly humorous people and partly because the collectors and compilers placed a *special value* on humorous items; they liked their jokes and saw the jokes as distinctively Scottish and as contributing to a timely and favorable portrait of Scotland. But jokes are popular and entertaining and saleable to a far greater degree than say trite proverbs, ancient superstitions, obsolete agricultural rituals and practices or the details of peat digging, midden construction, cottaging (in the original sense of the word) or the outer garments of maidservants. Folklore is pyrites, but jokes earn silver. The worthies who compiled the earliest books no doubt had an eye to this point and so did their publishers who were after all Scotsmen on the make. That there was a local market for such books (and one on which an international market could be built) is a further tribute to the Scottish sense of humor and the Scottish sense that their own humor was special, distinctive and a suitable vehicle for national self-promotion.

It is clear from the writings of the Scottish humor compilers that Scottish self-mockery is ambiguous in yet another sense. The Scots are a highly differentiated nation by region, social class and education. The cultivated, educated religious liberals and writers in standard English who compiled Scotland's early joke books clearly set themselves apart from the fundamentalist, Calvinist, Sabbatarian, dialect-speaking rustics who were the butts of their jokes. Yet the cultivated joke tellers did *not* reject these people but rather saw them in an almost sentimental way as an anachronistic version of themselves, as a relic of an older, more truly Scottish tradition now being eroded by secularization, Anglicization and bland civility. In recording and mocking the comic foibles of the latter the joke tellers are raising them up as well as putting them down. For the joke tellers the butts of the jokes may be clearly different from "people like us" but they are *also* still our ain folk (own people), our brother Scots.

The joke tellers are making fun of the very essence of Scottishness and yet they are in no sense denying their own Scottish identity; on the contrary they are proclaiming it. Social mobility and a degree of assimilation may increase social distance but they need not lead to estrangement for a strong sense of mutual belonging remains. Individuals in this situation telling jokes can always avoid making fun of themselves as individuals but they can still be reasonably described as mocking their own group. The jokers may be less Scottish than the ideal typical Scots who are the butts of their jokes but they are in no sense un-Scottish or anti-Scottish.

What happens when the jokes are purveyed to an outside audience is that these subtle internal differences cease to be perceived as part of or relevant to the joke. Jokes about a faction become jokes about Scots in general. Jokes about canny Aberdonians become jokes about canny Scots with Aberdeen being seen by non-Scots simply as a typical or an extreme case of Scots in general. The differences between Highlanders and Lowlanders or Aberdonians and whustlin' Fifers are neither apparent nor relevant to the English, the Welsh or the Irish, let alone Italians or Czechs. All dissolves into a single script of the canny Scot and in this way an undifferentiated self-mockery was established.

Yet the question remains, why are the Scots, together with the Jews, pre-eminent in self-mocking humor? What do the two groups have in common that set them apart from other peoples in this respect and, indeed, in many others?

Both the Scots and Jews are minorities, albeit in very different ways, and also the butts in many countries of jokes about their allegedly canny (crafty and stingy) qualities. Most minorities tell jokes about their own members such that it would at first seem that Jewish and Scottish jokes are merely a particular instance of a more general phenomenon, namely the asymmetry (Middleton and Moland 1959; Nevo 1986; Zenner 1970) between the humor of those who belong to dominant majorities and the humor of groups who are, in one sense or another, subordinate. The members of dominant groups tend to tell jokes *mainly* about minorities whose culture is peripheral to their own and they do not usually tell jokes about their own group. By contrast those who belong to minorities or to nations peripheral but similar to a larger national entity tell more jokes about their own group (and may well find them funnier) than about the majority.

Empirical studies of joking behavior and preferences have shown that the Irish in Britain tell jokes about Irish people (O'Donnell cited in Wilson 1979), that Polish Americans enjoy jokes about Poles (Kusielewicz 1969), that African Americans tell and enjoy jokes about members of their own group (Middleton 1959; Oring 1992), as do the Druze (Zenner 1970). In Israel where the Jews are in a majority and dominate the major institutions of the society, Arabs as well as Jews can show a preference for jokes that disparage Arabs rather than Jews (Nevo 1986; Ziv 1984:159).

By virtue of their social location the members of a minority have to live in two cultures that may have different languages, religions, values and ways of life (Glazer and Moynihan 1975:14). For all the lip-service paid to cultural pluralism members of a majority do not have to take account of minority ways of life to the same extent. Polish Americans know full well what mainstream America is about but Americans in general are, as indicated in chapter 8, completely ignorant of the history, culture and traditions of the Poles. The Scots of necessity have long known a great deal about England, its history, religion and mores because they have often needed to seek employment there or to influence British institutions run largely by English people. The English neither can nor need to return the compliment. Those who belong to an established majority are enclosed in a bubble of their own "normality" and, therefore, see the behavior of minorities as comic deviations from their own taken-for-granted world in which the universal is fused with the particular. Christian Americans are unable to see that their version of America is comic until someone like Philip Roth's (1969: 144) Alexander Portnoy stands outside their assumptions and complains about this self-contained majority's unawareness of the way in which, whatever the American Constitution may say, they act as if their religion is the core of and an officially established part of American national identity:

> I am into Irvington and it is simply awful: not only is there a tree conspicuously ablaze in every parlor but the houses themselves are outlined with colored bulbs advertising Christianity, and phonographs are pumping "Silent Night" out into the street as though— as though? it were the national anthem. (Roth 1969: 144)

Alexander Portnoy, as a self-consciously Jewish "complainer," can see that the Christians of Irvington (Irving's town) are ludicrous in their assumption that their entire nation is religiously as one, but it is not a humorous observation that most American Christians would or could have made for themselves, though no doubt they laughed at Roth's comic observations.

Nonetheless, most minorities are not noted for their creative capacity for self-mockery and, although they frequently do tell and enjoy jokes about their own group, they are but rarely the originators of the jokes. Sometimes those who are the butts of stupidity jokes are also noted for their skilled use of repartee and figurative language, and famous for their locally generated anecdotes as in the case of the Newfoundlanders discussed in chapter 6 or the Irish (Davies 1988A), but their jokes still lack the analytical skills and the self-awareness displayed in jokes invented about themselves by the butts of *canny* jokes such as the Jews and the Scots. But it is also the case that most groups who are the butt of canny jokes on a local basis do not display a Scottish or Jewish level of skill and degree of self-awareness in self-mockery. So far as the author is aware, these qualities are not to be found in canny jokes told by and about Gabrovonians in Bulgaria, Regimontanos in Mexico, Paisas in Colombia, Laihians in Finland, Isfahanis in Iran or Swabians in Germany, groups whose ethnic identity is unproblematically the same as that of the national majority. Such groups neither need nor have the advanced capacity for self-reflection found among the Jews and the Scots. They are the butt of canny jokes *only* because their local economic circumstances have given them a reputation for commercial acumen.

The Scots and Jews share this reputation but also display a sharp awareness of a distinctive and highly valued identity that is in one sense or another problematic, and that raises the questions "Who are we?" "Why are we what we are?" "How do we define ourselves?" Also both Scots and Jews have enjoyed a strong intellectual tradition that enables such questions properly to be explored. It is the questioning, disputing, argumentative quality of Judaism and of the Christian religion in Scotland and the corresponding requirements of literacy and study that have led both to the secular intellectual achievements of the Scots and the Jews, and also to their capacity for self-reflective joking. In both Scottish and Jewish jokes self-awareness extends even to the very process of being argumentative which makes the self-reflective jokes possible. As we have seen, Scottish jokes laugh directly at the Scots Presbyterians' national love of disputation, hair-splitting and schism, which is also, as we shall see in chapter 3, a strong theme in Jewish jokes and humor. Here lies the key to the humorous pre-eminence of the two peoples. The self-mocking Scottish humorous tradition that I have expounded and analyzed is not perhaps quite as rich, as profound, as extensive or as famous as that of the Jews but that will be true of *any* mode of thought in which the Jews have excelled. Perhaps an analogy will make the point clear. Jews of Eastern and Central European origin or ancestry have made a pre-eminent contribution out of all proportion to their numbers to demanding disciplines such as physics or philosophy; the Scots may not be able to rival them but they have produced Adam Smith and David Hume, Clerk Maxwell and Lord Kelvin so that they clearly come a good second and have the same *kind* of intellectual tradition as the Jews. There is also a very large corpus of Scottish jokes and a substantial proportion of them are directed against the Scots themselves. It is thus reasonable to compare Scottish and Jewish jokes and to seek common characteristics and origins for them. By doing so it is possible to provide explanations for *both* sets of jokes along the lines indicated above and also to refute some of the hypotheses that have been made about Jewish humor based on its supposedly unique qualities, qualities generated by the particular and peculiar history and social location of the Jewish people. That is the task of the following chapter.

3

The Balanced Jewish Sense of Humor

The Jews are the one group that can be said to excel the Scots in the production of jokes and humor and particularly of self-mocking jokes. However, even though the number of self-mocking Jewish jokes exceeds that generated by the Scots, the proportion of Jewish jokes that are self-mocking is probably lower than is the case with jokes of Caledonian origin. The Jews have been as successful in inventing jokes about outsiders, enemies and deserters as about themselves in a way that is not found among the self-deprecating Scots. For this reason I shall speak of the balanced Jewish sense of humor.

The idea that the Jews had a uniquely self-mocking sense of humor was most famously advanced by Freud (1960 [1905]) and endorsed by Diesendruck (1946: 46), Grotjahn (1970), and Mikes (1980). Freud (1960 [1905]: 112) wrote in *Jokes and Their Relation to the Unconscious*: "I do not know whether there are many other instances of a people making fun to such a degree of its own character."

The Scots, however, provide just such another instance of "such a degree" and it is necessary to seek a better, more elegant, more parsimonious explanation of these two instances of highly developed self-mockery that will supersede the previous limited and particular explanations of this facet of Jewish humor. These earlier explanations of Jewish self-mocking humor lacked a proper comparative dimension and got ensnared in irrelevant discussions of specific details of Jewish experience and character.

Freud seems to have known little of Scotland and its center of canny jokes—the city of Aberdeen. On the death of his former disciple, the excommunicated and much anathematized Alfred Adler (who was also an apostate, a convert to Protestantism), in Aberdeen in 1937, Freud wrote to Arnold Zweig:

I don't understand your sympathy for Adler. For a Jew boy out of a Viennese suburb a death in Aberdeen is an unheard of career in itself and a proof of how far he had got on. The world really rewarded him richly for his service in having contradicted psycho-analysis. (Quoted in Roazen 1976: 222)

On the face of it, Freud may have accepted that Aberdeen (the town of Clerk Maxwell and Robertson Smith) was no mean city, but he clearly did not know that it was *the* mean city or he would not have been able to resist including this in his offensive and unbalanced letter.

The existence of a self-mocking humor among the Scots whose recent history has been quite devoid of persecution or serious hostility from outsiders tends to undermine the thesis that the quality of self-mockery in Jewish humor is the result of anti-Semitic oppression. In the latter case the oppression was, of course, real but the Scottish comparison shows that it was not the key factor in producing a self-derogatory humor. The Scots have never had to endure this kind of malice and loathing yet their jokes indisputably "disparage" Scots. Nor can Scottish humor be seen as a defense-mechanism or as restrained aggression directed inwards (Saper 1991: 53). The Scots are the proclaimers of *Nemo me impune lacessit* or, more colloquially, "who daur meddle wi' me?" It is indeed very wise not to meddle with them or to quarrel with a man in a Glasgow bar who calls you James and enquires if you are all right or what you are looking at (for Scottish humor on this point, see Kington 1977: 155; Pattison 1990). But the members of this unco' aggressive nation are the same Scots who relentlessly make fun of themselves.

In particular, the study of the self-mocking Scottish jokes of the latter part of the nineteenth century and the earlier decades of the twentieth is a refutation of Grotjahn's (1970: 138) theory that "Aggression turned against the self seems to be an essential feature of the Jewish joke. It is as if the Jew tells the enemy: 'You do not need to attack us. We can do that ourselves and even better'" (see also comment by Novak and Waldoks 1981: xv-xvi). Martin Grotjahn (1970:137) describes a Jewish joke teller as "taking the enemy's dagger, splitting a hair in mid-air, stabbing himself and giving it back with the query 'can you do it half as well?'" The Scottish case undermines this thesis at two levels. First the Scots in recent times have not been attacked by outside enemies with daggers, whether real or metaphorical. The Scots have not had to respond to pogroms, mendacious ritual-murder accusations, segregation and exclusion, persecution and genocide nor to a hostile ideology demonizing them and interpreting their distinctive traits and traditions within a framework resembling a paranoid fantasy (on the Jewish experience in this regard, see Carmichael 1992; Cohn 1970; Dundes 1991, 1997: 92-119; Gurian 1946). Rather the Scots provided warriors for what was then the world's leading imperial power and were perceived by others as openly proud and aggressive. There are no social circumstances that would support the idea that the Scottish self-critical jokes are evidence of masochism, and the Scottish jokes are sufficiently similar in content to the corresponding Jewish jokes to undermine the idea that the latter are in and of themselves masochistic.

Secondly, the Scottish jokes can be read as a form of self-congratulation and self-promotion through self-mockery, a way of boasting without being immodest. Given that the Jews, despite vicious denigration from outsiders, had like the Scots a sense of being special, of being achievers, of being a moral example, and a light for others, why should self-mocking Jewish jokes not also be seen primarily as self-congratulation and self-promotion? The ambiguity of humor is such as to make this easily possible.

The existence and nature of the Scottish jokes negates altogether the idea that Jewish humor is in some sense pathological (Diesendruck 1946: 45-6). This thesis has been best summed up in Elliott Oring's (1992: 120) critical account of it:

> The conceptualisation of the Jewish joke as pathological, an irrational response to the Jewish condition, derives from an aside by Freud on the matter of Jewish jokes in *Jokes and their Relation to the Unconscious*: "A particularly favourable occasion for tendentious jokes is presented when the intended rebellious criticism is directed against the subject himself, or to put it more cautiously, against someone in whom the subject has a share—a collective person, that is (the subject's own nation for instance). The occurrence of self-criticism as a determinant may explain how it is that a number of the most apt jokes…have grown up on the soil of Jewish popular life. They are stories created by Jews and directed against Jewish characteristics…" Although Freud was not the first to conceptualise self-criticism as distinctive of Jewish humor, set within the framework of his psychology of the unconscious, his observation resonated with new meaning. The observation conditioned analysts Martin Grotjahn's and Theodore Reik's masochistic conceptualisations of Jewish wit. In truth both Grotjahn and Reik clearly recognized the positive psychological dimensions of Jewish humor, but their fundamental conceptualisation of Jewish humor was within the context of psychopathology. Such conceptualisations of the Jewish joke, of course, accorded very well with more general theories of Jewish self-hatred; and the notion that a pathological self-hatred underlies self-critical Jewish jokes is so strongly implied that it often has to be explicitly denied.(Oring 1992: 120)

Dan Ben-Amos (1973:119) has written, "perhaps the only validation of the Jewish masochism thesis is its mass acceptance by Jewish intellectuals for the actual evidence derived from the jokes themselves does not support it." The thesis might have had a superficial plausibility for intellectuals in Central and Eastern Europe who could perceive the impact of intense anti-Semitic hostility and hatred leading particular individual Jews genuinely to hate themselves for being Jewish (Diesendruck 1946: 45-6; Oring 1984: 106-113). What is more puzzling is that the theory should have had an appeal in America in the latter half of the twentieth century when anti-Semitism had become more of a nuisance than a threat. Yet as William Novak and Moishe Waldoks (1981: xvi), the editors of the justly celebrated collection, *The Big Book of Jewish Humor*, noted:

> The allegation of Jewish masochism (otherwise known as self-hatred) has been made with increasing frequency in recent years (especially against Philip Roth) and while there are certainly elements of it among other contemporary Jewish humorists, it is important to ask whether this reductive concept is the best way to describe an uninhibited and frequently critical treatment of Jewish life. Jewish humor, after all, is an extension of the Jewish mind, which has traditionally been a highly self-critical instrument, reluctant to accept anything at face value and not unwilling to search for evidences of the storm beneath the tranquillity of American life.... In addition the Jewish community in the absence of severe anti-Semitism in America has at times been overly sensitive to those Jewish artists and writers who are occasionally unflattering in their descriptions of Jewish middle-class life. It is sometimes suggested that such descriptions provide "ammunition" for anti-Semites but one suspects that the real sin lies elsewhere.... What may also disturb the official Jewish community is that some of the contemporary humorists such as Lenny Bruce and Wallace Markfield taunt not only the Jews but also the *goyim*...the real offense of the contemporary humorists is not in their dwelling on Jewish inferiority, but rather their revealing the more or less secret feelings of Jewish superiority. (Novak and Waldoks 1981: xvi)

The Scottish evidence suggests that a vein of superiority may well be present in such supposedly self-derogatory humor. Scottish self-mockery can be used as and read as a subtle form of boasting rather, like English understatement (Davies 1990: 250-53). What the Scots' humor of their golden age of jokes lacked, though, was the thorough trouncing of outsiders that is to be found in Jewish jokes and humor. Scottish jokes, in the same manner as Jewish jokes, often portray the canny Scotsman as victorious over an unsuspecting neighbor, but there are no distinctively Scottish jokes about non-Scots as such. There is no generic term for non-Scots equivalent to *goyim* for a group that could be made the butt of jokes about outsiders in general. Scottish jokes about, say, the English, the Irish, the Welsh, the

Americans, etc., are no different from those told about these same groups elsewhere; they are not distinctively Scottish. The distinctive quality of Jewish jokes that emerges from a comparison with the jokes of the Scots is not the existence of self-mocking jokes but of numerous and uniquely Jewish jokes that make fun of non-Jews.

Thus, Scottish humor and Jewish humor are similar in that they are both self-mocking, even though this *can* be used as a form of self-praise because of the ambiguous nature of humor, but Jewish humor is, *more balanced* in that it *also* aggressively makes fun of outsiders—the goyim, the Christians, apostates, etc. In contrast to the Scots, the Jews not only produce and own jokes about themselves, but invent distinctive jokes about others. Self-mockery is shared with the Scots, but the ability to create substantial numbers of excellent mocking jokes about large, powerful, encircling and often hostile majorities is uniquely Jewish. Far from being merely self-mocking and, by implication, pathological, Jewish humor is a means of playing with aggression that is launched *in all directions*, for it makes fun of everything and everyone. Jewish jokes are better balanced than those of other peoples.

Jewish humorous references to *goyische kop* (gentile head, stupidity), *goyische nachus* (trivia that give pleasure to gentiles), "*for goyim*" (a stupid statement that only gentiles would believe) or *shikses* are a way of laughing at outsiders as an undifferentiated generic category much as the Japanese laugh at *henna gaijin* (funny non-Japanese). Much of the humor of Lenny Bruce and more recently Jackie Mason repeatedly played with this distinction in a way that made fun of *both* groups. But as noted earlier there is no Scottish word for someone who is not-Scots, nor do the Scots have as clear a boundary between themselves and those who hold some other identity. In Jewish jokes and humor the goyim often have a purely negative identity; they are what the Jews are not.

Why did God make goyim?
Somebody has to buy retail. (Novak and Waldoks 1981:92)

Watch the gentile tourists come to this neighborhood from out of town. Just look at their faces. Did you ever see such placidity, such comfort, such serenity? They don't know where they are. They have no idea. No matter what they see, it's better than nothing.
"Hello Clyde, nice to see you. What's over there? A building? Good. What's over there? Nothing? Good."
"Where are you going?"
"Nowhere."
"Good. I'll go with you." (Mason 1987: 79)

Two gentiles met in the street.
"How's business? "
"Fine, and thank you for asking."
(Jewish, American, Chicago 2000)

Modern American and British Jewish jokes in particular poke fun at Christians and even laugh at the central mysteries of their faith which again indicates a very balanced Jewish sense of humor, one that is by no means limited to self-mockery:

An old Jew is run down in front of a church. A priest runs out and whispers in his ear, "Do you believe in the Father, the Son and the Holy Ghost?"
The Jew opens his eyes. "I'm dying and he asks me riddles." (Eliezer 1984: 26; see also 30, 58, 87)

An elderly Jewish man walks into a jewelry store to buy his wife a present. "How much is this?" he asks the clerk, pointing to a sterling silver crucifix.
"That's six hundred dollars, sir," replies the clerk.
"Nice," says the man. "And without the acrobat?" (Novak and Waldoks 1981: 219)

Two poor and elderly Jews, looking for a warm place on a cold day, made their way into a Catholic church. They found seats at the back of the sanctuary and looked around in astonishment at the ornate fixtures. In the front a ceremony was taking place as a hundred white-robed nuns were being inducted into the order. Noticing the unusual visitors a young priest went over to the men.
"Excuse me gentlemen," he said, "but what exactly brings you here today?"
"Not to worry," said one of the visitors, "We're from the Groom's side." (Novak and Waldoks 1981: 96)

Shlomo took a job in a shop selling religious artifacts to Roman Catholics. As his supervisor was about to leave for lunch, he told him that they were running low on crosses and asked what should he do to order some more. "Easy," said the supervisor, "just ring the number on the wall and ask for another batch of 103s." There was brisk business during lunch time and the shop came close to running out of crosses altogether. Shlomo rang the wholesaler and asked for another twenty-six 103s. "Certainly," said the voice at the other end of the phone, "mit Jesusle or mitout?" (Jewish, American, Chicago 1999)

A Jew visits his gentile friend and notices on the wall a picture of a man, woman and child barefoot and in rags. "Who are they?" he inquires.
"Why, it's the holy family," answered the gentile.
"How come they are so bedraggled?"
"No money to buy clothes."
"Why barefoot?"
"No money for shoes."
"Just like the gentiles," said the Jew, "naked, barefoot but they still have money to hire the best photographer to take a colored picture!" (UCBFA Blason Populaire American Jewish File. Collected by Natasher Doner 1968)

Because many of these jokes were published in best-selling compilations of Jewish jokes, the language is somewhat bowdlerized. Why, for example, should an elderly Jewish man want to buy a crucifix as a present for his *wife* (rather than for, say, a Roman Catholic neighbor)? However, the full force of Jewish humor about the Christians can be seen in the work of Philip Roth, ironically the author whom Novak and Waldoks (1981: xvi) suggest has been accused particularly of self-hatred. It is not surprising that most of his targets are Jewish (after all he knows more about them), but even in *Portnoy's Compaint* he is scathingly funny about the idiocies of the Christians and what seem to be their graven images:

> ...in the snowy lawns (of a gentile suburb) are set up little cut-out models of the scene in the manger—really, it's enough to make you sick. How can they possibly *believe* this shit? Not just children but grown-ups, too, stand around on the snowy lawns smiling down at pieces of wood six inches high that are called Mary and Joseph and little Jesus—and the little cut-out cows and horses are smiling too! (Roth 1969: 144, emphasis in original)
>
> Tucked above the Girardi sink is a picture of Jesus Christ floating up to Heaven in a pink night gown....when it comes to tawdriness and cheapness, to beliefs that would shame even a gorilla, you simply cannot top the *goyim*. What kind of base and brainless schmucks are these people to worship someone who, number one, never existed, and number two, if he did, looking as he does in that picture, was without a doubt The Pansy of Palestine. In a pageboy haircut, with a Palmolive complexion—and wearing a gown that I realize today must have come from Frederick's of Hollywood! (Roth 1969: 168)

Even the set piece, three-part minister, priest and rabbi jokes (jokes of inclusion as well as contrast) in which the rabbi alone has a realistic sense of the material world can, likewise, take on a hard edge, sometimes in ways that have nothing to with religious differences:

> A minister, a priest and a rabbi who are playing golf get held up by a very slow group playing ahead of them. On enquiry they discover that the tardy golfers up ahead are all blind.
> "What a wonderful display of human courage in the face of adversity," says the minister. "I shall preach about them in my next sermon."
> "It is truly a miracle that they can play golf," said the priest. "God must have inspired them. I'll speak about this to the faithful."
> "Huh," said the rabbi, "Why can't the schmucks play at night?" (Jewish, American 1990s)

The joke has at least two laughter-provoking aspects to it. First, it displays levity on the subject of blindness, which defies a strong social convention and thus plays with the forbidden. Second, it has, as in many other jokes, the rabbi as the realist, the one in touch with the immediate material world in contrast to the sentimentalism of the two Christians. But it is also the rabbi who comes out as tough-minded, as the terse, aggressive one for whom blind golfers are inconsiderate schmucks.

These modern American jokes are quite contrary to the idea that Jewish humor is inwardly directed. It is worth also examining them against Nathan Ausubel's comment in A *Treasury of Jewish Humor* that

> When Jewish humor turns harsh and cruel, as unfortunately it sometimes does, it is out of line with the folk tradition of laughter among Jews. That tradition grew out of Jewish ethical values which direct the individual to laugh *with* people rather than *at* them. (Ausubel 1951: xvii-iii, emphasis in original)

Now Ausubel's comment may well be true of the materials in his collection that have been chosen to illustrate the particular folk traditions and ethical values that he wishes to affirm, but it does not do justice to the full range of a balanced Jewish humor. There has also always been a harsh Jewish humor, a humor written "out of spite" (Oring 1992: 119) and it will not do to exclude it from the canon as in some sense inauthentic because it seems to offend against deeply held ethical values. We have a duty to act with mercy, charity and fairness in our serious dealings with other individuals, but there is no reason why humor should be constrained by this, for humor lives in a domain of its own to be judged on its own terms (in much the same way as Kant (1951: 37-8) divorces aesthetic judgments from moral and social ones). There is no reason why a people with a fine ethical tradition should not have a humor that can be harsh and cruel and which laughs *at* people rather than *with* them. That the purveyors of Jewish humor can play vigorously with aggression and laugh *at as well as with* is, in no sense, a shortcoming of the people who produced it or an occasion for criticism. On the contrary we should be grateful for this distinctive addition to the mirth of nations.

It is possible that Jewish humor has become bolder, and the playing with aggression rougher, in countries like contemporary Britain and America where the non-Jewish population is far less hostile and oppressive than was the case in Central and Eastern Europe; yet if this is the case it also creates problems for those who see Jewish humor as defensive or retaliatory (see comment on Adler and Freud in Oring 1992: 119). Furthermore, against whom is the joke about the blind golfers retaliating? It is simply a case of playing with aggression for its own sake. Nonetheless, there is also an older and strong tradition of jokes directed against those who were, or were seen as, the enemies or underminers of the Jewish people, individuals and groups whom it is reasonable to assume were resented.

The first genre of these jokes to be considered are those about apostates, those who left Judaism for another religion. Given that Judaism is a non-proselytizing religion the loss of a Jew by conversion was a threat to those who remained steadfast and to the integrity of the group. Such desertions were often in the past provoked by a desire to escape the anti-Semitic pressures of Christian societies that unfairly saw the Jews not as a religious minority with whom they had much in common but as an affront and as the betrayers and murderers of Christ.[1]

In this particular case there is a good match between a very real problem and a related seriously held fear and sense of resentment, on the one hand, and a set of jokes on the same topic that *could* (not do, but could) be a means of expressing these negative sentiments. In the face of this particular threat to Jewish identity, Jewish jokes have tended to play with two related if, in some ways, contradictory themes. First, the jokes depict the converts as having gone over to Christianity for reasons of self-interest that are far from being religious, and then often, after they had changed sides, as taking on the anti-Semitic prejudices of their new co-religionists. Second, the jokes represent the conversion as ineffective; the convert retains an indelible Jewish identity, habits and characteristics and can never become a fully confident, fully accepted, fully fledged Christian.

Three Jewish converts to Christianity are sitting in a country club, each explaining how he came to convert.
"I fell in love with a Christian girl," the first man says. "She wouldn't marry me unless I became a Christian. I loved her and so I did."
"I wanted to get a promotion at my bank," the second man says. "I knew there was no point in even applying for a higher position if I was Jewish. So I converted."
"And I converted," the third man says, "because I became convinced of the greater truth of Christian theology, and of the ethical superiority of the New Testament's teachings." The first two men glare at him: "What do you take us for, a bunch of goyim?" (Telushkin 1992: 136-7; also in Novak and Waldoks 1981: 95; and an older version in Mendelsohn 1935: 115-6)

A Jewish missionary in London put out a sign that on a certain evening he would deliver a lecture in which he would prove to the satisfaction of all that Christianity is the only true religion for the Jew. A goodly number of people assembled including several Jewish boys who prided themselves on their Jewish knowledge. After the lecture the boys began to fire questions at the speaker, quoting verse after verse from the Bible to disprove his thesis.

The discussion, which was conducted in English, grew terribly heated. After more than an hour the missionary became impatient and shouted at the boys in Yiddish:
"Rascals, get out! Give a poor Jew a chance to make a living." (Mendelsohn 1935: 120)

A Jewish young man called to see a Catholic priest and informed him that he had decided to embrace Catholicism. The priest beamed upon him and said:
"My son, I am indeed happy that the light of the new day has finally dawned for you. I cannot see you tomorrow, but if you will call the day after tomorrow I shall begin to instruct you in the true and holy faith."
"But the day after tomorrow will be too late, Father," insisted the young man. "I should like to change my religion at once."
"Well, then," conceded the priest, "I shall make a special effort in your case and see you tomorrow."
"But Father, I should like to become a Catholic today."
"Why are you in such a terrible hurry? A great faith like ours cannot be imparted in a few minutes."
"You see, Father," replied the young man, "I have just had an awful scrap with my Dad and I want to disgrace him immediately." (Mendelsohn 1935: 184).

A Jewish banker of Vienna accepted Christianity and joined the Lutheran church. When asked why he did not give preference to the dominant Catholic religion the banker replied:
"The Viennese Catholics already have too many Jews in their midst." (Mendelsohn 1935: 119)

For the past five years Neidel had been a Christian Scientist. One Sunday morning as he was leaving the house to go to church, his wife seized his arm. "What's the matter with you?" she cried. "You're wearing a *yarmulkah*!"
"Oy I forgot!" groaned Neidel. "It's my *goyisheh kop*!" (Wilde 1986: 167, there is another version in Telushkin 1992: 136).

A Jewish girl called to see Paul Cassel, well-known Jewish apostate of Berlin and director of a mission house for his former brethren. The girl was about to be married to a German for whose sake she had decided to be baptized, but her future husband's pastor told her that although she wished to be married within a month it would take her three months to learn the catechism. Since Herr Cassel was a former Jew he would perhaps help her out in her present dilemma, the girl said.
"Don't worry, my child," answered the *meshumad*, "you come to me and you will be married within a month. I am sure that you with your Jewish head will have no difficulty in learning the catechism in three weeks." (Mendelsohn 1935: 119)

A Jew converts to Catholicism and eventually becomes a priest. He is invited to speak in a church. After the service the local bishop congratulates him. Everything was fine he says. "Only next time, maybe you shouldn't begin by saying 'Fellow goyim'." (Novak and Waldoks 1981: 94; Telushkin 1992: 136)

In the 1920s two (men)... were walking along 5th Avenue. The first one was Otto Kahn a patron of the Metropolitan Opera. The second was Marshall B. Wilder, a hunch-backed scriptwriter. As they walked past a synagogue Kahn turned to Wilder and said, "You know, I used to be a Jew," and Wilder said, "Yeah and I used to be a hunchback." (Lee 1998: 170)

The late Dr. Theodor Herzl relates that at a dinner party in a fashionable home in Vienna a young son inquired of his baptized father:
"Papa, how old must one be before he becomes a Jew?"
"Don't talk nonsense," replied the impatient father. "To be a Jew or not to be a Jew has nothing to do with one's age."
"But that's not so," insisted the boy. "Just look here: I am twelve and I am a Christian; you are forty-five and you are still a Christian; but grandpa—he is old enough to be a Jew." (Mendelsohn 1935: 119)

The theme that true conversion is impossible is expressed in folklore with a serious message in the proverb, "*A meshumed iz nit keyn goy un nit keyn yid*" (An apostate is no Goy and no Jew), (Kumove 1986: 70), and the jokes could easily be used as a vehicle for a moral comment. Yet it is quite possible to make such a comment directly and in a bluntly critical way. Why disguise it by wrapping it up in a joke? Such a joke can be a more pleasing way of conveying disapproval, but it does so at the price of ambiguity since the main purpose of jokes is to play with aggression rather than to act as a vehicle for it.

Jewish jokes about anti-Semites which (with justification) depict them as brutal, irrational and dupeable can likewise be treated as an instance of an outwardly directed Jewish humor at the expense of a very real enemy. It is worth studying a subset of these jokes, the rich and varied collections of jokes about Soviet anti-Semitism on this point. Rabbi Joseph Telushkin (1992: 118) has commented on these jokes that

> Unlike almost all other Jewish humor, Soviet-Jewish jokes were almost *exclusively* directed against others; they had little to say about Jewish foibles. For dissidents it made no sense to turn such a weapon against oneself; after all, the Soviets already had the KGB, informers, guns, prison camps and even insane asylums for sane people. The only weapon in the dissidents' arsenal was ridicule (emphasis added). (Telushkin 1992: 118)

It has already been shown that several other genres of Jewish jokes contain *many* jokes directed against others and if, in addition, the Jewish dissidents' jokes are directed *exclusively* at others, then Jewish humor is very clearly balanced in character with as much humor directed at outsiders as in the direction of one's own group. Many of the Soviet-Jewish jokes like earlier jokes about religious and National Socialist anti-Semites and, indeed, like Eastern European jokes in general (Davies 1998: 77-81, 87-96) depict the politically powerful as remarkably stupid.

Abramovich was summoned to OVIR (the office issuing exit visas from the U.S.S.R).
"Why, Abramovich? Why do you want to leave us, to leave the land that nurtured you?"
the official inquired.
Abramovich remained silent.
"Don't you have a job?" the official asked, as he began enumerating with his fingers.
"I do," Abramovich whispered.
"And don't you have a place to live for a very cheap rent?" the official continued.
"I do," mumbled Abramovich.
"And free medical care?" the official noted.
"That too," sighed Abramovich.
"And schooling for your children?" the official confronted Abramovich.
"Uh-huh," the poor Jew agreed.
"Then why could you possibly want to leave, you dirty Jew?" bellowed the official.
"You've just reminded me, comrade. Thank you," smiled Abramovich. (Harris and
Rabinovitch 1988: 10-11)

At the opening of a public concert, the master of ceremonies announces from the stage:
"The People's Friendship String Quartet is going to perform for us tonight. Let us
welcome Comrade Prokopenko, Ukraine; Comrade Karapetian, Armenia; Comrade
Abdurashidov, Uzbekistan; and Comrade Rabinovich, Violin." (Draitser 1998: 136)

A decree was issued that all Jews and left-handed hunchback bicycle mechanics had to
pack their belongings and be prepared for deportation to Siberia within twenty-four
hours. The Russian people were puzzled. Why the left-handed hunchback bicycle
mechanics also had to prepare their things was simply beyond comprehension. (Harris
and Rabinovich, 1988: 122-3)

Abramovich arrived in Odessa from Kiev and wanted to call his friend, but he didn't
have the number handy. So he went to a telephone center and asked to see the telephone
directory.
"Sorry, but the city telephone directories have all been taken away by our glorious secret
police," explained the clerk.
"But why?" Abramovich asked in dismay.
"They discovered that the directory was really a complete listing of Zionist agents in
Odessa with full names, addresses, and phone numbers indicated for each. To disguise
the list, addresses and phone numbers were also given for non-Jews," the clerk revealed. (Harris and Rabinovitch 1988: 144)

A long queue outside a meat shop in Poland had been waiting for over an hour for the
doors to open. The manager came out and said "We don't have as much meat as we
expected. The Jews among you can go home." The Jews left. Two hours later the
manager emerged again and said "Meat stocks are very low. No meat can be sold to
anyone who is not a member of the (Communist) Party. The non-party members left.
The manager now spoke to the Party faithful and said "I know I can trust you with the
truth. Owing to unforeseen circumstances there has been no meat delivery. We won't be
selling meat this week. The Party members dispersed. One said to another in a disgruntled way "You see. Another bloody Jewish conspiracy." (Told in Poland in the
1980s. For another version, see Telushkin 1992: 121)

After a political class in an army division, the following exchange took place.
"Comrade Major, I must report to you that the damned Jew Khaimovich asked an
extremely provocative anti-Soviet question during our class today," the teacher in-

formed his commanding officer.

"What did he ask?" the officer inquired.

"He asked: 'Can you tell us, please, how many republics there are in the Soviet Union?'" replied the instructor.

"And what did you answer?" the officer continued.

"It wasn't easy, but I managed to get out of it. I told the Jew bastard to go screw himself," said the teacher proudly. (Harris and Rabinovitch 1988: 134)

Yet contrary to Telushkin's assertion that these jokes are directed *exclusively* against others such is the ambiguity of humor that many of these jokes can be read as portraying the Jews as victims and mocking them for it ; one more case of Jewish self-mockery. Indeed an unsympathetic and bloody-minded listener to the jokes might understand quite clearly that the teacher of the political class in the army or the bureaucrat in the visa office is a brutal idiot and yet still revel in hearing Abramovich called a "dirty Jew" or "the Jew bastard" being told to "go screw himself." Jokes rarely have one simple straightforward meaning and we can never be sure exactly why someone laughs at a particular joke. The same problem arises even in an extended work of comic genius such as Jaroslav Hašek's (1974 [1921-3]) *The Good Soldier Švejk*, which is full of brilliantly funny cameos of official brutality that can be laughed at in (at least) two ways (Davies 2000). Jokes about and against oppressors often turn out also to be about and against the oppressed. Telushkin's suggestion that the Soviet Jewish jokes are directed exclusively against others is thus false but at the same time the jokes are not directed exclusively or even primarily against the Jews so they provide no support for the Jewish masochism thesis either. What this demonstrates is the unsatisfactory nature of analyses of humor that posit a simple dichotomy between jokes directed against one's own group and jokes directed against others.

Humor is far too complex and ambiguous a phenomenon to be contained within such a simple scheme as can be seen from the further examples of Jewish humor cited below which mock the evasive action that Soviet Jews were forced to take in order to survive in a thoroughly anti-Semitic society.

A telephone is ringing in the communal apartment.

"May I talk to Moishe, please," the voice says.

A neighbor responds: "We don't have anyone like that here."

Another phone call: "May I talk to Misha?"

The neighbor shouts: "Moise it's for you." (Draitser 1998: 130)

A school principal walks into a class and announces:
"Finkelshtein, Shapiro and Ivan by your mother's surname should not come to school tomorrow. A delegation from Syria is visiting." (Draitser 1998: 137)

A Jew fills out one of the official applications:
"Have you been a member of any party other than the Communist Party?"
"No."
"Have you remained on any territory occupied by the enemy?"
"No."
"Have you been convicted or are you currently under investigation for any criminal activity?"
"No."
"Your nationality?"
"Yes." (Draitser 1998: 125)

They proposed a new penalty for traffic violators. For the first offense, the offender gets a hole punched in his driver's license. For the second violation, he gets another. After the third offense, the fifth item in his passport is to be changed to "Jew." (Draitser 1998: 125)

(In the Soviet Union the fifth item on a person's passport, a document needed even for internal travel within the country, was "nationality," which for many people referred to their republic of origin as "Russian," "Ukrainian," "Georgian," etc., but it could say Jew since the Jews were called a nationality, even though they lacked any of the rights and powers that being a nationality implies. It was simply one more way of identifying them and discriminating against them.)

It would be very difficult to argue that there is not a strong element of self-mockery in these jokes. The jokes are as much about Jewish weakness in the face of overwhelming oppression as about the idiocy of the oppression and the oppressors. Such jokes are *not* unequivocally weapons in the arsenal of Jewish dissidents as described by Telushkin. Indeed, it is difficult to see how Telushkin could sustain his argument that "it made no sense to turn such a weapon against oneself" (Telushkin 1992: 118), given that those in charge of the Soviet system controlled all the other levers of power, since the same argument would apply to all the other cases in which Jews have told self-mocking jokes at times of anti-Semitic persecution. Indeed, this is the basis of Grotjahn's Jewish masochism thesis. It may have "made no sense" to tell such jokes, indeed, it has been called an irrational response (see Oring 1992: 120) to the Jews' real situation, but joke tellers are neither obliged nor expected to make sense or to be rational. It is best not to speak of such jokes as weapons at all, since it is impossible to specify who is deploying them against whom. Jokes are best seen as a means of playing with aggression not of committing it, for the former conceptualization alone can cope with all these ambiguities and uncertainties whereas the latter view is bound to run into irresolvable contradictions.

If any Jewish jokes at all could be plausibly construed as an indication of a masochistic Jewish sense of humor as Grotjahn (1970) has suggested, it should not be those that ascribe qualities such as canniness to the Jews (after all the Scots do the same), but the jokes cited above that dwell upon a helpless Jewish victim-hood and that have few parallels among the jokes other peoples tell about themselves. The same point can be made in relation to an interesting observation made by Julia Ann Roth (1970) in her interesting study of the multinational airplane joke in which three volunteers are asked to jump out of an overloaded aeroplane in order to save the others. Two volunteers, usually British and French, jump out of the plane from a sense of duty and noblesse oblige and then a member of a third nationality who usually belongs to the *same group as the joke teller* throws out a member of a fourth nationality whom he dislikes with a suitable derisive epithet. The American, for example, throws out the Mexican, shouting "Remember the Alamo." In other versions of the joke the Greek throws out a Turk or an Italian, a Persian throws out an Arab, a Romanian throws out a Russian, and so on. Given the long history of conflicts between America and Mexico, Persians and Arabs, Greeks and Turks and in the twentieth century between Russians and Romanians and Greeks and Italians, it is easy to construe these jokes as the joke teller enjoying with some glee a tale of one of his fellow countrymen throwing a hated enemy out of a plane. When told in this way the overloaded airplane jokes are about as close as one is likely to get to a joke of conflict and hostility. Indeed, Roth (1970: 37) argues in the case of her Greek narrator telling the joke in which the Greek throws an Italian out that "for all the rationalizations in the joking form, it is strong hostility towards Italians which is being expressed." In relation to this particular telling she may well be right but you cannot generalize from particular performances.

However, the Jewish version in the University of California Berkeley Folklore Archive collected from Yahudi Aaron 'E', a Jewish-American lawyer is quite different (Roth 1970: 99):

A Frenchman, an Englishman, a German and a Jew were flying together across the Atlantic in a four-engine plane. Suddenly the captain came on over the public address system and announced that they had lost one engine and could only hope to reach land if one of the passengers was jettisoned. The Frenchman stood up, shouted "Vive la France!" and jumped out. The plane continued, but soon the captain came over the public address system again and again announced that they'd lost an engine and could only hope to reach land if another passenger were jettisoned. The Britisher arose, shouted "Rule Britannia!" and he jumped out of the aircraft. The crippled plane flew on, but soon a third engine failed, leaving the plane remaining aloft upon only one engine. The captain announced that they would be able to reach land only if another passenger was thrown out. At this point, the German stood up and shouted "Heil Hitler!" and threw out the Jew. (Roth 1970: 99)

Roth (1970: 38) comments that

It is significant that in 19 out of the 22 versions of this joke, the nationality of the teller is related to that of the character who pushes the victim from the plane. Clearly most narrators identified with the aggressor. However, the Jewish-American narrator has the Jew being pushed out by the German, the *only* example of a person from the victimized group telling the joke (emphasis added). (Roth 1970: 38)

Yet even this very striking contrast between the Jewish version of the joke (which the teller had learned at synagogue school) and the others is not proof of Jewish masochism, merely of a long history of being persecuted. Jokes draw on experience and the Jewish experience is one of being persecuted. To go beyond this and to suggest that because the other versions seem directly aggressive the Jewish version is a form of inward-directed aggression is unjustified. The Jew rather than the German gets thrown out of the plane in the Jewish-American version because it is true to an unpleasant history that we cannot alter. The image of the Jewish victim is to be found in all manner of other jokes that are simply using the familiar rather than being tendentious:

A Jew was walking down the street in Belfast when someone stuck a gun in his back and demanded aggressively in a strong Northern Irish accent "Are you a Protestant or a Catholic?" With great relief, he replied, "No, I'm a Jew."
"In that case," said the voice, "I'm the luckiest Arab in Belfast." (British 1970s)

The joke is simply based on an absurdity. It is a well-made joke that could not be rephrased without weakening it. Like the earlier Jewish airplane joke, *it plays with* Jewish victim-hood; it *does not endorse it*.

Jewish jokes in the face of adversity are and have long been extremely varied, sometimes self-mocking, sometimes outwardly directed precisely because they are not tendentious, not consistent, not part of a thought-out response to perceived difficulties. Jewish jokes do *not* have clear functions for the group that can be specified in advance rather than invented ex post. Jewish humor is balanced not merely in the crude sense that we can place some Jewish jokes in a category (such as self-mocking) and others in an opposed category (such as mocking outsiders) but in the deeper sense that many Jewish jokes have multiple possible meanings and can be fitted into either category or both. Jokes are ambiguous, humorous utterances not tendentious statements that can be reduced to single clear serious messages to be classed either as directed against one's own group or as weapons against others.

What is clear is that the Jewish jokes that have emerged from the long and vicious oppression and persecution of the Jews by anti-Semites, whether Christian, Nazi, Soviet or Arab in nature, bear a problematic relationship to that oppression, for they are extremely varied and cannot be reduced to a single category or dimension, nor used to deduce some kind of collective personality or outlook. Indeed, only one Jewish characteristic consistently emerges from the jokes and that is intelligence. Adversity has not led to a pattern of jokes embodying a particular philosophical outlook, but rather to a diversity of ways of playing with that experience of adversity in a humorous fashion. If adversity were in and of itself the force producing a self-mocking humor then we would expect the humorous runners-up to the Jews in self-mockery to be drawn from other much and long suffering nations not the secure and striving Scots.

Rather it is speculative intelligence and an awareness of contrasts between the ways of one's own people and those of numerous, varied and changing other peoples that are the key to Jewish humorous preeminence. It is a preeminence rooted in self-reflection and a love of arguments that make fine distinctions, putting things together and taking them apart again (Berger 1997: 93) much as we have already seen in the case of the Scots, only on an even greater scale. The Israeli humor scholar Avner Ziv (1988:115-6) and the sociologist of religion and tobacco, Peter Berger (1997: 93) have argued that Jewish humor is an outcome of the distinctive role of argument for its own sake and even without outcome within traditional Jewish education. It is a training in looking at each question from every possible angle, seeking out contradictions and looking for unlikely consistencies and relationships. Leo Rosten (1970: 295) cynically describes this kind of disputing or casuistry, the *pilpul* as "An inflated form of analysis and debate used in Talmudic study: i.e., unproductive hair-splitting that is employed not so much to radiate clarity or reveal meaning as to display one's own cleverness" and as being used colloquially to mean "Any hair-splitting or logic-chopping that leaves the main boulevard of a problem to bog down in the side streets." It is difficult to think of a better training for the production of jokes which *are* after all about displaying cleverness rather than advancing clarity and whose very structure depends on a narrative that suddenly and unpredictably switches from the boulevard to an unexpected side street.

We can see support for this argument in the way Jewish jokes are often based on disputes about patterns of required behavior and ritual shaped by religious tradition that are quite possibly incomprehensible to most outsiders (as in the case with Scottish jokes about doctrine and metaphysics).

A wealthy Jewish businessman went to see an orthodox rabbi and told him "I want to become a Kohen."

"I'm sorry," the rabbi replied, "but that is quite impossible."

"Listen," said the businessman, "it's important to me. I'll give your synagogue $100,000 if you make me a Kohen."

"Look," said the rabbi, "I can't do it. I do not have the power to do what you want. I literally cannot do what you ask."

"It it's that difficult, I'll make it $10 million," said the businessman. "I've made up my mind."

"It's no good," said the rabbi, "you're asking for something that no one can do for you. But why is it so important for you to be a Kohen anyway?"

"It's very simple," said his visitor. "My grandfather was a Kohen, my father was a Kohen and I want to be a Kohen." (American, Jewish, Chicago 2000)

A Misnagged (vehement opponent of the Hasidim): It is impossible to imitate a Hasid.

Reb. Schus: Why?

Misnagged: How would you imitate a Hasid?

Reb. Schus: I would grow a beard and peyes (sidelocks), put on a kapote (gabardine) and a shtreimel (fur hat), and white socks and when I pray tie a gartel (special belt) round my waist.

Misnagged: But if you did that you would not be imitating a Hasid. You would be a Hasid. (East European Jewish traditional, but alive in Chicago in 2000)

Jewish jokes about the importance of keeping the Sabbath have the same feel about them and are curiously similar to the corresponding Scottish jokes cited earlier:

Three Hasidim are boasting about their Rebbes. The first says, "My Rebbe is so great. One Friday afternoon he was in his carriage an hour's ride from home, with just an hour to Shabbes, when a terrible storm arose with hail and thunder and lightning, and they couldn't move. The Rebbe got up and said "Storm to the right and storm to the left, and clear in the middle." And a miracle happened: the storm continued to his right and to his left, but a clear path opened up in front of them and they got home just in time for Shabbes.

The second says, "That's nothing. One Friday afternoon *my* Rebbe was in his carriage an hour's ride from home, with just an hour to Shabbes, when a terrible fog came up. You couldn't see your hand in front of your face. They couldn't see which way was home. The Rebbe got up and said, "Fog to the right, and fog to the left, and clear in the middle. And a miracle happened: the fog continued to the right and to the left, but a path of visibility opened in front of them and they could drive through the fog and get home just in time for Shabbes.

The third says, "That's nothing. One Friday afternoon *my* Rebbe was in his carriage two hours' ride from home, with just one minute to Shabbes, and the Rebbe got up and said "Shabbes to the right and Shabbes to the left and Chol (any non-sacred day) in between." And a miracle happened; it was Shabbes to his right and Shabbes to his left but in the middle it was still Friday and he managed to get home without violating the Shabbes. (Eastern Europe traditional, but alive in Chicago America 2000)

What is most interesting about the above classic three-part joke of East European origin is the way in which it has been modernized and adapted in America and in Britain to become a minister, priest and rabbi joke that is accessible to gentiles as well as Jews:

A Protestant minister, a Roman Catholic priest and a rabbi were talking about the miracles they had experienced. The minister said, "I was once travelling on a plane when all the engines cut out one by one and we were falling out of the sky. I prayed and prayed to God and then one of the engines began to work again and we were able to land safely. It was a miraculous response to my prayers." The priest then said, "Once I was walking along the edge of a cliff when I stumbled and fell down towards the beach. I cried out "St. Anthony save me, I'm lost" and to my amazement I landed on a holiday maker's trampoline. The rabbi listened with interest to his colleagues' stories and said, "I was walking to synagogue one Saturday, when I saw a large bundle of bank notes lying at the side of the road and as you know I'm not allowed to carry money on the Sabbath. So I prayed and prayed and suddenly for a hundred yards around me it was Tuesday." (Jewish, British and American 1990s)

The new version has the same punch line as the old but the mainspring of the joke is no longer the credulous devotion of disciples but the conventional Jewish canny script. As usual the minister and the priest are merely part of the build up of their joke, a way of establishing a sequence of three but they also provide a means of conveying to the non-Jewish listener the vital information that Orthodox Jews must not carry money on the Sabbath. Because the rabbi has to enlighten the minister and priest on this point, the joke teller is able to slip in this vital fact without being didactic and disturbing the flow of the joke. In this way the joke has become a piece of deliberate Jewish self-mockery not just for an audience of insiders but also for gentiles. Indeed, in its new form the gentiles can add it to their repertoire and tell it among themselves thus further enhancing the reputation of the Jews as a humorous people.

A Scottish parallel is to be found in the text of an English cartoon of the 1930s:

> Tourist: (*after a long discussion with Station master on the subject of catching a steamer*) "So you would advise me to come back by the Sunday night train in order to catch the boat on Monday morning?"
> Station master: (*Severely*). "A wud advise nae mon tae profane the Sawbath; but a'll just repeat—if ye wait till the Monday ye'll nae get the connection." (*Mr. Punch in Scotland* 1933: 225)

The joke is indubitably Scottish and can be placed alongside the Sabbatarian tales collected by the learned compilers of classic Scottish anecdotes but it now contains *an outsider*, a tourist, to whom everything must be explained, thus making explicit the clash between sacred Scottish time and the mundane mechanical time of the railroad. It is a joke for non-Scots and Scots alike, a Scottish joke in an English magazine.

The argumentative origins of the Jewish joke are even celebrated within the jokes themselves. As in the Scottish jokes Jewish self-awareness extends even to the very process of being disputatious and to the love of hair splitting and tendency to schism that makes self-reflective jokes possible:

> A new rabbi comes to a well-established congregation.
> Every week on the Sabbath a fight erupts during the service. When it comes time to recite the *Sh'ma Yisra'el*, "Hear, O Israel the Lord is Our God, the Lord Is One" half of the congregation stands and the other half sits. The half who stand say, "Of course we stand for the *Sh'ma Yisra'el*: It's the credo of Judaism. Throughout history, thousands of Jews have died with the words of the *Sh'ma* on their lips." The half who remain seated say, "No. According to the *Shulkhan Arukh* (the code of Jewish law), if you are seated when you come to the *Sh'ma* you remain seated." The people who are standing yell at the people who are sitting, "Stand up!" while the people who are sitting yell at the people who are standing, "Sit down!" It's destroying the whole decorum of the service, and driving the rabbi crazy.
> Finally, it's brought to the rabbi's attention that at a nearby home for the aged is a ninety-eight year old man who was a founding member of the congregation. So, in accordance with talmudic tradition, the rabbi appoints a delegation of three, one who stands for the *Sh'ma*, one who sits, and the rabbi himself, to go interview the man. They enter his room, and the man who stands for the *Sh'ma* rushes over to the old man and says: "Wasn't it the tradition in our congregation to stand for the *Sh'ma*?"

"No," the old man answers in a weak voice. "That wasn't the tradition."
The other man jumps in excitedly. "Wasn't it the tradition in our congregation to sit for the *Sh'ma?*"
"No," the old man says. "That wasn't the tradition."
At this point, the rabbi cannot control himself. He cuts in angrily. "I don't care what the tradition was! Just tell them one or the other. Do you know what goes on in services every week—the people who are standing yell at the people who are sitting, the people who are sitting yell at the people who are standing—"
"*That was the tradition*," the old man says. (Telushkin 1992: 97-98)

It is a wonderful joke that reveals the social circumstances that made its own production possible. It indicates both why the Jews have been preeminent as inventors and disseminators of jokes, including jokes about themselves, and why the Scots have been their nearest rivals and closest to them in patterns of joking.

However, much can also be learned by making an opposite comparison and asking the question, "Which people also distinguished by remarkable economic, cultural and intellectual achievements has the fewest jokes?" There are as the author has shown earlier (Davies 1998) remarkably few modern Japanese jokes of any kind, no Japanese ethnic jokes about other nations, and no self-reflective jokes about the Japanese themselves or their relations and interaction with other peoples. There are no collections of contemporary indigenous Japanese jokes and it is extremely difficult, if not impossible, to obtain jokes from Japanese informants; with Jewish informants this problem is somewhat rare.

Julia Ann Roth (1970: 28) noted this difficulty in her cross-national study of jokes involving multiple ethnic groups, when she tried with great success to collect such jokes from foreign students studying at the University of California, Berkeley. Her success did not extend to the Japanese from whom "one joke was collected from a Japanese student after repeated requests" (Roth 1970: 28). It is not that the Japanese lack a sense of humor, as may be seen from the success of modern kabuki, notably the Red Buddha theatre or of *rakugo* (the stylized narration of a long humorous tale by a professional story-teller). Rather Japanese humor is context dependent and in conversation consists of *share* (witticisms and play on words) that do not subsequently get detached from their original context and turned into jokes (Davies 1992B) as they would in other parts of the world. There are very few modern Japanese set piece jokes with a tightly crafted punch-line designed for informal performance which is, of course, the crowning sudden glory of Jewish humor. Traditional Japanese humorous anecdotes do not display any degree of self-reflection about Japanese identity or mock distinctively Japanese traits and in Blyth's (1959 and 1963) very substantial collections of these anecdotes only two are about other national or ethnic groups.

The lack of Japanese joking in general and ethnic joking in particular extends to Japanese Americans as may be seen from Kimi Oshima's (2000) excellent study, "Ethnic Jokes and Social Function in Hawaii." Hawaiian society is made up of many ethnic groups with no ethnic group exceeding a quarter of the population, including native Hawaiians and many persons of Japanese, Chinese, English, Filipino, German, Irish and Portuguese descent. Ethnic joking is very popular among most groups but less so among the Japanese (Oshima 2000: 46). None of the jokes about the Japanese refers to a particular alleged trait of that people, unlike jokes about native Hawaiians, Filipinos, Portuguese, Haoles (people of European ancestry in general), Samoans, Koreans or Chinese. The Chinese, rather than the Japanese, are the butt of "canny" jokes, (Oshima 2000: 50-1) even though the jokes recognize that the Japanese are a dominant economic group on the islands (Oshima 2000: 46, 49).

One Hawaiian fellow said to another, "I heard the Arabs are going to buy up all the property and land of Hawaii." The other said, "Don't worry, the Japanese will never sell them."(Oshima 2000: 49)

What is true of Japanese Americans in Hawaii is true of Japanese Americans in general and, indeed, of the Japanese in Japan. They are neither a source of mirth nor a subject of mirth in others. There are very few jokes about the Japanese and very few Japanese jokes. Neither ethnic tensions in the labor and housing markets in California and Hawaii nor World War II with its accompanying hysterical and unjustified deportation of American mainland citizens of Japanese ancestry to internment camps led to much in the way of ethnic jokes about the Japanese—so much for the conflict theories of humor.

The absence of jokes and other humorous items from Japanese and Japanese American folklore and their *preponderance* in Jewish folklore is illustrated in table 3.1, based on a very rough measurement of the number of items in the folklore archives of the University of California, Berkeley. The absolute number of Jewish-American items is much larger than those collected from the Japanese and from Japanese Americans for obvious reasons but the table refers

Table 3.1
Proportion of Materials in Folklore Files Consisting of Humorous Items

	Jewish American	Iranian	Japanese American	Japanese
Proportion of total folklore files consisting of humorous items	28%	19%	5%	1%

not to absolute numbers but to the *proportion* of items that are humorous. The proportions of the Iranian folklore materials (Iranians are noted for their skill with jokes and humor) have been added to the table to put the Jewish/Japanese contrast in perspective.

Why then is there such a major contrast between the Jews, the people of the joke and the Japanese, the people without jokes? The Japanese are after all a people of remarkable intelligence and technical and business acumen who have created the world's second largest economy. Why have they not emulated the success of the Jews and the Scots in creating their own distinctive joking tradition?

The answer lies in part with the long isolation and relative homogeneity of the Japanese people. Unlike the Jews, they have not had to mix with a diversity of other peoples and come to terms with their mores nor to cope with internal and geographical differentiation. The Japanese can take it for granted that they are "we Japanese" and can blandly describe and explain their distinctive way of life as "Japanese uniqueness." The Iranians occupy a higher though intermediate position in the production of humor somewhere between the Jewish and Japanese extremes. Iran has never been a homogeneous or isolated society, but one in which non-Farsi speaking ethnic minorities—Arabs, Turks, Central Asians, Afghans and others—make up nearly half the population and are the subject of much Iranian humor. Likewise, each town and region has its own identity which, in turn, is a subject of humor. Far from being an island, Iran is a crossroads, a place where identities are problematic and disputed. Not only is Iran itself the home of jokes, but the Iranian Diaspora in America even has its own website for jokes in both Farsi and English. (http: www.jokestan.com)

By contrast conditions of homogeneity and stability do not generate jokes and the Japanese can be regarded as the opposite of the

Jews in this respect. The Japanese find non-Japanese, the *henna gaijin* (funny foreigners), comic but they do not have jokes about them. There is no tradition in Japan of logical disputation for its own sake nor of trying to approach a question from several antagonistic points of view. Rather, the Japanese value harmony, hierarchy and group agreement and from such a tradition jokes are less likely to emerge. Even the conventional courtesies and decorum of Japanese conversation and its lack of verbal aggressiveness and competitiveness make it difficult for them to exchange jokes, a problem that does not seem to exist for Jewish joke tellers. The absence of jokes thus confirms the reasons for the preeminence of Jewish joking that have been put forward.

By comparing Jewish joking with that of the Scots who resemble them and with that of the Japanese who stand furthest away it is possible to find an explanation both for the triumph of the Jews as the world's greatest joke tellers and for the supposedly self-mocking quality of Jewish joking. Jewish humor *is* self-mocking in the sense that the Jews have invented more jokes making fun of themselves than any other group. However, the Jews also have an enormous repertoire of jokes mocking outsiders and the Scots, their runners-up in self-mockery, have fewer indigenous jokes of this kind. Self-mockery is thus not a uniquely nor even a markedly distinguishing Jewish characteristic.

It is both insightful and misleading to describe Jewish humor as consisting of two antithetical types: disparagement and superiority (see Nilsen and Nilsen 2000: 173). It is important to emphasize the *balanced* nature of Jewish humor, containing as it does both these extremes; Jewish humor is not skewed in one direction. It is wrong though to treat these two types as pure antitheses since in humor the two are often merged or different facets of one entity, so that disparagement *is* superiority. The world of explanations is never dialectical but humor (like religion) often is (Davies 1999). Rather what is striking is the extent to which Jewish jokes mock *everything*, both insiders and outsiders. If it is the case that insiders are mocked more, it is to a large extent because more is known about them. It is much easier for Jewish joke tellers to invent jokes about Orthodox versus Reform Jews or rationalist scholars versus Hasidim than about different brands of Christian or jokes about Jewish rather than gentile women. Familiarity breeds jokes. Jewish jokes about Jews are very striking in their sheer diversity, but in that diversity there is balance.

Note

1. That many of the individuals who converted did so from genuine conviction and remained sympathetic to the people of their ancestors (Guinness 1985, Stelchin 1997) is beside the point.

4

Jokes about Jewish Women and Australian Men

One interesting subset of Jewish jokes of a self-mocking kind are those told about Jewish women, although once again it is important to note the significance of internal differentiation within the group. The butts of the jokes are women, but the inventors and tellers of the jokes are predominantly Jewish men, even though many Jewish women may well appreciate and enjoy such jokes. Jewish jokes about Jewish women are unique and jokes about Jewish mothers, Jewish wives, and Jewish American Princesses cannot be switched to other religious or ethnic groups or nations. Nor do other peoples, as far as is known, produce similar jokes either spontaneously or in emulation, even though the jokes are understood and enjoyed by gentiles. Gentiles have jokes about mothers-in-law, not mothers (Chanfrault 1992: 11-12; MacHale 1987).

It is not possible, therefore, to carry out a comparative analysis using similar jokes told by another group (as was done between Jewish jokes generally and those of the Scots), and so the approach adopted here is to seek out jokes based on an exactly opposite set of scripts and images and to contrast the two sets and their social origins and cultural backgrounds. The obvious contrasting group is Australian men who are also the subject of a self-mocking humor that is gender specific within their own society; Australian jokes about Australians are about Australian men. Australian jokes are also largely invented and told by men as may be seen from the distinctive coarseness of the humorous language used by the tellers. The purpose of the comparison is to complete and extend the general model of patterns of joking outlined in chapter 1, table 1.2.

The comparative strategy does not lead to a contrast between men and women as such (which is the basis of *other* kinds of joke about sex and sex roles that do not specify and do not need to specify national, ethnic or religious identities), but between two specific groups, one male and one female, who are the butts of very particular kinds of joke. It also enables us to contrast two groups of *men*, the Jewish men and Australian men who are the inventors and tellers of the two sets of jokes

All Jewish men owe their Jewish identity to a Jewish mother since conversion is discouraged and for the Orthodox, the children of a gentile wife who has not converted are not Jews. Likewise, in order to have Jewish children, a Jewish man must marry a Jewish wife or at the very least have children by a Jewish woman to whom he *could* be married (otherwise they would be *mamzerim,* the product of incest or adultery and excluded from the community). In order to have Jewish grandchildren he must either have daughters or be sure that his sons marry Jewish wives. Women, thus, are the key transmitters of Jewish identity and, given the strong relationship between humor and identity, this may well be why women are so important in Jewish humor as representations of the group itself. Other groups have generic jokes about all women but Jewish jokes are specifically about Jewish women, who by implication differ from all other women and have a power and significance that all other women lack; they alone have the power to confer the Jewish male identity for which Jewish men thank the king of the universe every morning of the year.[1]

It is then appropriate to begin an analysis of jokes about Jewish women with jokes about Jewish mothers, the mothers of Jewish sons. Behind the Jewish mother jokes lies the long-established script of the bossy, over-possessive Yiddische Momma

> The Yiddische Momma...is doting on her son and expects an equally all-devouring devotion on his part, while pretending to be self-effacing; she is very ambitious for her children (or their children); she is a fanatic about her children eating well; she is demanding and nagging. (Raskin 1985: 217)

According to the script, she is never willing to let go of her children and especially her male children. Even in middle age they remain in a state of emotional dependence and blackmail. The jokes speak for themselves:

> How many Jewish mothers does it take to change a light-bulb?
> None. Don't you mind about me. I'll just sit here in the dark. (American 1970s. See also Naiman 1981: 99; Raskin 1985: 217)

(After being away for more than a year, Ira phoned home.)
"Hello, Ma, how are you?"
"Just fine, son. When're you coming home? I'll fix you some chopped liver and chicken soup and a beautiful pot roast."
"I'm still pretty far away!"
"Oh, son," cried the desperate woman. "Just come home and I'll fix you your favourite—oatmeal cookies!"
"I don't like oatmeal cookies!" said the boy.
"You don't?" asked the woman.
"Say," said Ira, "is this Century 5-7682?"
"No!"
"Then I must have the wrong number!"
"Does that mean you're not coming?" asked the woman. (Wilde 1974: 37)

Jewish novel: a story in which boy meets girl, boy gets girl and then worries what his mother will say. (Bowles 1984: 38)

Two Yiddish mothers are talking and one says, "Oy have I got *tsouris*!" She says, "my son, my son he's going with a boy, he's a fairy. On the other hand I've got *nachus* because his boyfriend is a doctor." (U.C.B.F.A Jewish American jokes, file S6. Collected by William Jordan 1964)

One summer day Mrs. Saperstein took her little boy Alan to Jones Beach. As soon as she settled under a beach umbrella she cried out to her son:
"Alan, Alan come here! Don't run into the water. You'll get drowned! Alan don't play with the sand. You'll get it in your eyes! Alan, Alan don't stand in the sun. You'll get sunstroke! Oy Vey! Such a nervous child." (Novak and Waldoks 1981: 30)

Mrs. Schwartz drives up to the Fontainbleau Hotel in her limousine and gets out. Three busboys meet her at the entrance to take her things. She says to the first one, "Oh, you can take my luggage." "Yes, Mrs Schwartz." She says to the second one, "Oh and you can take my jewels." "Yes, Mrs Schwartz." She looks at the third one and says, "You can take my son." "What's the matter Mrs Schwartz, can't your son walk?" "Yes, but thank God he doesn't have to." (U.C.B.F.A, Jewish American Jokes, file S6, Jokes, Social Status and Social Matters. Collected by Ellen Diamond 1971)

What did the Jewish mother tell her son the air-force pilot?
Be sure to fly low and slow. (U.C.B.F.A., Blason populaire Israel file. Collected by John MacArthur 1968)

The Jewish mother scripts are the oldest of the comic scripts about Jewish women, as may be seen from Victor Raskin's (1985: 217) use of the term Yiddische Momma and the use of Yiddish words in the text of some of the jokes. Nonetheless, the jokes persisted throughout the twentieth century and are not simply the product of the experiences of first or second generation Jewish immigrants in America or Britain. Jewish mother jokes are unique to the Jews. The gentile neighbors of the Jewish joke tellers do not tell jokes about mothers, only about mothers-in-law. Because of the ubiquitousness and popularity of Jewish joke tellers telling Jewish jokes, gentiles obviously know the comic Jewish scripts about mothers and may even themselves tell jokes about Jewish mothers but they do not apply the script to the mothers in their own community, nor do they turn these scripts into generic jokes about all mothers. For those gentiles who understand the jokes it would from a purely technical point of view be very easy to make such a switch, but they never do so. This lost opportunity is proof of the absurdity of the thesis that the jokes are an expression of some kind of general misogyny; if they were then male gentiles would surely have exploited this Jewish invention for their own ends.

The Jewish wife script like the Jewish mother script is about an intensely controlling and manipulative person, a woman who demands an endless supply of luxurious status symbols and is obsessed with displaying them to impress other women (see Raskin 1985: 218), and who (possibly in furtherance of these goals) avoids and withholds sexual relations. Central to the jokes is a degree of calculativeness and materialism and indeed a loss of spontaneous pleasure in general that fits very well with the canny humorous scripts in general that are the basis of many ethnic jokes (Davies 1990: 28-39).

> When Harry died his wife had him cremated, brought the ashes home in an urn and tipped them on to the table. "Well, Harry," she said, "You always wanted me to give you a blow job…" (American Jewish 1980s)

> The most dreaded plastic surgery is performed by husbands cutting up their wives' credit cards. (Burns and Weinstein 1978: 24)

> My wife divorced me for religious reasons. She worshipped money and I didn't have any. (Novak and Waldoks 1981: 257)

> Whatsa matter, Harry? Ah, my wife is allergic to fur. Every time she sees another woman wearing a mink coat, she gets sick. (Wilde 1974: 31)

> While Mr. and Mrs. Blumstein were gaping at the gorilla in the cage the huge animal became sexually aroused, reached through the bars, pulled Mrs. Blumstein into the cage and began ripping off her clothes. "What should I do?" she screamed hysterically to her husband. "Do what you do with me," replied Mr. Blumstein. "Tell him you got a headache." (Raskin 1985: 218)

> What is Jewish foreplay?
> Thirty minutes of grovelling. (American Jewish 1970s; also Dundes 1987: 71)

In these jokes there is a tension between *two* kinds of canny materialism, that of the Jewish husband who cuts up his wife's credit cards to reduce her expenditure and that of the Jewish wife who seeks to gain status through ostentatious expenditure. The old canny jokes about avoidance of expenditure have been supplemented by a new and specifically Jewish genre of jokes about exultant female consumers. However, either way the jokes are characterized by a joyless and obsessive materialism (Davies 1990: 28-39), which is characteristic of many canny jokes; another version of this may be seen in Scottish jokes that combine sex and stinginess:

> A couple of Scottish newlyweds feel romantic and start making love on the living-room floor of their brand new house. In a little while the man says, "Don't fret so, love."
> "Fret?" his wife asks in surprise, "Don't you like it when I do it?"
> "Oh yes, very much so. In bed, it's a different matter. But here you will wear the shag off the carpet!" (Raskin 1985:190)

> The stingiest Scotsman is the one who slept with his mother-in-law to save the "wear and tear" on his pretty wife. (Legman 1968: 471)

In the Scottish jokes the wife's sexuality is not called into question and it is the man who is being canny, canny about expenditure in a way characteristic of both Scottish and Jewish men in other jokes based on the canny script. Indeed, the Scotsman is so stingy as to have sex with a woman who is usually the butt of British working-class jokes about her supposedly repellent characteristics, namely, his mother-in-law. The Scottish wife's enthusiasm for sex contrasts markedly with the calculative reluctance ascribed to Jewish wives in the jokes. The Scottish wife is merely an incidental victim of her husband's canniness and appears in the joke only to give us a chance to laugh at a canny Scotsman in a sexual context. Both sets of jokes, the Jewish and the Scottish, share a canny script but the relation between the sexes is quite different.

The Jewish American Princess jokes that boomed in the late 1970s and early 1980s share many themes with the jokes about Jewish wives. The jokes about the Jewish American Princess depict her as "vain, pampered, spoiled, sexually manipulative, materialistic, bossy, uncultured, loud, overdressed and bedecked with jewels, a bubble-head" (Alperin 1988: 4), a younger version of the Jewish wife and spoiled by a doting father (Raskin 1985: 218). Thus, the J.A.P. is the third kind of Jewish woman comically portrayed as having power over Jewish men, in her case over two kinds of Jewish men. First, she has power over her "doting father," who provides the money for her extravagance, particularly in regard to her obsessively fashionable appearance. In Jewish jokes the Jewish mother has power over her sons, but the Jewish daughter has power over her father, and her mother is less important to her than shopping. In the relationships between the generations it is the Jewish men of the jokes who always end up in a position of weakness relative to their women-folk. Second, the J.A.P. has power over the Jewish males who are her potential sexual partners, since she is depicted in the jokes as already being an over-controlled and over-controlling begrudger. Symbolically, this is expressed in her refusal now and also later as a wife to countenance the giving of oral sex, presumably because the one giving the oral stimulation is perceived as yielding power and control to her partner. Giving is the opposite of calculativeness.

Q. Why can't a Jewish American Princess get a colostomy?
A. She can't find shoes to match (the bag). (U.C.B.F.A., Jewish American Jokes, R5. Collected by Lee Greenberg 1983)

How many Jewish American Princesses does it take to replace the light bulb?
Two—one to pour out the Tab, the other to call daddy. (Novak and Waldoks 1981: 126)

What do you get if you cross a French whore with a J.A.P.?
A girl who sucks credit cards. (U.C.B.F.A., Jewish American Jokes File A5. Collected by Alia Aghia 1981)

What do you call a JAP on a water bed?
A Lake Placid (or) The Dead Sea. (U.C.B.F.A., Jewish American Jokes, file S6. Collected by Paul Rosenbaum)

Q. What do J.A.P.s most often make for dinner?
A. Reservations. (Rosten 1983:168)

What is the difference between a J.A.P. and a Puerto Rican woman?
The Puerto Rican has fake jewellery and real orgasms. (Jewish American 1980s)

What is the ideal house for a Jewish Princess?
6000 square feet with no bedroom and no kitchen. (Berger 1993:80)

How does a Jewish American Princess commit suicide?
She piles up all of her clothes on her bed and jumps off. (U.C.B.F.A., Jewish American jokes, file J2. Jewish American Princess. Collected by Mark Chambers 1986)

What do you get if you cross a J.A.P. and a PC?
A computer that won't go down on you. (U.C.B.F.A. Jewish American jokefile J2, Jewish American Princess. Collected by Susan Wyshak 1986)

Did you know that all Jewish girls are bisexual?
Whenever you ask one if she wants to have sex, she says "Bye!" (U.C.B.F.A., American-Jewish Joke File. Collected by Herlan Edelman 1980)

Once again it must be stressed that the jokes are not men's jokes about women in general; they are uniquely Jewish jokes specifically about Jewish women. Indeed, there could not be a greater contrast between Jewish jokes about Jewish women and Jewish jokes about shikses, the forbidden (the word shikse literally means female abomination (Telushkin 1992: 139-40)), alluring gentile women:

What are shiksas good for?
Shiksas are good for practising but not for marrying.(U.C.B.F.A., American Jewish Blason Populaire miscellaneous jokes file. Collected by Reginald P. Calaguas 1992)

Why does a Jew need legs?
To school he must be forced, to marriage he must be led, to burial he is brought, to the synagogue he won't go and after the gentile girls he crawls.
So why does he need legs? (Kumove 1986: 142)

A Jewish travelling salesman in a small town hotel calls in the red-headed chambermaid, and without a word throws her on the bed and has intercourse with her. Afterwards she says, "You know, I'm not mad, but how is it you Jewish drummers never ask a girl, the way the other fellows do? It's been the same way with the last six Jewish drummers. They just throw me on the bed. What's the big idea?" He takes her by the hand into the bathroom, and silently swings open the door of the medicine cabinet. Written in soap along the bottom of the mirror in Yiddish is the legend: *"Die röyte shicksa trennt* (The red-headed gentile screws)." (Legman 1968: 281)

A guy's mother died; he feels bad because his father's left all alone. So he sends his father to Kutscher's in the Catskills where he'll be fed kosher food, he'll meet nice eligible older Jewish women, and he won't be lonely. So after his father's been there a week and he hasn't heard from him, he tries to get in touch with him, keeps calling and calling but his father's not there. So he gets in his car and drive's up to Kutscher's and runs around looking for his father but nobody's seen him. Finally someone says he's seen him go off with a blonde women to another hotel. So the guy goes off to the other hotel and he asks for the room of this woman. And so he goes up to the room, bursts open the door; there's his father embracing this beautiful blonde bombshell, 45 years his junior, and clearly a shiksa. The guy cries out, "Father—what are you doing? What's going on here? I send you to Kutscher's where there are kosher meals and Jewish women, and here you are schtupping this shiksa! "His father turns around and says, "I don't eat here!" (U.C.B.F.A., American Jewish Joke file. Collected by Ruth Charloff 1986)

The shikse is depicted, indeed one might say constructed, in the jokes as *röyte* (red-head) or as "a beautiful blonde bombshell" with the adventurous sexual availability of the blonde in the Blonde Girl jokes (Davies 1998: 186-7). Indeed, the J.A.P. jokes and the Blonde Girl jokes can be regarded as antitheses, for the J.A.P. calculatingly withholds sex and particularly forms of sex that imply confusion or pollution whereas the Blonde Girl is recklessly and polymorphously promiscuous (Davies 1998: 183). The shikse is a forbidden fantasy, devoid of all the usual Jewish constraints, rules and inhibitions, a woman who is all *tuchus* and no *mikva*. Her situation and imagined characteristics have been well summed up by Marsha Richman and Kate O'Donnell (1978) in their humorous advice-book *The Shikse's Guide to Jewish Men*:

> To a Jewish man, the shikse is:
> Desirable because she is non-Jewish
> Inferior because she is non-Jewish
> Wonderful because she is non-Jewish
> Forbidden because she is wonderful
> Wonderful because she is forbidden.

With illusions like that someone is going to be disappointed. We are now in a position to suggest that the Jewish jokes about Jewish (as distinct from non-Jewish) women are not misogynistic in the way that Mimi Alperin (1988) and Esther Fuchs (1986) have alleged. Unlike the universal jokes about females told by Gentile and Jew alike, the Jewish jokes are not *primarily* about women or sex. Rather the jokes are about the conflict between duty and choice experienced by the virtuous Jewish man and about his sense that his life is more controlled and constrained than that of his gentile counterparts and that the controllers are the female members of his own family. The women are powerful partly because as outlined earlier they are so crucial to Jewish identity and partly because Jewish life is familistic and for most Jews during the last half-century middle class; there are no wild, delinquent Jewish all-male groups to escape to, no equivalent of Paddy's Bar or a sleazy pool room where all rules can be relaxed and evaded. In such a world the mother's authority and protectiveness and the wife's powerful influence receive few challenges from outside.

When it comes to choosing a wife, duty and ethnic loyalty should prevail for the would-be Jewish husband over a free choice based purely on personal characteristics. In the past such marriages might well have been arranged by a *shadchen*, a Jewish marriage broker and there is an entire genre of *shadchen* jokes based on the broker's incompetent attempts to foist an undesirable Jewish bride on a reluctant suitor. Most of the older East European jokes about marrying centered around the shadchen, that is, it was assumed that marriages would be arranged within the community. In America marrying out was rare in the first half of the twentieth century and met with strong disapproval. The earlier jokes about intermarriage in America tended to reflect the antipathy with which it was regarded. Some Orthodox Jews even observed the laws of mourning for a child, a brother or a sister who intermarried.

> One story tells of a man who married a non-Jew, whereupon his brother sat seven days of *shiva*, mourning him as dead. On one of these days his intermarried brother paid him a condolence visit! (Telushkin 1992:138)

> David came from an Orthodox family. One day he announced, "Mama, I'm going to marry an Irish girl named Maggie Coyle!"
> "That's nice, David," she said. "But don't tell your papa. You know he's got a weak heart."
> "And I wouldn't tell your sister, Ida. Remember how strongly she feels about religious questions."
> "And don't mention it to your brother, Louis, he might give you a bust in the mouth."
> "Me, it's all right, you told. I'm gonna commit suicide anyway." (Wilde 1978:143; see also Telushkin 1992:137-8)

Columnist David Schwartz told this one in the *California Jewish Voice*:

> A Jewish boy was in love with a girl of another faith. The boy's father was against the marriage but the son married her anyway.
> The son was employed in his father's store and on the Sabbath following the honeymoon, the bridegroom failed to show up at the place of business. He explained to his father that his wife would not allow him to work on *Shabbes*.
> "Aha!" exclaimed the father. "Didn't I warn you not to marry her?" (Spalding 1969: 390-1. Unless the wife was a Seventh Day Adventist, Spalding's wording of the joke suffers from internal contradictions. See Telushkin 1992:140 for a more consistent version)

However, except in very Orthodox circles, this kind of strong negative response has become rare. Rates of intermarriage have risen sharply (Norden 1991: 36-43) and this striking (and from the Jewish community's point of view destructive) social change coincided in America with the first major cycle of J.A.P. jokes in the late 1970s and early 1980s (Dundes 1987: 62). In the early 1960's only 10 percent of Jews intermarried with 20 percent of the gentile partners going over to Judaism. By the late 1980s the rate of intermarriage was over 50 percent and only 10 percent of the partners converted (Norden 1991: 41, based on the National Jewish Population Survey). The clash between duty and individual choice has intensified.

Duty says that each Jewish male should seek a Jewish wife in order to create a Jewish marriage and to ensure that his children are Jewish. It may well be that even from the purely egoistic point of view of individual Jewish men that Jewish duty is preferable to, better than, more conducive to happiness than giving way to the temptation offered by taking a non-Jewish wife, but that is beside the point. The point is that duty is a community-generated and community-imposed constraint on a choice that the wider society claims should be made on the basis of individual romantic attraction of which sexuality is an important component.

The jokes do not so much mock Jewish women as *Jewish duty*, namely the J.A.P. whom it is the Jewish man's duty to marry but whom increasingly he does not (Norden 1991: 36-43), the Jewish wife whom it is his duty to retain at a time of high divorce rates, and the anachronistic Jewish mother who is a key source of moral pressure to stay loyal to the group. Jewish women represent order, duty and control in a Jewish culture that still favors order, duty and control but today against a backdrop of Western societies that have become egoistic, anomic and hedonistic and that advertise endless sexual pleasure and adventure. Within wealthy modern societies the central socioeconomic reality for many people, perhaps especially in the United States, often consists of the undertaking of alienating work in order to achieve status by purchasing and displaying frivolous but expensive baubles. It is unfair, but hardly surprising, that this should lead to Jewish women becoming the butt of jokes that reflect this reality. The shikse who represents a free choice from a much larger sample of women to the neglect of duty is by definition the antithesis of constraint and control; she represents beauty, excitement, adventure, a *fictitious* world in which a man can eat what he likes, drink too much and indulge in sex as he chooses, and she costs less.

Jewish women are to some extent caught in the same dilemma but they do not tell distinctive jokes about Jewish sons and lovers, husbands and fathers. There are two reasons for this apart from the obvious point that men are more likely to invent and tell jokes. First, men are more likely to experiment and to invite relationships and, indeed, to marry out. Women are more likely to have an internalized sense of family and community duty and are less likely to kick against the pricks (Acts 26:14), whereas men see duties of this kind as a set of external pressures to be joked about; once again joking involves *playing with the forbidden*. Second, whereas Jewish women are likely to see their lives as constrained in much the same ways as other women, Jewish men, when comparing themselves to male gentiles, are likely to see their own lives as (for better or worse) subject to a greater degree of control, control by their families and women folk and control by their community.

What is lacking in the Jewish tradition is the existence of a legitimate life without marriage and the family in which a reckless bachelor culture could develop within a secular, hedonistic all-male group from which women and their restraining influence are excluded. A Jewish bachelor is not, as he may well be in other cultures, a heroic figure celebrated in male folklore for his wild exploits. For Orthodox Jewish men "marriage is…a mitzvah, a religious duty…. An unmarried man is only half a man, abiding without joy, without peace, without good" (Feldman 1974: 297). Once this is understood not only does the reason for the distinctive Jewish jokes about the ubiquitous control of women become clear but we can also see why there are no Jewish jokes about male drunkenness and violence of the kind that are popular among the Irish and the Australians, two peoples who have long had a strong bachelor culture. Also the Jewish male tradition is one of restraint, moderation and control, avoiding both asceticism and excess; the tradition is to some extent independent of but also totally congruent with the central importance of family life for Jews.

Even when there was a poor Jewish proletariat it was still the case, as Nathan Glazer (1960: 1690) noted that in America (and indeed in Britain):

> Jews did not drink; Jewish students were docile, accepting—as lower class children rarely do—today's restraints for tomorrow's rewards; Jewish workers stayed out of jail. When we look at the working class Jewish neighborhoods of the great American cities of the 1920s and 1930s it is clear that we are not dealing with ordinary workers. It was not dangerous to walk through the New York slums at night when they were inhabited by Jews.

Again, as the African American economist Thomas Sowell (1981: 94) has observed:

> Even when the Jews lived in slums they were slums with a difference—lower alcoholism, homicide, accidental death rates than other slums or even the city as a whole…the Jews had the social patterns of the middle class even when they lived in slums. Despite

a voluminous literature claiming that slums shape people's values, the Jews had their own values, and they took those values into and out of the slums.

In consequence there are no Jewish jokes about male violence. There is no Jewish equivalent of Andy Capp the working-class comic strip hero from the tough North-East of England who is equally ready to start a fight in a bar while inebriated or to attack his wife Florrie when he comes home. There is no Jewish version of Rab C. Nesbitt (Pattison 1990). Indeed, Jewish jokes are apt to mock and yet also to celebrate Jewish men for not being violent (Davies 1990: 222-225), as in the sketch by Jackie Mason (1987: 42):

> I never saw four black people walking down the street saying, "Watch out, there's a Jew over there!" Well, let's be honest about it. Did you ever see anybody afraid to walk into a Jewish neighborhood because he might get killed by an accountant?
> In this country Jews don't fight. I don't know if you noticed that. In this country they *almost* fight. Every Jew I know *almost* killed somebody. They'll tell you, "If he said one more word....he would have been dead today. That's right. I was ready...one more word...." What's the word? Nobody knows what the word is. (Mason 1987: 42)

The above analyses and descriptions also have a relevance for a further point about jokes about Jewish men, the *relative absence* of jokes about their getting drunk (Spalding 1976:180-1). There is an enormous wealth of jokes in Christian societies about male drunkenness, and there are distinctive ethnic jokes about the drunkenness of male Australians, Finns, Germans, Irish and Scots, all of which national groups contain larger than average numbers of problem drinkers and display distinctive modes of drunken comportment. In the past drunken or alcoholic Jews were rare (Glad 1947: 408-10) and the minority of Jews who are now increasingly abandoning the traditional moderation of their community (Glatt 1973: 268; Rosten 1983: 283-84) have no distinctive model of Jewish drunken comportment to follow—they are merely as shikker as a Goy. Most Jewish jokes and comic references to alcohol refer to inebriated gentiles and particularly to those whose violent tendencies are inflamed by alcohol, as in the song "Shikker iz a Goy because he is a Goy!" (Bermant 1986: 71-72; Rosemarine 1962; Snyder 1962: 206-7). For Jews drunkenness within the community is unacceptable rather than comic, but Jews have been reported as having a particular liking for jokes about gentiles being the worse for drink (Wolff et al. 1934: 357).

Likewise there is an absence of Jewish jokes about the (often female) temperance fanatic of the kind commonly found in the jokes of American, Australian, Scottish and Welsh Protestants (Davies 1998: 126-130). Ethnic jokes including jokes concerning alcohol are about excess in either direction; Jewish moderation generates few jokes. Even the Jewish holidays on which it was customary to drink more heavily, namely Purim and Simchat Torah at the end of Sukkoth (Kumove 1984: 153, 155) have not given rise to an extensive, distinctive Jewish humor of drunkenness. These holidays do not end in the kind of drunken brawling common on holidays, fairs and festivals in Russia, Ireland or Australia, especially in the past. The author carefully observed a, by gentile standards, decorous Purim carnival in Israel in 1997 and the disgusting drunken celebration of St. Patrick's Day in Savannah, Georgia in 1987 (Davies 1998: 119; see also Stivers 1976: 170). They had nothing in common. Yet Purim, though peaceful, is not an alcohol-free, teetotal occasion except in the descriptions of Jewish festivals in the writings of Protestant evangelicals (Buksbazen 1984: 67-8).

Jewish rational moderation can even be seen in the occasional joke about Jewish drunkenness, a rarity which has to be justified in a well-reasoned way:

> An old Jew was arrested for drunkenness and taken before a judge. The judge could hardly believe what had happened. "How did this happen?" the judge asked sympathetically. "Nothing happened," answered the old man," I'm not drunk at all." "Now listen here," said the judge, "it's perfectly obvious that something happened to put you in this state. Now tell me in your own words what happened." "It's very simple," started the old man, "I took one drink. There are many Biblical authorities for such conduct. One drink anyone may take. Now this drink made me a new man. Naturally, the new man was entitled to a drink. So he had one. Then we were two. As all the world knows it is permissible for them to have a drink. By this time we were joyous. And on a joyous occasion, one must drink." (U.C.B.F.A., Jewish-American joke file. Collected by Michael Estrin 1975)

There cannot be a greater contrast with the Jewish patterns of joking than the patterns of joking to be found in Australia. Australian jokes and jokes about Australians are about Australian men, with women only appearing in an (often literally) supporting role. Jewish women are mocked for supposedly being powerful. Australian jokes celebrate women's subordination as victims of the male excess, coarseness and crudity of the Australian ockers (the rough working class) and larrikins (hooligans).

Exhilarated male drunkenness and love of drink is as central to Australian as it is to Irish humor which is not surprising given the high proportion of Australians who are of Irish descent (Partington 1994). In either case it stems from the strong development of a *bachelor culture*, in Ireland caused by the very late age of marriage after the famine (Stivers 1976: 57, 76-79), and in Australia by selective migration. "In 1820 men outnumbered women (in Australia) by ten to three in the towns and by five to one in the country. As late as 1842 the overall ratio was still roughly three men to every one woman. Among these female members of the young society only the minority were genteel or possessed of the softer accomplishments of their sex" (Conway 1974: 29). Australia was a bachelor society and especially in the outback. Relatively few Australians lived in the outback but those who did were regarded as the carriers of a distinctively Australian tough, masculine outlook. In the absence of women and families a cult of "mateship" developed around the culturally important all-male groups whose central values were "male solidarity and equality" and the "superiority of men over women" (Oxley 1977: 95).

Whereas Jews typically drink in moderation and at meal-times with their families and under the eyes of their women-folk, Australian men drink as a group of men in a men-only bar, standing drinks for one another on a mutual basis which results in heavy drinking as each man is expected to and, indeed, demands to have his own shout (buy his own round) (Oxley 1977: 79; Sargent 1979: 24-31). The Australian drinking group came to form a cohesive if shallow brotherhood and persisted and continued to exclude women long after the initial demographic reason for its existence had disappeared (Conway 1974: 32, 141). The all-male drinking group in Australia as in Ireland began as a substitute for the family and remained as a rival to it, a group whose ethic far from being orderly as the presence of women would have demanded, was one of ''fraternal anarchy" (Conway 1974: 77). It has given rise to a pattern of jokes that are the antithesis of those found among Jews. In Australian as in Irish jokes, a man's ability to drink and brawl are more important than his ties with women:

An Australian queer is a man who prefers girls to beer. (Bowles 1984: 56)

An Aussie loves his beer, his mates and his wife—and in that order. (British 1970s. See also O'Grady 1965: 97)

Most married men approve of wife swapping in Western Australia. Most of them want to swap theirs for a catamaran and a snorkle. (Cagney 1979: 28)

A bluff Australian tradesman walked in unexpectedly and found his regular girl friend on the couch with an Italian cook from the short-order café along the street. There was a heated argument and the Italian said, "Angela, she no longer like-a you. She my girl now. She like lover with Latin blood in his veins. I got-a Latin blood in-a my veins." The Aussie said, "Not for long you ain't, Casanova. I'm gonna spill most of it on the floor." (Cagney 1979: 80)

In the Wild West they like their womenfolk weak and their liquor strong. In the frozen North they like their women strong and their drink heated up. In New Brunswick they like their liquor straight and their women wavy. In Australia they like their women only when they've got to the state when they can't see any more liquor. (Cagney 1979: 25)

Australian drinking is extra-familial as may be seen from the long rows of cars parked outside outback pubs with disgruntled but dutiful women in the driving seat waiting for their tipsy husbands to condescend to be driven home safely. There is bound to be tension between family men who spent long years of apprenticeship in the hard-drinking bachelor culture before they married and their wives who wish they could break away from it altogether. The same tension between bar and family is, of course, central to many Irish and Irish-American jokes about drinking for exactly the same reasons:

A man goes into a bar with his wife and immediately on sitting down said to the bartender, "Give me a drink before it starts." The bartender pours him a beer. The man drinks it.
"Give me another beer," he says, "before it starts."
The bartender is puzzled. "There's no entertainment here tonight, sir. The strippers come on Fridays."
Again the man demands, "Another drink before it starts."
Whereupon his wife interjects with, "I think you've had enough to drink, dear."
And the man says to the bartender, "See! It's started." (Adams and Newell 1994: 325)

"Did you hear the news?" asked Reardon of his pal at the saloon.
"Harrigan drank so much, his wife left him!"
"Waiter! Give me six boiler-makers!" (Wilde 1979: 56)

"Have a drink, quick, before me wife comes in, Cassidy!" said Casey.
"What would she do if she caught ye?" enquired Cassidy. "Break every bone in me body!" explained Casey, adding "eternal vigilance is the price of liberty, Cassidy!" (Harvey 1904: 176)

Gaffney staggered into a bar crying.
"What happened?" asked Brady the bartender.
"I did a horrible thing," sniffed the drunk. "Just a few hours ago I sold my wife to someone for a bottle of scotch."
"That is awful," said Brady. "Now she's gone and you want her back, right?"
"Right," said Gaffney still crying.
"You're sorry you sold her because you realised too late that you love her, right?"
"Oh no," said the Irishman, "I want her back because I'm thirsty again."
(Wilde 1978: 110)

What is clear from both the Australian and the Irish jokes is that the existence of the all-male drinking group as a rival pivot to the family both enables men to enjoy a dominant position and provokes overt conflict between the sexes. It is the antithesis of the Jewish situation in which Jewish males, bound into a much more grid-like family life, tell jokes about their own alleged subordination to and control by Jewish women. By contrast, the bachelor boys of Australia and Ireland are violent and reckless drinkers, free from the restraints of married life and exult in this in their jokes. In Australia alcohol is known as lunatic soup (Crooked Mick of the Spewa 1986: 35). Australian jokes and humor about male drinking, drunkenness and its aftermath are very similar to those of other hard-drinking cultures with a bachelor and larrikin tradition. However, male Australian humor goes even further than most in its defiance of the more ordered, controlled and fastidious world preferred by women, notably in its celebration of rude, coarse vomiting after a bout of manly drinking.

> Why do Australians piss in the bushes at parties?
> Because there's always someone chundering (being sick) in the toilet. (Ocker 1986).

There are or were even Australian Internet sites (December 1999) devoted to the comedy of chundering (Australian for vomiting, from the warning to those down under the puker to "watch under"). One particularly notable one is the *The Great ChunderPageThepagewithCarrotsinit* (homepages.tig.com.au/~McGarry/paul/chunder. See also the *Chunder and Alcohol Links*)."Some great 'action shots' are viewable from here as well as some great vomiteurs." There are also pictures of projectile vomit, "a truly exceptional photo of a spontaneous vomit" and "simulvom" or "simulpuke," a photo of "two people showing one of the signs of true friendship, the simultaneous vomit."

It is images like this that must have inspired the *Monty Python Australian Table Wine Sketch* (montypython.virtualave.net/text/austwine.txt) which speaks of:

> Chateau Chunder…an Appelachian controle specially grown for those keen on regurgitation—a fine wine which really opens the sluices at both ends…real emit fans will also go for a "Hobart Muddy" and a prize-winning Cuiver Reserve Chateau Bottled Nuit San Wogga Wogga which has a bouquet like an aborigine's armpit.

The strongest piece of evidence concerning the dingo-like tendency of Australians to return to their vomit for humor lies in the

Australians' more extensive and far more picturesque vocabulary on the subject of vomiting (known in the United Kingdom as Australian diarrhea) than is the case with other speakers of English. The Australian authors and editors of humorous guides to Australian English provide many terms for vomiting that are not in the Oxford English Dictionary which has only ninety-nine, on the whole, rather boring entries under "vomit" (liberty.vc.wlu.edu/~hbllack/oed/vomit December 1999). Australian English glories in phrases such as to air the diced carrots, the big spit, to bring fluorescent Christmas cheer, to call Ralph on the big white telephone, to chuckle, to churn the China sea, to cry Ralph, to drive the dunny, to drive the porcelain bus (brrrrrooooom!), to growl at the gravel, to have a long conversation with Armytage Shanks, to kark, to laugh at your shoes, to liquidate your assets, a liquid laugh, to make love to the lav, to make an offering to the great porcelain god, to make pavement asterisks, to make a pea and carrot kaleidoscope, to park a Tiger, to play the whale, to pop a gastric zit, to scream in Braille, to serve a message to the waste basket, to shout Europe at the sink, to sing the national anthem of Bulimia-God Save the Princess of Wales, a technicolour yawn, a three dimensional burp, a thunder-chunder rainbow, tuna salad swimming upstream, upward nutritional mobility, to use the chunky mouthwash, the yellow tornado, to yodel in technicolour (Blackman 1991; Bowles 1986; Crooked Mick of the Spewa 1986; Hudson and Pickering 1987; Humphries and Garland 1988; *The Vomit Dictionary* on artemis.eng.monash/edu.au/~mills/waterski and *Chunder Synonymous* on proximity.com.au~brian/chunder December 1999). Many of these synonyms and images may well exist in other forms of English, but in aggregate (and Australian editors, writers and publishers are far more likely to aggregate them than their colleagues in other countries) the Australians win on numbers, crudity and inventiveness. The comic quality of Australian chundering is also indicated by the way it is linked to laughing or chuckling in some of these expressions and this quality is also present in the Australian chundering song *Bondi Pier,* which is almost as internationally famous as the song of the wandering swagman, *Waltzing Matilda*. Other countries have distinctive ethnic drinking songs such as *Bread from Evans's* or *I belong to Glasgow* or the songs sung by the scar-faced members of German duelling corps, which celebrate the elation, exuberance, intoxication and even violence

induced by alcohol, but Australia almost alone possesses songs that
revel in drinking's vomiting aftermath:

Bondi Pier

I was down by Bondi Pier,
Drinkin' tubes of ice cold beer,
With a bucket full of prawns upon my knee,
When I swallowed the last prawn,
I had a technicolour yawn,
And I chundered in the old Pacific Sea.

Drink it up, drink it up,
Crack another dozen tubes and prawns with me.
If you want to throw your voice,
Mate you won't have any choice,
But to chunder in the Old Pacific Sea.

I was sitting in the surf, when a mate of mine called Murf,
Asks if he can crack a tube or two with me.
The bastard barely swallowed it,
When he went for the big spit,
And he chundered in the Old Pacific Sea.

Drink it up, drink it up, etc.

I've had liquid laughs in bars,
And I've hurled from moving cars,
And I've chuckled when and where it suited me.
But if I could choose the spot,
To regurgitate me lot,
Then I'd chunder in the Old Pacific Sea. (cs.cmu.edu/~mleone/
gdead/dead-lyrics/Bondi_Pier.txt December 1999)

The Australian humor of chundering within the hard-drinking,
all-male group is a way of celebrating disorder, reversal and confusion which are both descriptions of the act and consequences of
vomiting itself and of the social characteristics of the group in which
it occurs. Its members are deliberately shocking and defying those
"others" who stand for order, refinement and control, namely *women*,
respectable Australia including the wowsers (we only want social
evils remedied) and their descendants (we acknowledge no known
ethnic rivalries), and the upper-middle class English, the pommie
bastards, Australia's polite, intellectual and hierarchical rival and
former mentor.

The force of this defiance is best seen in the work of the Australians' greatest comic genius and superstar, Barry Humphries, the creator of the Barry McKenzie cartoon strip (1988) and films and of the internationally famous theatre and television personalities Dame Edna Everage (Lahr 1992) and Dr. Sir Leslie Colin Patterson, the cultural attache to the Australian High Commission in London, and author of *The Travellers Tool* (1986). Barry McKenzie is an unsophisticated, good-hearted Australian visitor to England who unleashes his simple authentic, spontaneous chundering over pretentious English intellectuals who seek to exploit him. He always does so in a way that undermines or exposes the inadequacy of the English victims' use of English, that very symbol of their superior orderliness.

A good example of this occurs when the yartz-ridden BBC television producer Dominic Fry invites Barry McKenzie to chunder on camera. McKenzie who has recklessly mixed alcohol and amphetamines before his live broadcast instead drops his daks (trousers/pants) and flashes what he calls his nasty, his one-eyed trouser snake, his beef bugle, his old mutton dagger (the male member) at millions of British viewers (Humphries and Garland 1988: 39-40). Dominic Fry is ecstatic at this television breakthrough and offers Barry his own television series, but the by now nauseous and shaken McKenzie is sick all over him. The besicked-on television producer is last seen running away, gibbering:

> I think I'm going mad—hear no evil—see no evil—smell no evil...
> You've chundered on me for the last time...out, out damned spot...
> Will the multitudinous seas incarnadine...he took water and washed his hands
> ...Aghh!!...my soul is white but oh my suit is orange. Omo washes whiter—clean—clean—white—pure white! Wings winging. (Humphries and Garland 1988: 40)

In this speech the familiar words of Lady Macbeth from Shakespeare and in the description of the actions of Pontius Pilate in the Gospel according to St. Matthew (27: 24) in the King James' Authorized Version of the Bible (1611), the very basis of English literacy, order and tradition, dissolve into an advertising slogan for soap powder which then fragments into pseudo-poetic nonsense. A speech involving the destruction of order, language and meaning is singularly appropriate coming from a television producer who has just been the victim of a chunderer. Television is to complex thought and speech what puking is to eating for it breaks them down and spews them out again as a shapeless colloid of pictures decorated with words. The media is the mess age, for what we eat becomes what we are and what we think becomes what we say, except in puking and television where there is an unnatural reversal of these normally one-way processes bringing us back to disorder (Davies 1990: 302-3).

At a previous time during his stay in England, Barry McKenzie had been seized, taken to a lunatic asylum and confined in a straight-jacket. While trapped in this completely helpless position he is forced to listen to the Freudian psycho-babble of a British Jewish psychia-trist, Dr. Meyer de Lamphrey, who suggests that McKenzie's diffi-culties with the mother country, Britain, stem from problems in his relationship with his own mother. There is only one form of counter-attack available to a nauseous man trapped in a straight jacket. McKenzie threatens Dr. de Lamphrey that he will "chunder on his wall to wall," "throw the voice," "play the whale," and "laugh at the ground," but the wretched psychiatric expert trapped in his own jar-gon cannot understand good, plain, down-to-earth Australian En-glish. Barry McKenzie entices him close enough for a chunder and is sick all over his hair shouting triumphantly, "cop that, you Pommy Bastard" (Humphries and Garland 1988: 26). Once again order and authority have been degraded.

Many chunders later McKenzie while travelling between England and France on a ferry is sick over the rail on the upper deck of a ship onto a nice old English lady, who is jabbering in baby-talk to her rat-sized small dog. In some way she is evading the health regulations designed to stop the spread of what she describes to her dog as "those horrid rabie wabies." Her nonsensical infantile chat with her pet is suddenly silenced when Barry McKenzie entombs her and the dog in "tepid chuck" (Humphries and Garland 1988: 80). Barry McKenzie now returns to the dog and his vomit and says medita-tively to his Frenchified Australian associate "Col the Frog," "Isn't it funny when you come to think of it? A bastard tucks away a few jars of ice cold, it's only in his Ned Kelly for a few jiffs and then when he has a decent hurl it comes out all thick and different somehow." At this point the old lady becomes nauseous from listening to McKenzie's musings about his own vomit and is herself sick over the side of the ship. Barry McKenzie encourages her by shouting, "Go on lady, play the whale, but I'll bet you a greenie it won't look nothing like what you had for lunch" (Humphries and Garland 1988: 80).

It is significant that this victim of McKenzie's chundering is female and, like all the others chundered on in Humphries and Garland's cartoon strip, fastidiously English and middle class; in some cases they are Jewish (Dr. Meyer de Lamphrey and Lou Silver) as well. Each category is placed in opposition to the hard-drinking, male Australian ocker and bachelor culture of Barry McKenzie whose representatives revel in their rejection of order, categories and control.

Perhaps significantly, the creation of the Barry McKenzie cartoon strip was rooted in the Dada experiments of their Australian writer Barry Humphries when a student at Melbourne University in Australia (Allen 1984: 14; Brissenden 1981: xii; Coleman 1990: 26-32; Lahr 1992: 44-49). Humphries describes two such artistic but revolting episodes from his student days in the 1950s in his autobiography, *More Please* (Humphries 1993: 118-9). That middle-class and suburban Australians were shocked by their experience of Humphries' antics is not remarkable; what is significant is that it is Australia that produced Humphries, the artist and comedian, the cultured and revolting aesthete, and in consequence is responsible for the shocking scenes he describes:

The firm of H J Heinz had an excellent product called Russian Salad. It consisted largely of diced potato in mayonnaise with a few peas and carrot chips. Surreptitiously spilt and splashed in large quantities on the pavement of a city block, it closely resembled human vomit. It was a simple and delightful recreation of mine to approach a recent deposit of salad in the guise, once again, of a tramp. Disgusted pedestrians were already giving it a very wide berth, holding their breaths and looking away with watering eyes. Not I, as I knelt beside one of the larger puddles, curdled and carrot-flecked. Drawing a spoon from my top pocket I devoured several mouthfuls, noticing out of the corner of my eye, and with some satisfaction, several people actually being sick at the spectacle.

Even more entertaining by far were the two Dada exhibitions held in the Women Graduates' Lounge in the Old Union building, and our lunchtime revue, Call Me Madman! These are the highlights of my short University career. The "art" exhibitions occurred on consecutive years but have merged in my memory. One of the most notorious exhibits consisted of a large tub filled with old books, one about Cézanne and another called *The Book of Beauty*. Over these volumes a large industrial-sized can of Heinz Russian Salad had been poured. By consulting their catalogues, curious art lovers could discover that this exhibit bore the title, "I was reading these books when I felt sick." (Humphries 1993: 118-9)

Humphries even took his pranks aimed at inspiring "a chain reaction of irrational behaviour" (Lahr 1992: 49) onto an airline and "got himself temporarily banned from Qantas flights for tipping a tin of Russian salad into a sick bag, loudly feigning illness and then eating his "vomit." "If an air hostess sees you," he said, "it can produce what I call the Chain Chunder. Five minutes later the pilot is throwing up" (Lahr 1992: 49). The Australian airline Qantas, however, had a more general problem with untrammeled Australian males and in the early 1980s new and extra-ordinary regulations had to be introduced by the Flight Stewards Association of Australia, impounding all duty-free liquor in order to prevent in-flight violence by drunken Australians on their planes. These regulations dated 30 November 1980 were publicly posted at Heathrow Airport, London, and at all other airports where Qantas operated. Rationality is soluble in alcohol and Australians have distinct forms of drunken comportment of which vomiting is only one aspect. In this case it was not their dangerous in-flight behavior that was seen as comic but the image invoked by Qantas *alone* of all the world's airlines having to post such a public prohibition for all to read.

The language of Barry McKenzie, like that of Barry Humphries' even coarser creation, Dr. Sir Leslie Colin Patterson (Patterson 1986), is characterized by distinctively Australian crude but creative colloquialisms. (It is instructive that in Australian English foul language is referred to as colloquialisms, that is, colloquial to Australia). In doing so, Barry Humphries was merely improving upon, making public, and putting into print an oral tradition of male Australian bar-room humor that had until then been constrained by censorship. Hyram Davis and Peter Crofts (1988) in their famous essay on Australian humor note that:

> The hotel functions as a vernacular museum for verbal Australian humour. Beehives of indigenous oral comedy—Oz-lingo, rhyming slang, ockerisms, and larrikin language—are integral parts of the speech patterns of Australians. The most popular is strong language, otherwise known as swearing, and its use is ambivalent. One use is as a term of endearment: "G'day you bloody old bastard" is a common form used by Australians when they greet one another. The other is a form of abuse, particularly *against people in authority.* Censorship has been the main obstacle in the past preventing Australian humour surfacing because its essence is unprintable. Australians have a certain sense of shame about the crudeness of their humour. It is both a giving and sharing experience—*but only for males.* It is a thread of commitment that has developed into an entire subculture, which to this day remains largely untapped. Being highly coloured, its one-dimensionality effectively maintains this humour as a *male preserve.* (Davis and Crofts 1988: 8; emphasis added)

The Australian filth that dared not speak its full range of names was only hinted at in the earlier humorous books about Australian

English, such as Afferbeck Lauder's (1965) *Let Stalk Strine* (Let's talk Australian) and *Nose Tone Unturned* (1966) combined in *Fraffly Strine Everything* (1969), or John O'Grady's *Aussie English* (1965) and *Aussie Etiket* (1971), which circulated mainly in Australia. Lauder's work contains passages that read "Blank blank and blank but blank" and in the F section of O'Grady's dictionary is a word referred to as **** in the manner of the later four-star barrel punning advertisement for Castlemaine beer that tells us "Australians wouldn't give an XXXX for any other beer." O'Grady mysteriously warned Americans visiting Australia not to root for their favorite team on the grounds that in Australian English the word root has a fundamental biological extremely vulgar application (O'Grady 1965: 75), as in "wouldn't it King Farouk you?" (O'Grady 1965: 88). Perhaps he should also have warned American tourists not to ask a nice Australian girl for a date even if she is wearing a calendar coat. O'Grady spoke of "bloody" as the great Australian adjective and of "bastard" as an extremely useful noun, as valuable to Australians as the coconut is to Polynesians (O'Grady 1965: 40; see also Crooked Mick 1986: 7). The noun "bugger" he regarded as a substitute for bastard (O'Grady 1965: 26) though he does not explain why Australians never tell one another to go to bastardy. Such words were, O'Grady claimed, never used by or in the presence of women (O'Grady 1965:26) and he even speculated that women did not know the words existed (O'Grady 1965: 40). This kind of coarse, sexsegregated pattern of speech would have been found in many working-class communities elsewhere as in the "pit language" of English mining villages, but only in Australia was it seen as nationally typical, as characteristically Australian. Australian women and clergymen were thus excluded from their own national language.

It could also appear to uncomprehending outsiders a very tedious form of English, composed of a limited and endlessly repeated set of banal obscenities. Indeed, an English mathematician calculated that an Australian in full spate would be able to use the word bloody 18,200 times in a lifetime (de Witt 1970: 95), while Eric Newby 1975: 143) described with surprise an Australian who, while ploughing a field, continuously shouted "fuck, fuck, fuck." There are many Australian anecdotes and anecdotal jokes that have as their theme the sheer monotony of this kind of Australian English:

"Full of intercoorsin politicians I'd sooner have in me nostrils the smell o'deadmen than the smell of intercoorsin hope-they-die bloody politicians.... Had to drive fifteen intercoorsin miles to get a carton of milk on Sundy." (Small town Australian recently returned from Canberra, quoted in O'Grady 1965: 97)

An Arab Sheik found it impossible to learn to speak English. He hired tutors from the best universities in Britain and America but failed to make any progress. Eventually in desperation he hired an Australian to teach him English and after his first fifteen minute lesson emerged delighted.
"I have learned half the entire English language," he said proudly.
"How is that possible?" asked his courtiers in amazement.
"Very simple," replied the sheik. "I now know that every second word is 'fuck'."
(Australian 1981. Told to the author by an Australian radio producer)

Australian rigmarole: I was walking along this f**king morning, f**king sun, f**king shining away, little country f**king lane and I meets up with this f**king girl, f**king lovely she was, so we gets into f**king conversation and I takes her over a f**king gate into a f**king field and we has sexual intercourse. (Paros 1984: 7)

In the late 1980s though, a new generation of guides to Australian English emerged notably Colin Bowles, *G'Day, Teach Yourself Australian* (1986) and Bob Hudson and Larry Pickering's *The First Australian Dictionary of Vulgarities and Obscenities* (1987), which were published and sold widely in England as well as Australia and which provided a much more complete picture of the creative, complex and innovative use of obscenity in Australian language and humor. The *authentic national origins* of the forms of speech given by Barry Humphries to Barry McKenzie and Dr. Sir Les Patterson were now clearly established for all the world to see. It is striking also that these books of Australian compiled and edited colloquialisms were successfully sold in Britain; no British publisher or distributor would ever try to market an American, Canadian, Irish, Indian, New Zealand, Newfoundland, Nigerian, Scottish, Singlish (Singapore English), South African or Wenglish (Welsh English) dictionary of local and nationally typical vulgarities and obscenities. Only the Australians have both the material and the reputation to form the basis of a lexicon of crudities that will sell in Britain. Similar collections of rude antipodian colloquialisms are also sold in Singapore (Aitchison and Chan 1995 and 1996), where the local people are familiar with the coarse Australian speech patterns of expatriates from that nearby country or have been to Australia as tourists. There is a striking richness of imagery, simile and metaphor in humorous Australian vulgarity. The words and the ideas are available to those who speak British or American English but the Australians are able to string them together with a verbal skill all of their own. Crude phrases such as "to be up there like a rat up a pump," "a bootsie" (a crawler so far up the boss's arse you can only see his boots), "carpet burns," "to choke a darkie," "to chuck a brown eye," "done up like a pox doctor's clerk," "dry as a nun's nasty," "eating hair pie," "go and dip your left eye in hot cocky shit," "go and stick your head up a dead bear's bum," "hair like a bush pig's arse," "hose down the cassowary", "I hope your chooks turn into emus and kick your shit house down," "I wouldn't want him to fart in my last pound of flour," "if it were raining virgins I'd be washed away with a poofter," "lipstick on the dipstick," "the map of Tasmania," "the one-eyed trouser snake," "opening your lunch," "a packapoo ticket," "pissing in someone's pocket," "pushing shit uphill," "rare as rocking-horse shit," "skidmarks on underwear," "to smell like a lubra's loincloth," "sparrowfart," "to spear the bearded clam," "a Thirty Four— I'll owe you one (34 x 2 +1 =69)," "a vegemite driller," or "to yodel up the valley" (Bowles 1986; Crooked Mick 1986; Hudson and Pickering 1987; Humphries and Garland 1968, 1972, 1988; Johansen 1988; Patterson (Humphries) 1986; Rushton 1983: 109-16) are very Australian. Some of the phrases may well exist elsewhere but no other country has such a collection of calculated coarseness, and so many and such skilled expositors and inventors, notably Barry Humphries (Ingrams 1971:18), or so many unique local items. Also editors and publishers of forms of English other than mainstream English and American do not produce dictionaries of obscenities as national icons. Mockeries and self-mockeries of New Zealand English (Buzo 1994) and South African English (Malong 1972) speech lack that instinctive Australian feel for filth. The distinctively masculine Australian language wins yet again.

Australian men also win within their own jokes. In Jewish jokes invented by Jewish men, Jewish women are represented as feared and powerful, but when Australian women appear in Australian jokes they tend to be disregarded and derided as sad losers (see also Wannan 1995: 134):

> "I've got to dash—I'm on a promise tonight. I'm going to use the rodeo position!"
> "What the hell is the rodeo position?"
> "Well, you get her down on the bed and start giving it to her doggy fashion. As soon as she starts to enjoy it you whisper in her ear 'That's how Tracy at the pub likes it'. Then you have to see how long you can stay on!" (Unknown Australian publication 1990s. Accompanied by an extremely graphic and cleverly drawn cartoon)

Australian foreplay: 1. Nudging his sheila in the ribs: You awake? 2. Brace yourself, Raelene. 3. Make yer a cuppa after. (Ocker 1986. See also Bowles 1986: 87)

Two ancient battlers of the backblocks were sitting in a brown study on the veranda of the local pub when one broke the silence, "Ya know, Arthur, if they'd had electric blankets and ready-cooked tucker when I was a boy, I'm darn sure I'd never o'got married." (Howcroft 1977: 31)

An Englishman, an Irishman and an Australian are at the beach together and see a mermaid sunning herself alluringly on the sand. They are all overcome by her charms. The Englishman marches up to her with great dignity and says, "My dear, you are an exquisite creature and you must tell me if any man has ever kissed you." The mermaid demurely answers, "No, I've never been kissed." So the Englishman bends down and plants a reverential kiss on her cheek then goes back to his colleagues, blushing with happiness.
The Irishman sidles over to the mermaid and says, "Sure and you're the most beautiful little morrmaid I ever saw. Tell me, my beauty, has any man ever touched you gently on your perfectly formed, firm young breasts?" The mermaid lowered her gaze and admitted that she'd never been touched there. The Irishman bent down, gave her a feel and went back to the others beaming with satisfaction.
Then the Australian strode over to the mermaid. "You ever been rooted?" he demanded. "Actually, no," said the mermaid. "Well, you're rooted now, because the tide's gone out." (Adams and Newell 1994: 158-9)

Woman: "Officer, I've been half-raped."
Policeman: "What do you mean half-raped?"
Woman: "It was a wharfie and it started to rain."
(A wharfie is an Australian longshoreman or docker. They were a tough lot but always trying to avoid work so that if it rained everyone would stop work.) (Adams and Newell 1994: 299)

During the Second World War a group of Australian soldiers stationed in the Pacific miles from any woman were watching an English (or American, it matters little which it was) film. The hero and the heroine of the film had quarrelled and the hero said angrily to the heroine: "I'd like to tear you into a thousand little pieces." At that point an Australian voice from the audience shouted: "Good on yer, mate. Throw us the cunt, will yer." (Told to the author in 1985 by an English Professor of Sociology and folklorist who thought it was probably Australian 1950s in origin)

Motto of the Royal Australian Navy:
No sea too rough, no muff too tough. (Told to the author by an Australian radio producer 1981)

There is no sense in even considering whether or not there is a "kernel of truth" in the Australian or the Jewish jokes about sexuality since we do not have anywhere near enough reliable evidence to work with. Nor is there any point in speculating about the motives of or satisfactions derived by the joke tellers (who are also bit by bit the inventors and polishers of the jokes) and those who enjoy the jokes since these are going to vary not only between individuals but between occasions and contexts and cannot be aggregated. To try to infer the motives of tellers and the tendencies and functions of jokes merely from their content and then to use these to explain that very some content is circular and like all circles leads nowhere. It is simply not possible to explain why a particular joke or genre of jokes exists in terms of its or their possible pay offs for the jokers or for the groups to which they belong. The two sets of jokes and other humor that have been discussed here (the Jewish and the Australian) and most important of all the differences between the two sets have to be treated as social facts and an explanation sought in terms of other independent social facts.

The central contrast between the Jewish and Australian jokes and humor that have been examined above in much detail concerns "control." The Jewish women in the jokes are shown as over-controlled and over-controlling and the Australian men as uncontrolled in their language, drinking and sexuality. For outsiders, namely those who are neither Jewish nor Australian, both sets of jokes are funny for the same reason that other ethnic jokes based on opposed extremes, notably those about the canny versus the stupid and cowards versus militarists (i.e., those who are too controlled by material or military life and those who are too loosely attached to them), are *universally* popular (Davies 1990 and 1998, and see chapter 1). In all these cases people who have a rough idea of some kind of desirable and achievable, if less than golden, mean and some sense of what is reasonable in relation to the central pressures of the modern world, laugh at those who are portrayed in the jokes as markedly departing from these in either direction. The Jewish and Australian jokes reveal another central aspect of the modern world that is a source of jokes, namely the historic growth of control over impulses and behavior (Elias 1982: 230-3, 278-90) which also has its downside and which has, in turn, been partly reversed in the latter decades of the twentieth century (Davies 1994; 1994A; Himmelfarb 1995) to produce a very anomic situation. Just as there is a tension between work and leisure and between national obligation and personal safety in a contradictory modern world that forces individuals to seek a balance between competing demands, so, too, there is a tension between indulgence and control, both of which receive encouragement in complex modern societies (Bell 1979). Too much of either is funny because it taps a central tension in modern societies. By contrast there are now few jokes about other more peripheral kinds of excess, for example, in regard to too much or too little piety or learning, neither of which is salient for or even accessible to modern jokers (but see also Oring 1992: 67-80). Even though everyone can laugh at Jewish and Australian jokes for these reasons, it should not surprise us that the prime inventors and circulators of such humor should be respectively the Jews and Australians themselves. They after all are in the best position to observe, to exaggerate and to laugh at cultural differences between themselves and their neighbors.

The contrast between the jokes about Jewish women and Australian men in regard to control and indulgence can be related to three factors: cultural traditions, sex roles and social class. First, the Orthodox Jewish tradition is one of the minute control of everyday life and this is, in turn, closely connected to the maintenance of Jewish identity. Jewish rules, rituals and controls are, of course, a subject of much disagreement, dispute and schism as we saw in chapter 3, but this only confirms how important they are. Jewish jokes are about momentum and collisions, Australian jokes are about chaos and heat.

The central theme of the Jewish rules of conduct is the need for the preservation of a proper orderliness of boundaries and categories and an avoidance of mixing things that should be kept apart (Leviticus 19: 19; Deuteronomy 22: 9-11). It is easy to see why even for modern secularized Jews in America this should lead to strong doubts regarding the permissibility of fellatio and in consequence to jokes about it. Fellatio brings together categories that should be kept apart, the upper and the lower body and the entrance and exit of digestion. Likewise vomiting is unseemly not simply because it is a sequel to drunkenness but also because it *reverses* the natural process of turning orderly, rule-governed food into the reconstruction and maintenance of the structured and orderly human body and turns the mouth, the natural entrance to the body, into an exit. The food thus returned is a formless mess, an aspect of vomit that is expressed in Australian jokes and comic musings about viscosity and diced carrots. Such jokes could not be fitted within the Jewish tradition of order. Likewise there are many Australian jokes about the loss of control by those who are shikker (Australian English as well as Yiddish for being drunk) but no Jewish jokes. If being civilized is defined in terms of personal control over impulse then by comparison with most of the citizens of Western societies the Jews appear over-civilized and the Australians under-civilized.

Norbet Elias's (1982) study of the civilizing process cited earlier laid great stress on the development of personal control, courtesy and etiquette, and the absence of the latter and thus of civilization is a common subject of Australian jokes and humor about Australia, as in John O'Grady's (1971) *Aussie Etiket*.

Belch: The Australian national anthem. (Bowles, 1984: 8)

Aussie etiquette:
Got a match, Tom?
No, but I got a lighter.
How'm I gonna pick my teeth with a lighter. (Ocker 1986)

Australian journalist interviewing Mrs. Gandhi. "Excuse me you've got a dirty mark on your forehead." Licks finger and wipes it off. (Collected by author from an Australian radio producer 1981)

It seemed like an appalling affront to the dignity of the upper class bank in an upper class area of Melbourne when a scruffy-looking male, about 25, walked in. Noses sniffed in disdain. He approached the upper class, snooty-looking female teller and said, "I wanna open a fuckin' cheque account." Her surprise was barely contained by her practised dignity. She told him she would most certainly not serve a man so rude and would he please leave the establishment. Instead, he repeated his request, "I wanna open a fuckin' cheque account, ya bitch." She left her cage with icy decorum and fetched the grey-suited, silvery-haired manager who approached with a supercilious expression. In an accent appropriate to the suburb, he chastened the young guy and impressed upon him the bank's strong belief in manners, decorum, cleanliness and presentation.
In spite of this the scruff repeated, "I just wanna open a fuckin' cheque account, arsehole." The manager raised an eyebrow and asked, very icily, "And how much would your initial deposit be, perchance?"
The reply came, "Three-and-a-half million dollars. I just won Tattslotto."
To which the manager said, "And what cock-sucking little slut refused to serve you?" (Adams and Newell 1994:288)
(There are many jokes in which the manager changes his attitude when he hears of big money, but only the Australian version revels in coarseness and the dragging down of the tall poppy head to the coarse one's level such that he abandons his posh upper class speech and rivals him in crude abuse of the respectable female bank teller. Only in Australia.)

On the train bearing him and an MCC team across the Nullabor Plain from Perth to Adelaide, when Swanton (the late E. W. Swanton the great writer on cricket) asked for a pink gin at the buffet, the Ocker barman replied: "In this country our gin's white, pom." (Heffer 2000: 11)

Australian society has been humorously described as a "rugby-match without a ball" (British 1970s), a hooligans' game played without its purpose and by implication its rules. Such a description of average everyday life in Australia is both unfair and inaccurate, for the everyday life of Australians differs very little from that of those in the other affluent English-speaking societies. (Davis and Encel 1965). However, if we were to construct an "ideal type" Australia in which all the quite small differences between Australia and other comparable societies were pushed to their logical (and extreme and unattainable) conclusions, we would, indeed, find Sir Les Patterson's and Barry McKenzie's Australia.

As indicated earlier, the Australian tradition that extols and jokes and laughs about hard-drinking, vomiting and the extensive use of obscenity, all aspects of a weakly regulated (or a deliberate loss of control over) everyday behavior is a male tradition and one associated with the lower social classes—the ockers (working class and full of it) and the cockies (small farmers in the outback). In most Western societies self-control is stronger among and more strongly expected from women than men and among and from the middle classes than the classes below them. In Australia early patterns of migration, settlement and employment emancipated men from the refining and civilizing influence of women and the lower classes were able to establish a more equal and influential cultural relationship with the classes above them than was true in other similar societies. A male egalitarian bachelor culture was created whose influence survives in a society where "men habitually desert their women at social gatherings and crowd around the beer keg swapping yarns, laughing raucously, literally wallowing in the rituals of mateship" (Conway 1974: 141) and in which "Drink, sports-talk, blue-stories and male solidarity prove effective levellers" (Oxley 1978: 111).

By contrast the Jewish tradition is strongly family centered and women as mothers and wives are both an example of control and a source of control, the women who, in the past, kept kosher households and controlled their own and their husbands' sexuality and avoided defilement through self-examination and the use of the *mikvah* (ritual bath). Jokes about Jewish women are about the secular heiresses of this tradition of control.

Jewish women are also, as indicated earlier, the controllers of Jewish identity and at a time when this identity is being eroded by intermarriage, particularly by Jewish men, they have become the subject of new kinds of jokes to add to an older tradition. Rules become a source of humor when their legitimacy is still accepted but they are in practice frequently broken. Jewish men break the rules and joke about the women who uphold them.

Jewish self-control as well as learning and ambition has led to social mobility (again a great source of Jewish jokes) and in the English-speaking countries to the creation of predominantly middle-class Jewish communities, where Jewish ideas of social control are, of course, further reinforced by the pressures of social class. Many of the American jokes about Jewish wives and the very concept of the Jewish American *Princess* are linked to the concern with visible wealth and status associated with those newly arrived in the American upper-middle class; J.A.P jokes are as much jokes about *class* as about ethnicity and as much about American materialism as about Jewish women. The J.A.P. is American and a princess as well as being Jewish. Her position depends on the ordered use of wealth in the pursuit of status.

Thus, a variety of cultural and historical forces have placed Jewish women and Australian men in social positions such that each has come to be humorously regarded as residing at the extremes of the social dimension I have described in terms of the contrast between control on the one hand and absence or loss of control on the other, between the over-civilized and the under-civilized. Both groups are in consequence mocked by Jews, Australians and outsiders alike; the best humor comes from within but the audiences are far more universal.

Note

1.   The following blessings from Birkot Hashachar, the Morning Blessings are recited every morning of the year by Orthodox Jews, including Shabbat and holidays:

(a) is recited by males, (b) by females.

(a) Blessed are You, HASHEM, our G-d, king of the universe, who has not made me a woman.

(b) Blessed are You, HASHEM, our G-d, king of the universe, who has made me according to His will.

5

Canadian Jokes about Newfoundlanders: Neighborly, Bilingual, North American

There is a marked contrast between the self-mocking jokes told by the Scots and the Jews in chapters 2, 3, and 4 and the American jokes about Poles that are largely imposed on Polish Americans by other Americans for reasons analyzed in chapters 7 and 8. The Poles do not own, indeed, are not even important to, the jokes that are told about them. They simply happened to occupy a position in the American class system that made it likely that they would be the butt of stupidity jokes.

Canadian jokes about Newfoundlanders occupy an interesting intermediate position. The American Polish joke cycle of the 1960s soon spread to Eastern Canada where the jokes were pinned on the inhabitants of Newfoundland, Canada's island province in the Atlantic Ocean. It would seem at first sight as if the Canadians had lost control of yet one more part of their culture to the Americans, as indicated in the jokes:

> What is the capital of Canada?
> Mainly American. (Kelly and Mann 1978)

> What wars did Canada take part in?
> Oh, the same ones. (Kelly and Mann 1978)

> When will Canada legalize marijuana?
> The day after. (Kelly and Mann 1978)

> What do you get when you cross a Canadian and an American?
> An American. (Kelly and Mann 1978)

> Canadian genius is ten per cent imitation and ninety per cent importation.
> (Mann 1977: 49)

Yet as the analysis of the Canadian jokes below indicates, the Canadians do own their own jokes, and Newfoundland jokes, though similar to their American counterparts, are distinctively Canadian.

When jokes are imported they are adapted to take account of local circumstances and in the case of Quebec the local language. Yet, at the same time, the essential script of the stupid and the dirty has remained the same and it is clear from archival material that the Newfie jokes told about themselves by Newfoundlanders do not differ significantly from those told elsewhere in Canada or those told about Poles in America. There is no difference between the jokes told on the outside and those told on the inside, and it is clear from the Newfoundland joke collectors' comments on the jokes the Newfoundlanders told about themselves that they did not feel in any way self-demeaned by telling them. They had become another form of accepted self-mockery alongside the older, indigenous tradition of self-mocking jokes about stupidity for which Newfoundland has long been famous and which will be the subject of chapter 6. These jokes have always been under Newfoundland ownership and the new Canadian jokes have simply been merged with the older anecdotes to form a composite Newfoundland humor. But, first, let us look at the wider Canadian situation.

Ethnic or regional jokes about the supposed stupidity of a particular people (or in some cases the inhabitants of a particular town) occur in most countries as can be seen from table 1.1 in chapter 1 (see also Davies 1988A, 1988B, 1990, and 1998). Canadian jokes about Newfoundland are unique to Canada, yet they can be regarded as simply one example of a very popular international joke, one that travels from country to country and can be switched from one appropriate group to another. Indeed, this very switchability has led some Canadian scholars wrongly to conclude that the ethnic stupidity joke cannot be identified with any particular people and can be shifted around with total flexibility (Downey 1986: 3; See also Mercer n.d. C.C.N.S). In practice, this isn't true; no one, for example, routinely tells "stupidity" jokes about the Jews (except those of Chelm) or the Scots or the Japanese or the Swabians or the Paisas, even though it would be easy in theory to construct such jokes simply by changing the identity of the protagonists of the stupidity joke. Indeed, as indicated in chapter 1 we can specify clearly the specific sociological conditions under which stupidity jokes are told about a group (and by extension not told about some other group). There are implicit cultural rules that decide who will be the butt of a particular kind of joke; they are not the product of some kind of politically correct censorship but are the result of the spontaneous perceptions and actions of the millions of ordinary citizens who invent and transmit jokes.

There also exist major differences in the content of the stupidity jokes circulating in different countries; for example, when Americans tell stupidity jokes about Poles or Italians they also treat them as being dirty, whereas this dimension does not exist in British jokes about the Irish nor in French jokes about the Belgians (Davies 1990, 1996). It will be interesting to see how the Newfie jokes (jokes about Newfoundlanders) from Canada, a country subject to British, French and American influences, fit into this pattern, a pattern which has important implications for our understanding of the deeper and more general differences between the relevant cultures.

Also although many of the jokes about ethnic stupidity have travelled from the United States to Canada, many Newfie jokes have clearly been invented in Canada and reflect specifically Canadian characteristics. One of these characteristics is that Canadian Newfie jokes exist in *two* languages: English and French; although many of the jokes have been translated from one language to the other, others clearly belong primarily to one or the other of Canada's two main language communities and the humor of many of these may even depend on an untranslatable pun or play on words. A further specifically Newfoundland and Canadian theme in the stupidity jokes can be inferred from the numerous references in the jokes to fish (especially cod) and fishing. However, it should be noted that these humorous fishy Canadian references to a distinctly Newfoundland food and activity do have close equivalents in the ethnic jokes of other countries, notably those which refer to food and footwear. Thus, Canadian ethnic stupidity jokes are part of a broad, almost worldwide pattern, and yet within that pattern there are items specific to Canada. It is also important to emphasize that the Newfoundlanders are a famously witty and humorous people with a very rich tradition of locally based jokes and anecdotes, and pride themselves on having a marked and distinctive sense of humor. It might be thought that this would make them an unlikely target for ethnic jokes about stupidity. On the contrary, as in the case of the Irish, the two kinds of humor fit together very well. *Both* kinds are the product of Newfoundland's distinctive geographical position, economic activities and cultural tradition.

The importance and popularity of Newfoundland jokes in Canada are now declining in the twenty-first century after the boom in such jokes between the 1960s and 1990s, much as has happened in other countries, but for a joke cycle to last for over thirty years is in itself remarkable. Edith Fowkes (1982: 53; see also Klymasz 1970) has noted in her study of Canadian folktales that jokes and anecdotes are the most familiar kind of tale told in the modern world.

> Tall tales depending on exaggeration for their humor, bawdy jokes, and tales of stupid characters, usually directed against some particular group—Newfoundlanders, Ukrainians, Pakistanis, etc.—are probably the most common forms of folktales told in Canada today (Fowkes 1982:53).

From Fowkes's assessment we can derive three important reasons for studying the Newfoundland joke. First, its importance as one of the most "common forms of folktales told in Canada," which justifies a detailed examination of both its international and specifically Canadian aspects. Second, the special position of the Newfoundlanders in the construction, shaping and reshaping of the Newfie joke in contrast to the relative passivity of the Ukrainians, who have been the butt of stupidity jokes in Western Canada (Klymasz 1970); this point will be explored in depth in chapter 6. Finally, there is Fowkes's strange and, as we shall see, quite invalid notion that jokes are "directed against" Newfoundlanders, despite the total absence of evidence that Canadians treat Newfoundlanders with the kind of disdain, hostility and discrimination imposed on many of those truly at the bottom of the ethnic vertical mosaic that is Canada. All these aspects of Canadian culture and humor also need to be explored.

The fact that Canadians (at least in Eastern Canada) tell stupidity jokes about Newfoundlanders rather than about some other group is part of a general pattern that can be inferred from the instances listed in table 1.1 in chapter 1. In each case the peoples about whom the jokes are told *share* a common country, culture or language with the joke tellers, but they inevitably live at the edge of that country or culture, whereas the joke tellers live at the center; the position of the edge in relation to the center may be defined in terms of geographical space or in terms of time, the butts of the jokes being relatively new but familiar and accepted members of the society. Newfoundlanders qualify under both headings but most clearly in terms of geography. Newfoundland is an off-shore island in the Atlantic at the very edge of Canada with its own time zone and is perceived by Canadians as a remote place, much as Ireland is perceived by the British, Kerry by the Irish, Tasmania by the Australians, Ostfriesland by the Germans or the west coast of the South Island of New Zealand by New Zealanders.

Perhaps because of the stretch of sea that separates Newfoundland from what the Newfoundlanders significantly refer to as "the mainland," the people of Newfoundland have retained a distinctive and separate provincial identity; indeed, for many years they were an independent self-governing country. Newfoundland refused to join the Canadian Federation in 1867 and in 1869 there were widespread popular demonstrations on the island celebrating the triumph of local independence over confederation (Chadwick 1967: 27; see also F. Jones 1990; Noel 1971). In the 1930s the Dominion of Newfoundland went bankrupt and returned for a time to a state of semi-dependence on Britain. Eventually the Newfoundlanders voted by referendum to become a Canadian province, but only by a very small majority on the second ballot. It was finally agreed that Newfoundland should join Canada on 1 April 1949; only at the very last moment was the date brought forward a day "to avoid holding the anniversary of confederation on April Fool's Day" (Noel 1971: 261). It would not be unfair to say that historically the Newfoundlanders were reluctant Canadians. The particular case of Canadians telling stupidity jokes about Newfies fits very well the general sociological model of those at the center telling stupidity jokes about those at the edge, for the Newfoundlanders can be said to be peripheral to Canada in terms of *both* space *and* time. Also there has been considerable out-migration from Newfoundland to mainland Canada. Before Newfoundland joined Canada the Newfoundlanders were immigrants having to adjust to the local mores of Canada; they were new arrivals from outside in Canadian society. Today Newfoundlanders simply migrate within Canada; in going to, say, Toronto or even Halifax they transplant to the center something of the way of life characteristic of a distant periphery.

As in many of the other cases listed in table 1.I in chapter 1, the economic situation of Newfoundland as an island at the very edge of Canada has also fuelled the development of stupidity jokes. Historically, Newfoundland depended heavily on fishing (especially for cod) and hunting (especially for seals) (Coish 1979; England 1969 (1924); Patey 1990); also berry picking was a useful supplement (Narváez 1991) to the root crops that are all that would grow on the inhospitable rock that constitutes the island. The Newfoundlander's traditional economic activities are, and long have been, a source of humor both for the local people and for outsiders who tend to contrast them with the advanced and sophisticated manufacturing and service industries of urban mainland Canada. Sidney Noel has written of the smaller Newfoundland communities, that the people there lived until, the second half of the twentieth century, in

> tiny isolated out-ports where their way of life was not essentially different from that led by their fore-fathers. The fishery with its antiquated technology and financial structure still remained their basic source of livelihood: Such amenities as motor roads and hydro-electric power were practically unknown; while in their homes a simple nineteenth century world of large patriarchal families, Victorian morals, oil lamps and wood stoves remained anachronistically alive. (Noel 1971: 262)

Given the dedication of most inhabitants of modern industrial societies to an ideology of progress, change and improvement, it is easy to see how those who are perceived by others as leading, or at least having led until recently, an "antiquated" and "anachronistic" way of life become the butt of stupidity jokes. For those who dwell in the more prosperous parts of urban Canada, Newfoundlanders must have appeared stupid to have chosen to live like that and to have only abandoned such a way of life after they had joined Canada and were dragged "kicking and screaming into the twentieth century" (Harold Hocking cited in Miller (n.d.) C.C.N.S).

This big gap between the economic position, the way of life and the social attitudes of the people at the edge and those of the inhabitants of the sophisticated urban centers gave rise to stupidity jokes about the Newfoundlanders even before Confederation. Within Newfoundland itself such jokes were told by the "townies" of St. John's, the capital city and trading center of Newfoundland about the "baymen" who lived in the remote out-ports, much as British jokes about the Irish are told in Ireland about the Kerrymen from the remote coasts of County Kerry. In the modern world where skills change rapidly with technology and where a person's knowledge has to be increasingly more general and abstract to cope with the changes, there is inevitably a further intensification of the view that there is something comically stupid about the way of life based on traditional and craft skills of those at the edge, relative to the way of life of those at the center, and this view will be shared by both groups. Those at the center know that they will never need the skills and knowledge possessed by those at the edge, while those at the edge are uneasily aware that the skills and knowledge held by those at the center are likely also to dominate the lives of those at the edge.

In fairness it must be added that there are other values, virtues and admired qualities more strongly characteristic of those at the edge who live in stable rural or small town communities ; they are likely to be more self-sufficiently practical, more friendly, more honest, more helpful and more devout. Those at the center, however superior they may feel, are likely to acknowledge and recognize this (Laba 1977). Also those at the edge have a more distinct collective identity based on residence, kinship and ancestry than the individuals living in an impersonal, cosmopolitan city. Indeed, viewed from this perspective the "baymen" are better Newfoundlanders than the "townies" who joke about them (Laba 1977), and the Newfoundlanders of today are more distinctively Canadian than those who live in the large English-speaking cities of central Canada, whose way of life is uncomfortably similar to that of the United States (Pocius 1994). Newfoundland, like Quebec, is essential to a Canada defined as non-American northern North America. There is scope for a "reverse" humor here, but in a world addicted to progress it is unlikely to prevail over the dominant humor based on the outlook of those who live in the urban center.

One striking feature of the long cycle of Newfoundland jokes that began in the 1960s is that the jokes exist in large numbers in Canada, both in English and French. This is relatively unusual for ethnic jokes about stupidity, since elsewhere almost every country and culture has its own version of the jokes, though as may be seen from table 1.1 in chapter 1, both the French and the Dutch tell such jokes about the Belgians. Also jokes about Sikhs exist all over India and Pakistan and are definitely told in Gujarati, Hindi, Urdu, Kashmiri, Punjabi and English.

So far as the jokes in English are concerned, what is striking is the *contrast* between the importance of the distinctive speech patterns of the Newfoundlanders in the traditional humorous narrative anecdotes generated within the province and their relative lack of importance in the most recent cycle of Newfie jokes which are told in many English-speaking provinces of Canada as well as in Newfoundland itself. The latter tend to be about some universal property of material reality rather than the local idiosyncratic quirks of Newfoundland English. In the latter jokes, Newfoundland speech is merely a shibboleth, an identifier, the means by which outsiders can tell who is a native of Newfoundland. The person telling Newfie jokes may well adopt a strong and, indeed, exaggerated Newfoundland accent, but is likely to employ only a few crude characteristics of Newfoundland speech such as the substitution of a "d" for a "th" sound (as in "dis" and "dat"), the dropping of "h" at the beginning of words and its strange re-emergence at the start of words that begin with a vowel, plus a tendency to address all and sundry as b'y (boy) (Mercer n.d. C.C.N.S). However, the very circulation of the jokes throughout the whole of Eastern and Central Canada precludes any detailed use of the rich and distinctive Newfoundland vocabulary, most of which will be unfamiliar to other Canadians. It is in this respect very like the Scots jokes discussed earlier.

In particular, the distinctive qualities of Newfoundland speech are likely to be unfamiliar to French-Canadians, who tend to have a dichotomous view of Canada as divided into Anglophone and Francophone segments. Rather it is noteworthy that many Newfie jokes told in French depend upon a play on words peculiar to the French language that cannot be easily translated into English:

> "Le 'Newfie' pensait que les crayons à mine (AMIN) venaient de l'Ouganda." (Allard 1976: 69)

> "Je suis allé dans un magasin 'Newfie' et j'ai demandé une robe de chambre... le 'Newfie' m'a demandé: 'Quelle grandeur la chambre?'" (Allard 1976: 91)

It is clear from jokes such as these, that the French-speaking Canadians have invented and circulated Newfie jokes independently of what was happening in English-speaking Canada. At the same time, many of the other Newfie jokes told in French in Quebec or New Brunswick correspond almost exactly to jokes told in English in other parts of Canada or to jokes told about Poles or Italians in the United States. The ethnic stupidity jokes told in French-speaking Canada as elsewhere in the world consist of a mixture of freely circulating international jokes together with those that have been invented locally and are unique to that locality.

It has sometimes been suggested that the enthusiasm for Newfie jokes to be found among French Canadians is rooted in malice (either towards Newfoundlanders per se or towards what was perceived as a particularly vulnerable group of Anglophones). However, during my work on Newfoundland jokes in New Brunswick and Quebec in 1994, French-Canadians often said to me, on learning of the subject of my research: "We (too) are Newfies." By this they meant that they occupied a comparably peripheral position in Canadian society or indeed within Anglophone North America to that of the Newfoundlanders and there are jokes that imply this in both French and English:

> "It is said that a Newfie is a Québecois who has never been to Ontario." (author's translation from Allard 1976: 112)

> Years ago a Scotsman came to work as an engineer with the A.N.D. company at Grand Falls. After living at Grand Falls for a few months, he decided he liked Newfoundland and the people. He wished that he could be a Newfoundlander and expressing his desire to a doctor one evening, the doctor said he could help him.
> "We can take you into hospital and remove one-quarter of your brain. You will then be a Newfoundlander."
> "You're sure it will work?" replied the Scotsman.
> "Quite sure," replied the doctor.
> "OK, I'll do it!" said the Scotsman. The next week he went into hospital for the operation. A few hours after coming from surgery, he was visited by his doctor. Before the patient could say anything, the doctor said, "I'm dreadfully sorry, but we've made a mistake. Instead of removing only one-quarter of your brain, we've removed three-quarters."
> "Mon Dieu," came the reply. (Sheppard and Noftle 1979: 30)

However, it might be more true to say that the French speakers *used* to be Newfies, but that the urbanization, secularization and commercialization of Quebec from the 1960s put them in a position where they were better able to tell jokes about Newfoundlanders as the rural periphery. Indeed, the rapidity with which short urban jokes (often in the form of a riddle) about Newfoundlanders or other ethnic groups in French have replaced the detailed humorous anecdotes of an earlier rural generation, which were often centered on the power of the local priest (see A.C.E.A. files), is a striking demonstration of the rapid social transformation of French Canada. The jokes have even changed the French language in Canada, for by 1979 Pierre DesRuisseaux noted in *Le Livre des Expressions Québecoises*, that *être Newfie* (to be a Newfie) had come to be used with the meaning *être imbécile, nigaud*, (to be an imbecile, a booby). He says that it is generally used without malice, much in the same way that Anglophones generally are referred to by the French as *têtes carrées*, (square-heads) (DesRuisseaux 1979: 178).

Fish and fishing have been central to Newfoundland's way of life for most of its history and humorous cartoons of the Newfoundlander tend to show him dressed and equipped for work as a fisherman (Allard 1976, 1978, The Tulks n.d.). Many traditional Newfoundland jokes are based on real or fictional incidents related to fish and fishing and the existence of many jokes relating to fishing in the most recent cycle of stupidity jokes suggests that these jokes are of Canadian origin, although it should be noted that similar Scandinavian jokes about cold climate fishing also exist:

Two Newfies were fishing on the ice at Venise-en-Québec. Suddenly a Ski-doo went past and one said to the other: "We ought to go trolling for fish, too." (author's translation from Lepage 1983: 64)

Did you hear about the Newfoundlander who pulled the plug from the bottom of his boat while returning from a fishing trip in order to get rid of the water already ankle deep? (M.U.N.F.L.A. file 68-24G. Collector H. Boyd Trask)

Why don't Newfoundlanders fish in the Winter time?
Because they can't cut a hole in the ice big enough to put the boat in. (M.U.N.F.L.A. file 69-1F. Collector, Bernice Bartlett)

A Newfie thinks that a fish caught on his hook wags its tail because it is happy. (author's translation of joke in A.U.L. file F 513: 19. Collectors: Francine Garneau and Lucie Levac 1978)

Newfy goes ice fishing and came home with 2 tons of ice.
His wife drowned trying to cook it. (Finnigan 1981: 29)

While the references to fish and fishing give a distinctive quality to Canadian jokes about Newfoundlanders, they also lock them into more general patterns to be found in jokes about stupidity throughout the world and into patterns of joking to be found in ethnic jokes about food throughout the Western Christian world.

The first of the links is occupational, in that the key occupational badge of the Newfoundland fishermen—and by extension Newfoundlanders in general—is their high rubber boots which figure in the jokes in a variety of improbable ways.

How do you recognise the groom at a "Newfie" Wedding?
He is the one wearing the new rubber boots. (author's translation from Allard 1976:97)

The fisherman's boots of the Canadian Newfie jokes have the same significance as the Wellington boots appropriate to building sites worn by the Irish in British stupidity jokes, the pattens worn by the woodmen of Tadley in Berkshire stupidity jokes about Tadley and the Chinese clogs worn by the Suaku (mountain tortoises), the people from the outlying rural districts who appear in Singapore jokes (see Chia, Seet and Wong 1985: 2, 8). Together with brogues (originally heel-less shoes), clod-hoppers, clogs, sabots and wooden shoes generally, they are the badge of those who work out of doors in mucky conditions in the primary sector of the economy or on construction sites, in contrast to the more elegant footgear of those who work indoors in higher status occupations in the cities. At an even more fundamental level, footwear is our link with the ground and has an effect on the way we walk, which is, in turn, an expression of orderliness, sex, age, occupation, social class and military or civilian status. The British guardsman who is expected to die with his boots clean, the Japanese censor who banned John Cleese's Ministry of Silly Walks as being subversive of authority, the mandarin's daughters hobbling on crushed feet, the goose-stepping Prussian, the Parisian whore mincing along in ultra-high heeled shoes, the skinhead lounging on a street corner in his Bovver boots, the furtive thief about to run off in his expensive trainers, and the down and out shuffling along the sidewalk in cracked shoes all tell us who they are through their feet.

Traditionally fish was not only the key source of Newfoundlanders' earnings but also a central item in their diet (England 1969 (1924): 173, 324). The eating of fish, and especially cod, and a keen appetite for such food are frequent items in Newfie jokes:

Question: What's the loudest noise you will ever hear?
Answer: I don't know. What is it?
Reply: A Newfoundlander and a seagull fighting over a cod-fish. (M.U.N.F.L.A file 69-25. Collected by Lionel Strong)
(Elsewhere in Canada this joke is also told about Icelanders [Klymasz 1970: 168. See also Instad 1966: 293])

Did you know that at the Earth Summit John Crosbie turned all the tree huggers into codfish lovers? Now there is a new national dish—cod fried in bay leaves. (Fahey 1993: 54)

How do you get ten Newfies in a Volkswagen?
Throw in a cod fish. (Tulk 1971: 80)

Such jokes are *both* characteristically attached to Newfoundland *and* part of a general pattern of ethnic jokes about food told throughout the Western Christian world, in which the Welsh eat cheese, the Scots eat porridge, the Irish eat potatoes, the Belgians eat *frites/frieten*, (chips/French fries), the Italians eat spaghetti, the Mexicans eat beans, and African Americans eat watermelons. In each case the implication is that the butts of the jokes cannot afford to eat meat, until recently the most prized and expensive food of the Western world (Barkas 1975: 68: Ziegler 1956: 11-16; Fieldhouse 1986), and that they even have a coarse zest for the humble food they are forced to eat. There are by contrast no Western ethnic jokes about meat-eaters (with the exception of guzzlers of sausages, an item whose meat content is unknown, uncertain and shapeless). Meat eaters are by definition, and by contrast, prosperous and powerful (Barkas 1975: 178; Walker and Cannon 1985: 72). They constitute the tall, beefy (though not necessarily healthy, which is why meat consumption has now fallen) dominant people of the center, in whose shadow the short stocky folk of the periphery are forced to live.

Indeed, such foods may become the basis of the nicknames of an entire people as with the Italians (spags, makaronás, loksh), Germans (krauts, patatucchi) or French (Frogs, Froschesser) (Roback 1944). Within Canada a Québecois may be termed a Pea-souper as well as the more generic Johnny Crapeau (toad) or Frog-eater; the name of the area called Cabbagetown, east of downtown Toronto, was derived from the supposed diet of its formerly impoverished inhabitants, while a person from the Maritime provinces, and particularly New Brunswick, may be termed a herring-choker (Canuck 1967; DesRuisseaux 1979: 178; Greenough 1897: 170). Likewise Gerald Thomas has noted that among French-speaking Newfoundlanders the people of St. George's are known as *Les Mangeurs d'belvets* or Blueberry Eaters, those of Stephenville as *Les mangeurs d'navots*, or Turnip Eaters, those of Stephenville Crossing as *Les mangeurs d'anguille* or Eel Eaters, the people of Port-au-Port as *les mangeurs de hareng* or herring-chokers, and those of Cap-St-Georges as *les mangeurs d'morue* or cod-eaters (Thomas 1976A). The Acadians who live in the North-East of New Brunswick are likewise known as *morue* (cod) by other Acadians (Ronald Labelle, Director A.C.E.A., personal communication).

All of these humorous *blasons populaires* fit the general model of meat = status and prosperity, while lesser foods = poverty, but in the case of a country such as Canada with a strong and diverse Roman Catholic tradition, the references to cod have a further significant dimension. The French-Canadian writer L'Abbé J. C.Massicotte and his brother Leo-Arsène Massicotte (Rev. Frère Ladislas) wrote (1951) that "*Les anglais* (English-speaking Canadians) love cod both fresh and salted. They love this penitential dish, this dish of Good Friday" (author's translation). It was a way of saying that the mainly Protestant Anglophones had an odd puritanical relish for a food that was (the rules no longer apply) consumed by Roman Catholics only as a periodic ritually demanded constraint on their appetite for meat. Paradoxically, where Roman Catholics have constituted a religious or ethnic minority, as with the Irish in Britain or America, it is they who have been the butt of jokes about the consumption of fish (albeit only or mainly on Fridays) (see Douglas 1970; England 1969 (1924): 45; Greeley 1972; Schmitz 1991), and these jokes (Macdonald 1915: 29-30; Wilde 1979: 99-103) are also to be found in Newfoundland.

Bread, on the other hand, very rarely appears in jokes in Western countries since, although it is a basic cheap food of the poor (indeed even a Giffen good), it is also a sacred food that is central to the religious rites of both Christians and Jews and is a potent image in prayers and in secular political rhetoric. It is perceived as a universal food and a food with shape and dignity (unlike, say, porridge) and one that should not be used in jokes that impute a lack of social status to a particular group. Perhaps the nearest thing to a joke that breaks this rule is one that comes from and refers to Newfoundland:

What's the definition of a Newfoundland sandwich?
A slice of bread jammed between two more. (M.U.N.F.L.A. file 69-25c. Collection Lionel Strong)

However, this is a one-off example, whereas references to the cod are very common in jokes about Newfoundland to the point that it is used in stupidity jokes even where another fish might be more appropriate:

The Cod (Newfie)

A Chinese travelling in Newfoundland visited an aquarium exhibiting fish, rather like Marineland, with great glass tanks full of cod fish. The Chinese pressed his face against the glass of one of the tanks, caught a great cod-fish in his gaze and made it come towards him.

The Newfoundlander looked into the tank and followed the cod with narrowed eyes just like the Chinese. But he could not work out what was going on. So he said to the Chinese, "What is going on here?"

"Well," said the Chinese, "it is an example of control by an intelligent mind over things that have no intelligence."

The Newfoundlander said, "Let me try." The Chinese stood back and the Newfoundlander pressed his face against the glass and caught a large cod in his gaze. Five minutes passed and nothing had happened. After ten minutes still nothing had happened. Then after a quarter of an hour the Newfoundlander began to open and close his mouth like a codfish. (author's translation from A.C.E.A. file B300; See also Dupont and Mathieu 1986)

One of the most significant differences between American and British ethnic stupidity jokes is that American jokes about Poles associate stupidity with dirtiness whereas British jokes about the stupid Irish do not. This key differences between the two sets of jokes is not based on any real differences in cleanliness between the groups who are the butts of the jokes, nor does it reflect any greater degree of ethnic hostility towards Poles or Italians on the part of the American joke tellers relative to their British counter-parts' feelings about the Irish. Also this is a *real* difference between the two sets of jokes as told in the two countries; it is *not* an artifact of some kind of social censorship forcing British jokes about the "dirty Irish" underground. A survey of joke-telling that covered both British and American school children revealed that the American children told jokes about "dirty Polacks," despite being forbidden to tell any kind of ethnic jokes by their schoolteachers, whereas the British children did not tell jokes about the Irish being dirty (McCosh 1976:64), even though their schoolteachers were not particularly concerned about what jokes they told (McCosh 1976: 71-2). An attempt was made on one occasion to introduce jokes about "dirty Paddys" into Britain, by crudely substituting Paddys for Polacks in jokes about dirty Polacks taken from an American joke book (Macklin and Erdman 1976) and publishing them in a book of Irish jokes published in England (Hornby 1978), but the jokes never caught on in Britain and jokes about the Irish being dirty have never been in general oral circulation.

The Canadian case is an interesting one and in a sense exactly the opposite of the British situation described above. Jokes about "dirty" Newfies have circulated orally in Canada in large numbers in both English and French and in Ontario, Quebec, and the other Maritime Provinces as well as in Newfoundland itself. However, these jokes are *rare* in published joke books and when they do occur they tend to have been altered and bowdlerized, often to the point where the jokes are crippled and distorted and deprived of their humorous essence. A study of Canadian Newfoundland jokes based *only* on published sources would wrongly come to the conclusion that Canadian ethnic stupidity jokes are very similar to those found in Britain (i.e., dirtiness jokes are to all intents and purposes lacking) and decisively different from their dirt-rich American counterparts. Now, as it happens, the jokes are a very important diagnostic marker of a key difference between American and British culture, namely that the Americans perceive hygiene as an aspect of rationality and as part of their technical mastery over ageing, human-imperfection and even decay and dissolution after death, whereas the British do not share this *Weltanshauung* (Davies 1990, 1995). A study of Canadian ethnic jokes about stupidity limited to published sources would have falsely concluded that the Canadians (both Anglophone and Francophone) resembled the British in their acceptance of a grubby and imperfect world as it is, rather than the Americans with their zeal to cleanse and purify it. Thus, the Canadian editorial self-censorship of jokebooks could well have misled the world into supposing that Canadians were characterized by the stolid limitations of the British rather than the boundless aspirations of the Americans.

Many jokes about "dirty" Newfies have been collected *within Newfoundland itself* (see chapter 6). Most are essentially similar to the corresponding American riddle jokes about ethnic dirt tagged onto stupidity, but they also contain local elements:

Why do they put a fish on the altar at a Newfoundland wedding?
To keep the flies off the bride. (M.U.N.F.L.A. file 68-251. Collected by Margaret Walsh)

Why did the Newfie, at Expo, look down the sewers?
Answer: He was looking for the Newfoundland pavilion.(M.U.N.F.L.A. file 69-1F. Collected by Bernice Bartlett)

How does a Newfoundlander wipe his mouth after eating?
He rubs his mouth along his shirt-sleeve, then takes his serviette and wipes off the sleeve. (M.U.N.F.L.A. file 69-1F. Collected by Bernice Bartlett)

What do you call a snotty-nosed Newfie?
Greensleeves. (M.U.N.F.L.A. file 70-22. Collected by Sharon Oliver)

What's the definition of air pollution?
Answer: Two Newfies jumping out of an aeroplane. (M.U.N.F.L.A. file 69-1F. Collector Bernice Bartlett)

How do you get a Newfoundlander out of your front yard?
Bring the garbage around the back. (M.U.N.F.L.A. file 68-14B, Collector Gary P. Marsh)

The importance of these jokes and others like them lies not so much in the details of their contents, but in the fact that the collectors found them scattered among other Newfie jokes being told in casual good-humored joke-telling sessions in Newfoundland itself. Indeed, these were the characteristic circumstances under which the Newfie jokes in the folklore archive at Memorial University were collected.[1] There are also a few recorded cases in which it seems that the jokes were used maliciously by individuals from other Canadian provinces to mock a small, outnumbered and beleaguered group of Newfoundlanders (e.g., during military training).[2] However, this was not a common use of such jokes; on the contrary most of the collectors describe the joke-telling sessions (both those held outside Newfoundland and those within the Province itself) in which Newfie jokes were told as friendly, and they themselves clearly found the jokes very funny. What is very striking, though, is that there are *no real differences in content* between the jokes told in these numerous harmonious sessions and those told on the few occasions when Newfoundlanders felt they were being got at. The difference between the two occasions lay purely in the *tone* with which the jokes were told. It was *not* the case that jokes about "dirty Newfies" were more likely to be told on ''hostile'' rather than harmonious occasions.[3]

In any case within Newfoundland itself the townies of St. John's had long since been telling tales and reciting humorous doggerel about their "dirty" neighbours from Torbay; dirtiness was not a new source of humor in Newfoundland:

> Down the street as thick as flies
> Dirty shirts and dirty ties
> Dirty rings around their eyes
> Dirty old Torbaymen!
> (Hiscock 1990A: 37)

Why then do jokes about dirty Newfies, which are clearly widely known and told in Newfoundland, not exist in print in published Canadian joke books, including those published in Newfoundland itself, in the way that the equivalent jokes about dirty Polacks do in the United States? In the Canadian Newfie joke books there are occasional humorous rural anecdotes about dirt, usually of a scatological nature, but the joke books' editors and compilers have avoided the riddle jokes about absence of soap and love of garbage, that occur so frequently among the oral jokes recorded both in Newfoundland and elsewhere. Also those jokes about dirt that do make it into print are censored and bowdlerized as can be seen by comparing the (earlier) oral and the (later) printed version of particular jokes:

Version in Oral Circulation
Do you know why there are only two Newfie pall bearers at a funeral?
There are only two handles on a garbage can. (M.U.N.F.L.A. file 69-1F. Collected by Bernice Bartlett; recorded as told by one Newfoundlander to another in Toronto before 1969. A very common ethnic joke in North America; it is also told about Poles in the United States)

Published Version
I know Henry wasn't well liked, but why was there only two pall bearers at his funeral?
There are only two handles on a garbage can. (Tulk 1971: 33)

Version in Oral Circulation
What is the best method to get a Newfoundlander out of a swimming pool?
...By throwing in a cake of soap. (M.U.N.F.L.A. file 69-25C. Collected by Lionel Strong; recorded 1969. A very common ethnic joke in North America. The author recorded the same joke but told about Poles in the United States in the United States in autumn 1965)

Published Version
Dirty joke: "The best way to get my buddy out of the bathtub is to toss in a bar of soap." (Tulk. 1971: 76)

The Tulk versions (from the collection *Newfie Jokes* that has gone through at least nine printings and which became the first volume in a very successful series of Newfie joke books) no longer make any direct mention of Newfoundland at all and a reader who does not know the original jokes or the script on which they were based (Raskin, 1985), or the joke cycle from which they came, will be puzzled as to what the jokes are about. Is the joke that refers to Henry's funeral a joke about dirt or a joke about unpopularity? They have ceased to be well-made jokes.

The reason for the censorship of this kind of dirt joke (though curiously not of lavatorial humor or jokes about sex) from Canadian joke books can be discovered by looking in each case at the cover, first page of, or introduction to these same books where there inevitably appears a uniquely Canadian (they are quite uncommon in other countries) contribution to humor: the opening introductory apology. A few examples will illustrate what these are like:

This book was published, not for the purpose of making fun of Newfoundlanders but to show that most of us can take a joke as well as give one. (Tulk and The Tulks, the same wording in each of several volumes.)

Our intentions are not to make fun of anyone but to show that Newfoundlanders are a fun loving people who can give and take a joke. (Fahey 1993)

It is not the intention of the author to poke fun at any person or persons or any ethnic group. (Standish 1984)

There was no intention to "poke fun" at any particular group of people. (Ralph et al. 1990)

Our intention in publishing this book was for your relaxation and enjoyment. (Sheppard and Noftle 1979)

C'est une étrange entreprise que celle de faire rire les honnêtes gens. (Molière)

Ce n'est pas drôle d'avoir à préfacer un livre comme celui-ci, mais il faut le faire...ne serait-ce que pour avertir ceux qui croient que ce livre est méchant, qu' ils ont tort.

Le rire est toujours un peu méchant...mais le rire est une méchanceté rose.... Pour réconforter nos amis "Newfies," disons que le rire est une revanche du faible sur le fort. (Allard 1976; the content of the apology is essentially trivial, much like the others, but the verbose, would-be literary-philosophical and high-falutin' style is distinctively French. It is best left untranslated)

The very existence of the last of these apologies is a further indication of the way in which the humor of Québec has become Canadian. Even Francophones in Montréal feel they have to defer to the hysterical pressures of Canadian political correctness. French-Canadians have also become part of the ultra-clean culture of North America generally, so that French language jokes about dirty Newfies *and* about dirty Italians (who are also a common butt of such jokes in the U.S.) are very common in Quebec:

Pourquoi c'est marqué C.M.I. sur les trucks de vidange à Montréal?
Cantine Mobile des Italiens (Why are Montreal garbage trucks marked "C.M.I."? It stands for Italian meals on wheels). (Author's free translation of French version in A.U.L. file F.513. Collected by Hélène Joncas)

Do you know why Italians put a lock on their garbage cans?
So that their children won't eat between meals. (Author's translation; A.U.L. file F.513. Collected by Hélène Joncas)

Why do Newfies have a piece of shit on their shoulders?
Because two heads are better than one. (Author's translation; A.U.L file F.513. Collected by Hélène Joncas)

A Newfie, who for the first time in his life, saw a man cleaning his teeth ran out to fetch his gun. He thought he had rabies. (Author's translation; A.U.L. file F.513. Collected by Hélène Joncas)

Similar jokes are also to be found in published anthologies of French language jokes in Canada, but in fairly small numbers. Nonetheless, the degree of self-censorship seems to be somewhat less than in Anglophone Canada, although far greater than in the United States, and the following French jokes have escaped the censor:

Hey, Newfie. We no longer allow people to pee in the swimming baths here.
I am not the only one.
Perhaps not, but you are the only one to do it before jumping off the diving board.
(Allard 1978: 102; see also Newbine 1984: 123)

The Newfie Father Xmas doesn't come down the chimney; he comes up the sewage pipe. (Allard 1976: 28)

It is striking that it is the ethnic jokes about dirtiness that have been censored out of the printed joke books in Canada, whereas the ethnic jokes about stupidity in general remain intact, despite the fact that the jokes are part of a general North-American genre of jokes in which dirtiness is treated as an extension of stupidity, and even though those telling these jokes (both Newfoundlanders and mainlanders) generally do not make a distinction between jokes based on dirt and jokes based on stupidity (see note 3). However, those in a position in society to put pressure on the compilers and editors are unlikely to be typical of joke tellers and joke-book readers in general. It seems likely that the censorious ones among the Canadians subscribe to the following mistaken beliefs: (a) that jokes can be reduced to their equivalent serious statements and that the humorous form of the utterance is merely a disguise for real accusations of dirtiness or stupidity, (b) that jokes imputing negative qualities to a group are necessarily an expression of hostility towards that group (even in the absence of independent expressions of real hostility towards Newfoundlanders by other Canadians in general), (c) that a serious statement to the effect that Newfoundlanders were dirty would be a stronger and more insulting expression of hostility towards them than saying they were stupid (even metaphorically, for to call someone a dirty bugger is stronger than calling the same person a silly bugger) and therefore jokes about Newfoundlanders being dirty express a greater degree of hostility towards Newfoundlanders than jokes about their being stupid. It is clear from an examination of jokes told in Britain, where, historically, there has been more conflict with and hostility towards the Irish than in America in relation to the Poles, yet where the Irish as butts of stupidity jokes are *not* treated as dirty (whereas Polish Americans are), that there is *no truth whatsoever* in the line of argument implied by (a), (b), and (c) taken together.

Whether or not those who live at the center, close to the places where political and economic power are exercised, come to feel and express hatred and contempt for those leading a traditional way of life at the edge of a modern society depends not on the circulation of ambiguous humorous items, such as jokes, but on whether or not there exists a direct political conflict about political issues as in the Punjab in India, in Kurdistan in Iraq, or in Ireland in the British Isles, where attempts at secession triggered by political disputes have led to bitter conflicts. The conflicts neither cause the jokes nor are they caused by the jokes; rather both are related to the distinctive relationships that exist between the center and the edge. Should this relationship *not* be inflamed by a political dispute, the *jokes* will *still exist* but not the conflict as, say, in the case of Turkish jokes about the Laz or Swedish jokes about Norwegians, at least up to the point where the self-righteous protesting Swedish urban middle-classes decided to object to Norwegian seal-hunting and publicly dipped the Norwegian flag in a bucket of blood in the Swedish capital, Stockholm. It was a clear political attack on the traditional way of life of those almost ideal-typical Norwegians, the sailors, hunters and fishermen who live on the rugged coastal edge of Norway and, indeed, of Scandinavia. Suddenly a traditional Norwegian way of life, based on hunting and fishing, and involving a direct confrontation between human beings and the sea, ceased to be merely comically backward in the eyes of Sweden's smug city folk and was demonized as evil and cruel.

A similar sequence of events occurred in Newfoundland, when outside protestors succeeded for a time in stopping the annual seal hunt, an event that had once been central to the local economy and way of life and was still a revered tradition (England 1969 (1924): 40, 324). In their letters to Newfoundlanders the protesters used a rhetoric of Newfoundlanders as stupid and backward, not in an ambiguous and comic fashion but in a direct, vicious and hate-filled way. There is no overlap at all between Canadian jokes about Newfies and the direct verbal and political attacks on Newfoundlanders made by the protestors, most of whom came from outside Canada and would not have known the jokes anyway. The only thing the two phenomena have in common is that they are both rooted in the economic, social and psychological gap between the "center" and the "edge." The quotations below from the protestors' viciously anti-Newfoundland hate mail sent to Newfoundlanders speak for themselves.

> Newfoundlanders from north to south are ignorant, primitive, stupid, cold-blooded people. I have many questions about the people of your town (St. Anthony, Newfoundland). Do you know that aeroplanes have been invented? Do you live in caves and eat raw meat?... Do you ride around in dog sleds? (Unsigned letter. Quoted in Patey 1990: 52. See also Lamson 1979)

> Don't you know that this is the twentieth century...the whole world is aware that, on this earth, there are still savages in Newfoundland who go around with their clubs killing baby seals.... I thank God that we live far away from you in a civilized world. (letter from Illinois, USA. Quoted in Patey 1990: 55)

> I guess it's true, Newfoundland is backward, ignorant and prehistoric. (Letter from Milwaukee, USA. Quoted in Patey 1990: 55)

> Savages wear skins. I take it you pander to savages... (Letter from South Africa to the Premier of Newfoundland. Quoted in Patey 1990: 63)

These accusations of backwardness are but a small part of the vile and malicious hate-mail that flooded into Newfoundland at the time of the protest, but that is beside the point. What is striking is that these accusations were made at all. If the protesters believed (whether rightly or wrongly) that the activities of the sealers were cruel, why should this lead them to accuse the Newfoundlanders of being stupid, backward, primitive savages? Cruelty is, after all, an eminently (though by no means exclusively) modern phenomenon, a visible characteristic of that twentieth century of which the letter writers were so proud. Cruelty was practiced in a massive, deliberate, rational, modern and systematically organized way by such great mass murderers and torturers as the governments and agents of German National Socialism and of Marxist-Leninist societies generally. The mildly old-fashioned way of life of the kindly Newfoundlanders is the antithesis of the theory and practice of those evil modern ideologies. More cruelty was and is practiced in Milwaukee, Illinois, and South Africa (where the quoted letter writers lived) than by Newfoundlanders. Also each of the letter-writers' home territories has been distinguished by social experiments far more stupid than anything ever tried in Newfoundland, namely the Milwaukee experiment, Prohibition and the war against drugs, and apartheid all of which displayed or display a crass refusal to face reality. However, the *rhetoric* of stupidity has been shaped by the almost universal perception of the edge as being a place of *greater social stupidity* than the center; it is a perception that regularly gives rise to humor, but if, as here, an appropriate provocation exists it can also be used in the service of hatred. What is certain though is that the presence or absence, the existence or non-existence, the knowledge or ignorance of Newfie jokes will have made no difference whatsoever to the degree of venomousness towards Newfoundland expressed by those protesting against the seal-hunt. The only people to use humor during the conflict over the hunt were the Newfoundlanders themselves (Burke 1981: 85; Lamson 1979; Wise Willy 1991); but then they are by long tradition a giftedly humorous people. Some of them even enjoyed the foolishness of the politically correct animal rights protesters using the word "savage" as a term of abuse. The author who went on illicit seal-hunts for food with the Inuit in Greenland during the time of Danish colonialism is aware that the Newfoundlanders' amusement as well as resentment at accusations of savagery is not a phenomenon confined to Newfoundland.

A similar point can be made in relation to animal rights terrorism against medical researchers in Europe which is, in some cases, combined with either hard left or neo-Nazi ideological sympathies (Foggo 2000: 5). The Nazis after all introduced a ban on medical experiments on animals in Prussia in 1933, with the threat that vivisectionists would be sent to concentration camps. In contemporary Germany one such group employs the slogan "End experiments on animals. Use Turks instead" (Palmer 2000: 35), the Turks being an unpopular minority whom some Germans would like to see repatriated back to Turkey. The Turks have also been the subject of jokes about dirty Turks, *Türkenwitze* similar to those told about Newfoundlanders.

> Why are the garbage cans in Köln made of glass?
> So that the Turks can go window shopping

It would be foolish to indiscriminately postulate "interconnections" between these two phenomena, for the key distinction remains that between ideology and humor. The jokes about the dirty Turks are a form of playing with aggression just as the Newfie jokes are in Canada, but the German jokes are invented in a society where there is *also* real hostility to the butts of the jokes. Interestingly though, the jokes differ in one respect from those told in Canada, in that in

Germany, whereas the stupidity jokes are, as expected, told about fellow Germans at the edges of Germany in Ostfriesland and more recently Saxony, the jokes about dirt are quite separate and pinned on a large and often disliked immigrant group. The jokes told about dirty Turks in Germany are also popular in the Netherlands (Kuipers 2000: 145, 169-72) where political attitudes to immigrants are markedly more liberal (Kuipers 2000: 157-8) , though as expected stupidity jokes are told about the neighboring and familiar Belgians most of whom speak Dutch and who are as it happens liked by the Dutch (Kuipers 2000: 145, 169-72; see also Kuipers 2001). Stupidity jokes then are pinned on "cousins," but jokes about dirtiness have a variety of targets. In either case the *content* of the jokes about people being dirty remains the *same* regardless of levels of hostility; there is no connection between the content of these jokes and levels of hostility.

It is rather the slogan, "End experiments on animals. Use Turks instead," that is problematic. Now it *could* be a joke and, indeed, similar jokes are told about lawyers in the United States:

Why have psychologists started using lawyers instead of rats in their experiments?

There are more of them, you cannot get fond of them and there are some things even a rat won't do.

The problem with the slogan lies rather in its *context*, namely in its use as a slogan by groups known for their ideological extremism and violence, who are the political descendants of the Nazis, who did use human beings as a substitute for animals in experiments in the past, and of those who pursued or supported the Soviet "experiment" (Courtois et al. 1999) that also killed tens of millions of individual human beings. For them the slogan may be utterly serious or at least utter seriousness conjoined with tasteless humor. Yet it is also easy to see how the slogan could be used both humorously and seriously to ridicule animal rights campaigners, whether extremists or moderates, and indeed to see how it could be used as a building block of a new set of jokes by someone with no particular axe to grind. It is the human propensity for ideological fanaticism that creates danger for us all not the human search for amusement.

Many Newfoundlanders were upset and in some cases frightened by the vehemence of the campaign against their province which was at times conducted so as to impinge unpleasantly and unpredictably on particular individuals. Foreign opponents of the seal hunt would even obtain copies of the Newfoundland phone book in order to make anonymous phone calls to individual Newfoundlanders whose numbers were taken at random from the book and abuse and even threaten them on the phone. It is difficult to imagine that such a campaigner would tell Newfie jokes about stupidity or even dirtiness or cod or rubber boots anonymously on the phone to unknown Newfoundlanders in order to insult them or make them feel afraid. Not only are jokes not suited to that purpose because they are primarily humorous utterances but also they would not fit the mind-set of the angry and bitter person making such a phone call.

It is, of course, possible to imagine jokes being used in such a way by an anonymous phone caller wishing to cause offense and fear. Shortly after the attacks on the World Trade Center in New York by Osama Bin Laden's Al-Qaeda terrorists on September 11, 2001, there were, as many humor scholars had predicted (Ellis 2001), substantial numbers of sick and shocking jokes in circulation in both America and Britain about this tragic event. It is a familiar pattern and previous disasters and tragedies, such as the explosion of the Challenger space shuttle, have generated very similar types of jokes (Davies 1990A, 1999).

> Have you seen the new Osama Bin Laden cookbook?
> It is called "How to make a Big Apple crumble."

> The American economy must be in as much trouble as in 1929. The stock-brokers are jumping out of windows on the eighteenth floor.

Were persons hostile to America or to free and democratic societies in general to have phoned up people randomly selected from the New York phonebook and told them sick and shocking jokes of this kind, they might well have achieved their political objective of spreading alarm and despondency, let alone its being a singularly nasty thing to do. Yet why should our enemies adopt such an indirect and uncertain method of attaining this goal? Straightforward taunting, scorn or derision would be more effective. Why confuse and soften the message with humor? Why risk being misunderstood and producing laughter rather than resentment?

Sick jokes about the bombing will have been circulating even in New York itself and indeed by phone; they always do, even after the most savage and tragic of events. They will have been exchanged just as jokes with no intention of harming anyone either directly or covertly. It is possible that one New Yorker might phone another whom he or she knows would not appreciate such a joke and indeed be upset by it and tell it for schadenfreude, rather as some people perpetrate malicious practical jokes, but that would be an oddity and not a representative case. What is more to the point, upsetting forms of behavior by particular individuals *do not explain why* such jokes come into existence. Likewise the circulation and further invention of such jokes by New Yorkers themselves (Ferguson 2001) are an indication that the jokes had become as much the property of the citizens of New York themselves as of anyone else. We have here a very extreme case but one that again indicates how all kinds of jokes can be used in many ways and annexed by anyone who wants to own them.

The war in Afghanistan that followed the terror bombing of New York and Washington, D.C., has also led to a new wave of generic ethnic stupidity jokes:

The Irish SAS (Special Air Services) have stormed the Battersea dogs' home (in London) and killed three Afghans. (In circulation in Britain by email in September 2001. The SAS are an elite special forces unit within the British army)

The police have arrested three Irish terrorists who had been working for Bin Laden— Bin Sleepen, Bin Drinken and Bin Liner. They are still searching unsuccessfully for Bin Worken. (In circulation in Britain 2001)

These new jokes about Irish ineptness will no doubt be told about Poles in America or Newfies in Canada as has often happened before. When a new wave of ethnic stupidity jokes does appear in Canada, it may well also incorporate references to dirtiness and to local Canadian themes, such as fishing for and eating the now somewhat scarce cod, and the distinctive patterns of Newfoundland speech.

Indeed, it may well be Newfoundlanders themselves who do the adapting and go on to invent new examples of their own. The Newfoundlanders have, as we shall see in chapter 6, a strikingly rich local tradition of humor, wit and joking. It has enabled them to take possession of the Canadian jokes about Newfies in the past and they will continue to do so in whatever circumstances arise. Their self-mocking humor deserves a chapter of its own.

Notes

1. See M.U.N.F.L.A. files Q68-69, Q68-104, Q68-188, Q68-274, 68-24C, 68-251, 69-1F, 69-25C.
2. See M.U.N.F.L.A. files Q68-14B, 68-30, 69-225.
3. In the study of the hostile use of jokes in file Q68-30 only one joke about dirt is cited and in 68-14B no more jokes about dirt were collected from outsiders as were collected from Newfoundland students. In Q68-69, on a harmonious occasion four jokes about dirt were told alongside eleven other jokes about Newfoundlanders. In file 69-1F, Newfie jokes are listed as being told (a) by Newfoundlanders in Newfoundland (9 about dirt, 19 other stupidity jokes, 3 possibly about dirt depending on definitions), (b) by Newfoundlanders living in Toronto (4 about dirt, 18 other stupidity jokes, and 2 possibly about dirt), and (c) by natives of Toronto (1 about dirt, 5 other stupidity jokes). There is no evidence here to support the view that Newfie jokes about dirt are selectively used in a hostile way or that they appeal to outsiders more than to Newfoundlanders.

6

Jokes about Newfies and Jokes Told by Newfoundlanders

In many of the types of ethnic stupidity jokes cited in table 1.1, the butts of the jokes may well tell and circulate these jokes among themselves and even add to the stock of such jokes but they do not pride themselves on, or have a reputation for, being a witty and humorous people. Indeed they may be perceived by others and even by themselves as heavy, dour, slow or stubborn people. Such is not the case in Newfoundland, where the contents of the folklore archive at Memorial University, the numerous publications within the province by collectors of local jokes and anecdotes and the works of local authors reveal both the ability of Newfoundlanders to be humorous and the degree to which such an ability is prized within Newfoundland society. Given that it takes intelligence to be witty and humorous, how is this compatible with Newfoundlanders being the butt of stupidity jokes? The paradox is easily resolvable if we look in turn at (a) ignorance stories, (b) tall tales, and (c) stories about the witty people of Upper Island Cove in Newfoundland, all of which are, in fact, about locally generated stupidity. It would quite wrong to assume that the Newfoundlanders are any less stupid in their own jokes than in those told by mainland Canadians from outside; rather the Newfoundlanders' intelligence is revealed by the verbal skill with which they mock their own stupidity.

A classic "universal" stupidity joke about Newfoundlanders, one that is elsewhere told about other peripheral peoples of the arboreal edge, such as the Finns, has been collected and published with comments by the eminent Newfoundland folklorist Gerald Thomas (1976: 144) who writes,

Newfoundland even today is more socially backward than many other parts of Canada and it is still possible to hear people claim with pride that the Newfoundlander's way of life has hardly changed over two hundred years. There is enough truth in such an assertion for folklorists and sociologists to view the island as a researcher's paradise.

There is a joke...which describes the problems faced by a man when he changes from an axe to a power saw to cut his tally of wood. He manages to keep up to the level of pre-power-saw production but finds it particularly tiring. He complains about the new tool and is frightened out of his life when the vendor presses the starter button.

The humorous item cited by Thomas in an essay on Canadian folklore exists in two forms. First, there is the version published in a collection of humorous, purportedly authentic Newfoundland stories:

Then there is the time the first chainsaw came to rural Newfoundland. The agent came round the community telling the loggers just how good the chainsaw was. He told them that he could cut five cords with the old buck saw, but that he was able to cut ten cords with this modern instrument called a chainsaw.
So the guy decided to give it a try. This could double his wages!
When the coastal boat came, he got his chainsaw and Monday morning he decided to test his agent's promise. He spent all day in the woods with his new saw and when evening came he left the woods disgusted and angry.
He had done no better with the chainsaw than he did with the buck saw. So he phoned the agent to come over and take the saw back.
The agent asked if he had put oil in it. "I have."
Then he was asked if he had put gasoline in her. "You know I did," came the reply.
"Did she make a lot of noise when you got her going?"
"I didn't set her going," came the reply. (Burke 1981: 92-3)

In contrast to this local version , there is the generic international stupidity joke told about Newfoundlanders, Finns, and even the treeless Irish, as in the joke:

An Irishman got a job as a lumberjack, but, try as he might, he couldn't meet his quota of fifty trees a day. By chance he saw an advertisement in a shop window for chainsaws "guaranteed to fell sixty trees a day." So he bought one, but the best he could manage was forty trees a day.
He took it back to the shop and complained that there must be something wrong with it. "Let me look at it," said the man in the shop and, taking the chainsaw, he switched it on. "What's that noise?" said the Irishman. (MacHale 1984: n.p.)

Now if asked the question, "what is the difference between the two stories?" the compiler and editor of the book containing the former version would no doubt say that his is the more genuine Newfoundland story, either because it is tied to a more realistic and local setting or because it illustrates the "Newfoundlander's unique way of telling a good story, and telling it with a flavor and taste that brings laughter rather than derision and ridicule" (Burke 1981). By contrast Professor Desmond MacHale, distinguished mathematician from Europe's irrational fraction that he is, probably chose to speak of forty, fifty, and sixty trees because it constitutes an arithmetical series with fifty in the middle rather, than from any pretense to an acquaintance with the lumberjacks of tree-free Ireland. This is the kind of distinction that people seem to have in mind when they speak of the difference between the real Newfoundland humor and the ethnic stupidity jokes. Yet, in fact, the core element in both jokes is the same—a risibly stupid ignorance of modern technology. It might be argued that in the first version the stupidity is confined to particular types of individual in rural Newfoundland, but then in practice that is how modern Newfie jokes generally are interpreted by their tellers in Newfoundland. The townies of St John's the capital and trading center of Newfoundland itself are able to think that Newfie jokes are about the baymen of Newfoundland's own periphery and the baymen pass them down the line to the remotest of outports (Hiscock 1990, 1990A; Laba 1977). No one is ever obliged to think the joke is about himself or herself. From this point of view it is the traditional tales that should be perceived as offensive for they often ascribe negative traits to particular named individuals in specific small communities who are singled out as being stupid, tedious or greedy. By contrast, in a Newfie or Irish joke no one need feel that they are being assailed personally.

Much more fundamental is that the first version of the chainsaw tale is longer and more discursive and repetitive whereas the second is a well-made joke with a familiar ethnic script, the deliberate creation of suspense and a sudden but indirect resolution of the joke through a skillfully constructed punch line. The punch line, "What's that noise?" tells us *indirectly* that MacHale's Irishman/Newfie did not understand how the chainsaw worked and does so using only three words. It is possible to decode the punch line quickly and precisely, because the use of Irish or Newfie at the beginning has provided the clue that something stupid will happen at the end. The change in the structure of the joke is not the result of the new style joke tellers wanting to "get at" the butts of their jokes, but of a much more general set of changes in the folklore of modern societies. Gerald Thomas, for instance, has studied changes in the telling of *Märchen* among the French-speaking Newfoundlanders of the Port-au-Pont peninsula, with the decline of the old public *veillée* and the

preference today for the (preexisting) private family tradition of narrating tales (Thomas 1979: 72-3; 1980: 343; 1982: 176,179; 1991:
61-2). Thomas has noted the same decline in repetition (and, indeed, a modern dislike of what has come to be seen as "excessive"
repetition) and the same growth in the use of mechanisms to produce suspense in the telling of traditional narratives that have been
discussed above in the case of jokes. Both of these he relates to the
growing influence of television and especially television soap op-
eras (which are fitted into short slots and which make great use of
techniques for generating suspense) and to the way in which the
average person's day in a modern society is governed by a series of
fixed deadlines which directly constrain and indirectly shape people's
tastes (Thomas 1979: 73-4; 1980: 343-4; 1982: 179-80). The same
point may be made about successful television comedies that work
well as half-hour units but whose scriptwriters are quite unable to convert them into successful feature-length films or stage shows based on
the same characters. Likewise, too, the change in the length and structure of jokes may well be a result of the shift to a society in which joke
tellers are likely to exchange jokes in short sessions with diverse groups
of individuals who may rarely meet each other again (Utley 1971: 3)
Each person wants to squeeze as much laughter out of the session as
possible and to have a lot of material to take away with them for use
elsewhere. This, as much as the influence of professional stand-up
comedians, has changed the very nature of joking.

The three different versions of the tale below can be viewed in the
same way:

> A certain postmaster in Bonavista some years ago had held the position for quite a long
> period of time, so much so that he knew practically every man, woman and child who
> came to the post office to inquire if there was any mail. In most cases, therefore, he
> would not have to ask the name of the person, because he knew most of them by long
> association. There were a number of persons who inquired for their mail by asking, "Is
> there arra letter yer for I?"

> The postmaster finally left this position and there was a young lady by the name of
> Smith from Flat Island in Placentia Bay, who arrived to take up the position of postmis-
> tress in Bonavista. Being a complete stranger, she had to ask people their names when
> they came for their mail.

> In Bonavista at this time there was a man by the name of Noody and each year around
> February he would write to Capt. Bill Winsor in Wesleyville—Capt. Winsor being
> captain of a sailing steamer—to inquire if he could get a berth to the ice for the coming
> spring. In this particular year Noody had written his letter or had got someone to write
> it for him and each day was expecting a reply. One day after the arrival of the new

postmistress, he went to the post-office and when the young lady, Miss Smith, who, of course, did not know who Noody was, came to the wicket, he said, "Is there arra letter yer for I?" She naturally inquired what his name was and Noody replied, "My Lard, all you got to do is look at the envelope." (Reader 1967: 3)

This version of the tale is long, authentically told, and is full of details about particular places and persons. Also everything is explained *en route* so that there is no build up of expectation or suspense to be resolved by Noody's foolish question at the end. What we have rather is a long exposition of the circumstances that have led to his stupid misunderstanding.

This tale exists in a drastically shorter and simplified version in the folklore archive at Memorial University as one of a series of "Dicky and Tibby" stories, told as true stories about the brothers Richard and Tobias Crewe by other elderly fishermen at Bird Island Cove, now called Elliston, in the late 1960s:

Tibby went to the Post Office at Deer Lake after a few months in the woods and asked the girl behind the counter if there was a letter for him.
"Your name, Sir"? asked the girl.
"My name is on the letter, stupid," replied Tibby. (M.U.N.F.L.A. file 69-17D Collected by Roger Hobbs)

This version is much shorter, no explanations are given and Tibby's stupidity as revealed in the punch line, is emphasized by Tibby's addressing the anonymous girl behind the counter as "stupid." Here is a real clash between the man who has been several months in the woods and the woman in charge of the local branch of a large bureaucratic system. Even this degree of reference to particular persons and places disappears in the French-Canadian joke quoted below, which is based on a similar contrast between the local and personal and the general and bureaucratic. Here the joke is expressed as an ethnic stupidity tale about Newfies:

A Newfie arrived in the main post-office in Montreal and asked the post-master:
"Have you a letter for me?"
"I think so. We have a letter here addressed like this:
'To my son Montreal'
and it comes from Newfoundland." (Author's translation of Allard 1978:119)

In all three cases the humor is about stupidity, the stupidity of a person whose social experience is limited to a small community and who cannot comprehend why a stranger doesn't know his or her identity. In the first case this is made explicit repeatedly and at length whereas the latter two cases have the form of a modern well-made joke culminating in a punch line. That one of the latter jokes should have as its butt a particular named bayman and the other *un Newfie de Terre-Neuve* is a much less important difference than the difference between the two modern jokes and the earlier anecdote.

The same point may be made in relation to Elizabeth Miller's essay on *Ted Russell: Newfoundland's Contribution to the World of Humor* in which she writes,

> Much of the humor in Ted Russell's stories derives from the limited and often naive perceptions of village residents. For example there is Aunt Paish Bartle who, when confronted with the inevitability of an aeroplane trip for a medical emergency, asked if she could sit by the door: "Because, if we don't get up there in the sky and anything goes wrong with that thing, I don't intend to run any risks. I want to be right by the door so that I can open it and walk out." Again, Bobby Tacker on first seeing a helicopter called it "a young airplane, not fully growed and not able to fly proper."(Miller 1982: 3)

These are *both* items derived from the charming well-crafted tales of Ted Russell *and* also the *very stuff that ethnic stupidity jokes are made of*. It would be very easy, indeed, to construct two conventional Newfie riddle jokes out of Aunt Bartle and Bobby Tacker's remarks.

As in many other "frontier" societies, such as those of the Australian outback the old American frontier or the earlier rural Jewish settlements in Palestine (Elliott Oring 2000, personal communication), tall tales are very much part of a Newfoundland tradition (Narváez 1983) of inventiveness and the skilled use of language, as can be seen from the following examples:

> Max went trouting and he only got one fish. He was pretty disappointed so he just threw it in the trunk of the car and took off. He was only about half-way home when he heard the siren coming up behind him. He pulled over and the Mountie came over and wanted to know what he had in the trunk. Max told him about the one trout.
> "Well I'm sorry, b'y," says the Mountie. "I got to give you a ticket. You should have had a red rag tied to his tail." (M.U.N.F.L.A. file 69-10G. Collected by S. Dawn Cox)

The Frozen Tear-drops

> Anyway another time I can recall my Grandfather. He's a person in the woods. I really wanted to go in the woods on Saturdays. So, in those years it was the old muzzle-loader gun. It wasn't the breech loading gun at all, it was the old muzzle loader. Powder and shot bag one ting and the other. Put your powder and shot bag over your shoulder and away you'd go.

> So we were in over the hills. It was late, late in November. Probably a day something like it was today, after it turned out. It was a lovely morning before we left. So, when we got in there we killed some partridges and rabbits and one ting. Finally, we ran out of

shot and Grandfather said, "Boy," he said, "that's all right," he said, "we're not goin' to see anything else today," you know he said, "we're on our way out," you know.

So anyway, it was cold. It began to get cold and freezing and one ting and the other. So I looked back over my shoulder and seen this coming towards me and I thought it was a black sheep, you know. And I said, "My God!" I said, "Grandfather, what's that?" "Where to," he sez. "Me son you're seein' tings," you know. "No my son, by God, Art," he sez, "that's a bear." Now I never seen a bear in me life, you know. My lord I was frightened. So, I sat down on a stump somebody had sawed off some years previous you know and I start to cry, you know. Grandfather said, "Now boy," he said, "keep up your courage," he said, you know. He said, "if it comes to that point I'll hit him with the back stock of the gun."

The bear was still coming on, so I had my hands up to my eyes like that you know, and when I looked, lord my hand was just full of ice-pellets! Right full, like that, you know. We had all our shot fired away now, and I said, "Grandfather," and he said, "What?" "I believe we've got the riddle solved." "What do you mean?" (asked Grandfather.) I said, "You got some powder there?" He said, "Yes, I got powder, boy." Look I said, "I got my hand right full of frozen tear drops!" So Grandfather wasn't long puttin' the powder down in the gun and rammed some oakum down, threw the hand-full of tear-drops down in the gun and he said, "What good is dat goin' to do?" He went up and shot at the bear and five minutes after dat the bear died with water on the brain. (M.U.N.F.L.A. file 79-37. Collected by Shirley Churchill, Betty Kean and Rita Stratton)

Such stories are entertaining and yet stupid. They are told by particularly well-known named individuals and although clearly absurd, they purport to be true, with the narrator deliberately bringing his relatives into the story, so that they could be potential witnesses to the truth of his tale. In Newfoundland, as in other parts of the world, the tale-tellers are involved in and speak about activities taking place in the uncontrolled and relatively unpredictable world of nature: hunting, fishing and berry-gathering, the activities of the edge. Precisely because there is an uncontrolled and unpredictable element to these *close to nature* activities, there is scope for tall tales using exaggeration and the stretching of the improbable, while those who work in the factories or the designing offices of the urban center are *closer to the laws of nature* and less inclined to tell tall tales that depart from their professional ethic of precision. In the world of the center, where everything is measured, co-ordinated and inspected in a comprehensive *méchanisation de la vie* [1] from which any departure is necessarily comic, tall tales are mere stupidity, an exercise of a wild and unnecessary creative flexibility in speech, rather like the undisciplined gesturing of *les vieux Français de France,* now abandoned by their well-programmed Newfoundland descendants. (Thomas 1979: 76: 1982:177. See also 1982:168-9)

Even in Newfoundland itself doubts are expressed about the probity of well-loved tellers of tall tales such as Uncle Tom Trask whose stories were well known in his home area:

> "In de spring 'v 1900 I runned shart 'v hay. I had no money to buy none. Der wez a lot a snow on de groun. Me arse [horse] wez almos starvin. I didn know what te do. Bime by I dought 'v me green goggles. I carred um out and put um on 'er. Den I ged 'er some shavins from Samson's carpenter shop. She eat um jes like twez 'ay. Das what I kept 'er on til the snow wez gone." (M.U.N.F.L.A. file 68-24G. Collected by H. Boyd Trask)

Varied opinions were held about Uncle Tom and his tales. As the collector put it: "Uncle Tom was looked upon by some, as a liar; others merely thought that he handled the truth carelessly; and, yet, there were those who considered him an expert story teller" (M.U.N.F.L.A. file 68-24G. H. Boyd Trask).

However, his stories could not have deceived anyone; wood shavings *cannot* be substituted for hay by fitting a horse with green goggles. A person who tells a story that is *obviously* absurd is *not* a liar in the sense that we would use that word to describe, say, William Jefferson Clinton, Jeffery Archer, a used car salesman, a realtor, or an EU bureaucrat. Tom Trask by contrast was merely *playing* with lies, not telling them; merely *playing* with stupidity, not lapsing into it; merely *playing* with aggression (against the aggrieved "deceived"), not committing it.

The inhabitants of a local Newfoundland community can be even more ambivalent about the qualities demonstrated by their own particular tall-tale teller as in the case of the French-speaking neighbors of the French Newfoundlander Albert Ding-Dong Simon. They appreciated his narrative talent and the *contes de mensonge* he formed out of his work as a fisherman and hunter, as when he claimed to have boiled a kettle on the back of a whale thinking it was an island (Thomas 1987: 230. See also pp. 234-5 for this and other tales), but there was also a "subtly unstated mockery" in their attitude towards him; indeed his nickname, Ding-Dong, implied they thought he was not quite "all there" (Thomas 1987: 231-2). There was a well-known riddle about him: "What walks on the road and goes east an west?"... "Poor Albert Simon—Ding-Dong—cos he told so many lies—an he used to put his left shoe on his right foot and his right shoe on his left foot. They used to say he's going east an west"(Thomas 1987: 232).

He was, like other tall-tale tellers, called a liar and, indeed, in an act of public legitimate but anonymous disapproval, someone wrote in paint on his boat, "Albert Ding-Dong *le Menteur*" (the liar) (Thomas 1987: 233).Yet if he were a liar, he was merely a stupid crazy liar. His tales were not petty believable swindles but crack-pot fantasies, and yet he would get very angry if anyone questioned his veracity; it was not good to laugh openly when he was narrating (Thomas 1987: 233).

From the detailed study provided by Gerald Thomas, it is clear that M. Ding-Dong had problems holding fast to reality. In a traditional world he might have been primarily described as imaginative but in the modern world he was taken to be a fool, for even on the very edge of the edge of a modern society tolerance for stupidity has declined.

Even if we turn to those Newfoundland jokes in which a quick-witted person uses repartee to take control of a situation, as in the Upper Island Cove Stories, it is not entirely clear that the Upper Island Cover isn't stupid, even then, as we can see in the following examples:

> A man was stranded on a remote road in the middle of Newfoundland. He sat down on a huge gravel box full of grit. Some time later he stopped an Upper Island Cove man driving a taxi and asked him, "Can you give me a lift?" "Yes," came the reply," but I can't take your suit-case." (Told to author by Gerald Thomas, Newfoundland, September 1994)

True to his community's reputation for wit the Upper Island Cove man's comment is both clever and funny. Yet to a prosaic literal-minded person from the "center" it might well appear stupid, because as a remark it is tangential to the immediate practical problem facing the stranded one, who may well not appreciate figurative language. When we laugh at this joke, can we be sure at whom we are laughing? It is not necessary to be pedantic or unsympathetic to the witty driver or his mode of speech to see that it can create problems.

Likewise, while it is amusing to hear someone speak of a machine as if it were an animal it also hints of stupidity. For someone *really* to think of machines as being persons is an infallible sign of primitive stupidity and of an inability to understand the nature of causality or to think in an abstract and general way (Hallpike 1976; 1979). Even to speak of machines in this way may feel uncomfortably close to stupidity; the person who does so may be skilled in his or her use of language, but can we be sure that such a person has a secure understanding of the underlying material realities? (see

Narvaez 1991: 80). It might also be added that a similar doubt exists in the converse case, as in the Upper Island Cove story below about the man who complained to Uncle John that his wife was ill:

> "Boy now I'll tell you, the woman got a cold and a quinsey throat and I had an awful job trying to get her to take her oil for the colds." Uncle John said, "that's only simple sure, if she won't take the oil she must have dirt in the carburetor." (M.U.N.F.L.A. file 79-375, collected by Peter Mercer)

Throughout the Upper Island Cove jokes and humorous stories there is always only a very fine line between the tales about the person who humorously plays with stupidity and the person whose stupidity is humorously played with by others. Let us consider some toothsome cases:

> Johnny Crane (was) nicknamed Johnny Crump. Johnny had a tooth-ache one day and he was going to Hr Grace (to Harbor Grace) to the dentist to get his tooth out. In the meantime money was scarce in these days. He was sittin' down in the chair gettin he's tooth pulled and he said, "Doctor, how much do you charge to pull teeth now?" The Doctor says, "Well John tis a dollar for the first one and fifty cents for the second one." Johnny says, "Okay then Doctor pull the second one." (M.U.N.F.L.A. file 79-375 collected by Peter Mercer. Also in C.C.N.S. *The Record*, 1957 n.p.)

> Two old fellows from Upper Island Cove when false teeth first came out. A fellow from Island Cove went away and worked in Halifax for a few years and finally decided to come home, so he bought a set of false teeth which was something new then. So after a while living in Island Cove he decided to get married and build a house but he didn't have any money because times were poor. So he said to his father, "I don't wear me false teeth now, father. I think I'll sell them." So he decided to put an ad in the paper and he asked his father what would be a nice way to put this in the paper. "Teeth too large for owner maybe." In the meantime he was livin' with his family which was a large family. So his father said no that wouldn't be the right way to say it. So, old man, what would you say in the paper. "Well meson," he said, "I'll tell you what I would say, 'One set of false teeth. Reason for selling, owner got nothing to eat with them.'" (M.U.N.F.L.A. file 79-375, p. 23. Collected by Peter Mercer)

In both tales there is a clever use of words, but to what effect. The Harbor Grace dentist is not going to be deceived by a piece of mathematical *stupidity* into losing his full fee; though he might be so amused by Johnny Crump's verbal *cleverness* that he would reduce his charges somewhat. Also there is no further meaning behind Johnny Crump's remark; he is no Hodja Nasrudin or Til Eulenspiegel providing a critical comment on the dubious practice of offering a discount for multiple tooth extraction. The false-teeth story reveals the poverty and backwardness of the toothless inhabitants of Upper Island Cove, who cannot afford the luxuries of big-city Halifax. Is the proposed change in the advertisement, written by the Upper Island Covers wit or a failure to understand the nature of the market in second-hand false teeth? Likewise in the story below is Uncle Joe a fool who is unable to understand the difference between the two meanings of "take" or is he a wit who plays on the two possible meanings of "take" in order to make fun of a stranger? The overall meaning of the story is as ambiguous as the verb to take; in each case we can only know which one to choose from the context in which we hear it.

> Uncle Joe was on his way up from Harbour Grace one morning when he met a man on the way down. "Is this the road you take to go to Harbour Grace?" enquired the stranger.
> "Yes, but have it back by tomorrow morning, because I want to go in the woods." (C.C.N.S. *The Record*, 1957 n.p.)

Some of the tales collected and classified as being distinctively related to the witty folk of Upper Island Cove are in fact classic ethnic stupidity stories that also exist in other countries, as in the case of the following tale about an Island Cove bayman (from the "edge" of Newfoundland), joining the St. John's police force and thus moving to the economic and political center of Newfoundland:

> There was this young fellow from Island Cove went in St. John's to join the police force. He didn't have a clue what it was all about but he was willing to give it a try. This was before they used to give them any training, and the first day he was in it the sergeant took him down on New Flower Street to get him on a beat. The sergeant said to him, "Now this is your beat from now 'till twelve o'clock tonight. You just walk from here to that red light up there (he pointed to a red light about a quarter of a mile up the street) and back again. If you see anyone hangin' around store windows or lookin' suspicious just tell them to move along. Now do you understand what you got to do?" "Yes skipper," the fellow said, "I understands all that plain 'nough. I'll look after this part of it. You needn't worry a bit." The sergeant said, "Okay I'll see you back at the station twelve o'clock." Well, twelve o'clock came and buddy didn't turn up at the station. The sergeant sent a car up New Flower Street but no sign of buddy anywhere. They phoned his boarding house; thought he might have gone home but nobody had seen him anywhere. The night passed and still no sign of buddy. Anyway sometime late that day he turned up at the station, just able to walk. When the sergeant saw him come in he went over to him and said, "Well, what happened? I thought you were supposed to report back here twelve o'clock last night."
> "Well skipper," he said, "You knows that red light you told me to go to?" The sergeant said, "Yes, what about it?" "Well, that red light was a tail light of a bus goin' to Carbonear." (M.U.N.F.L.A. file 68-23D. Collected by Harold Stroud)

This particular humorous story was told on the radio in New York about that classic comic figure, the dumb Irish cop, sometime before

1947 (Ford et al. 1947: 80) and has since been recycled as an American stupidity joke about Poles. It can only be cited as a joke about the wit of Upper Island Cove in the sense that if they tell such a story about themselves, it shows that they possess a good sense of humor and a love of telling a good story for its own sake. The story is about one's own stupidity, but the very skill with which the Upper Island Cove raconteur tells it denies the possibility of their really being stupid.

Upper Island Cove is perhaps a microcosm of Newfoundland in this respect. It is interesting in this context to note some of the Newfoundland collectors' comments on why Upper Island Cove was "known for its humor and wit":

> The fact that at one time, Upper Island Cove was isolated from other communities might lend an explanation for its wit because the main form of entertainment was social, informal gatherings in someone's house, where you would get a lot of old "stories" and "yarns" being told that always produced much laughter....Upper Island Cove was always looked down upon up until these past twenty years or so, by larger surrounding communities such as Harbor Grace. The people of such a community as Harbor Grace were better educated, while the people of Island Cove were not and led a very simple life. Due largely to this lack of education and the isolation of the community, the people developed their own dialect, which to the outsider was something to behold. I think that people built a defence against this difference by using wit as a weapon and in doing so strengthened the belief that Island Cove people were less aware of the world around them (than those from) other communities, which led to misunderstanding. (M.U.N.F.L.A. file 79-375: 21. Collected by Peter Mercer)

The relationship of Upper Island Cove to Harbor Grace is clearly that of the baymen to the townies and that of Newfoundland to Canada; out of each layer of edge-center relations comes a humor of stupidity, which perhaps has been part of Newfoundland humor since the very first settlements (see Hayman 1628).

The nature of the difference between the two styles of Newfie jokes can be well seen in a comparison of the jokes about fish 'n boots discussed in chapter 5 with those told in Newfoundland dialect. The general Canadian jokes about these topics whether in English or French tend to be short, often riddle-type jokes with a clear punch-line of the modern kind. They may well involve a switch in scripts in a story that begins with the Newfie and his boots and then shifts abruptly to a script involving an unexpected new and perhaps forbidden script such as sex. The Newfie is only the pretext for the joke, rather than the central character.

- Hé, le Newfie! où vas-tu avec tes bottes?
- Je vais voir Histoire d'eau (O). (Allard 1976: 97)

(Rough translation by author: "Hey, Newfie, where are you going in those boots?" "I am going to see 'The story of eau/O' ." *Histoire d'O* was a sadomasochistic film in which the long-rubber boots loved by fetishists and indeed other kinds of long rubbers might well be on display but not the fisherman's boots doubly inappropriately worn by the Newfie, who thinks the film is called *Histoire d'eau*, the story of water, and is going to be wet in a quite literal sense.)

We may contrast this pleasingly decadent joke from modern French Canada with a local Newfoundland narrative joke:

A Newfie in Toronto wanted to buy a car. He went to the nearest garage with his hip rubber boots on. The salesman tried to find something suitable for his customer. He showed the Newfie a Volkswagen. The Newfie was not interested and retorted: "No, she's too small, shur I'se can pass her long rubbers and all."
The salesman then showed his friend a 1966 Ford. The Newfie was still dismayed and answered , "No I'se can pass her long rubbers and all."
The salesman was losing patience with the Newfie and thus decided to show him a new LTD. The Newfie said twas a nice car but added: "I'se can still pass her long rubbers and all."
The salesman decided to take the Newfie up on this. So they went out on the highway and the salesman takes off in his car. He drives at 30 m.p.h., looks in his rear view mirror and the Newfie is right on his heels; he speeds up to 50 m.p.h., then 70 m.p.h. and the Newfie stays with him. He is coming to a hill and thinks to himself that this would be a good place to lose his friend. So the salesman speeds up to 90 and when he gets over the hill he sees no sign of the Newfie. Then he goes back to see what happened When he gets there, the Newfie is crawling up over the hill on his hands and knees, his face all cut up and the rubber boots bursted up. The salesman asks him what happened. The Newfie answers, "If you were going 90 m.p.h. and got a blow out on your long rubbers, you'd have to crawl, too."(M.U.N.F.L.A. file 70-27. Collected by Karl Sullivan)

Here we have a much longer, more discursive joke with a classic three-part structure and a rather unfocused punch-line in which the final main clause about crawling, perhaps unfortunately, comes after the key piece of information about the blow-out which in and of itself switches us from boots to tires. The joke's charm will have lain in its telling, in its use of the distinctive and attractive English spoken in Newfoundland, which is so much more appealing than the tedious flat J. K. Galbraithian sounds of Ontario and no doubt for many North Americans also in its innocent talk of long rubbers, thus confusing boots and lengthy erasers. It is a joke that needs a good narrator who might well choose to tie it arbitrarily but skilfully to a local fisherman and pretend that it really happened. In Newfoundland the impossible is often up-graded to the improbable for the sake of a good story.

Likewise even jokes about eating cod can be locally distinctive with a characteristic unresolved absurdity about them:

That was Jimmy Lynch one day, came down on the wharf lookin' for a meal of cods heads. So I started breakin' off a few for him. Anyway after I broke off four or five I asked Jimmy how many more he wanted and Jimmy said, "I'm only gonna have one more, Harris boy, because I'm drivin'."

Newfoundland jokes of this kind are anecdotes and remembered witticisms that would have to be reworked and detached from their particular setting if they were going to be repeated as jokes outside the province and the style of performance would also need to change. Nonetheless, the joke is clearly cousin to the other fishy jokes cited in chapter 5.

It is then absurd to argue that there is a dichotomy between popular Newfoundland humor and Canadian ethnic stupidity jokes, as if these constituted polarized forms of humor. Rather they are very similar, though even the same *identically phrased items* can carry a very different set of sentiments depending upon the tone, context, aim and purpose for which they are used.

Curiously, there are many jokes about the stupidity of those at the center that could be told by Newfoundlanders, but are not. Occasionally the ethnic stupidity jokes are told in Newfoundland in reverse with a Mainlander or a citizen of Toronto substituted for the Newfie in an ethnic stupidity joke about Newfies. However, the jokes don't really work; not only are they but rarely collected by folklorists, but also no one is inventing or has invented any new ones that did not previously exist with a Newfie in the title role. Everyone knows that this kind of stupidity joke can *only* be told about those who live at the edge of a society, since this is where ignorance of modern artifacts and technical knowledge is likely to be concentrated. However, the dominance of the center is based as much on bureaucratic as on technical knowledge and much of this is either bogus or alienating. It is alienating where it has created efficiency by destroying the quality of life that is the purpose of that efficiency (Davies 1988A). There is no shortage of officially sanctioned stupid and mendacious tall tales in this brave new Canadian world and they do far more damage than anything ever imagined in Newfoundland. Idiocies such as the techno-moral panic about saccharine or the absurd Lalonde doctrine (Neal and Davies 1998: 58; Luik 1994; Wildavsky 1995) dedicated to the promotion of tall tales about health and safety scares that run wildly ahead of the evidence have made Canada the laughing-stock of statisticians, scientists, and economists throughout the world. The Newfoundlanders, as an island of old-fashioned common-sensical skepticism whose inhabitants regularly face up to and are willing to take real risks, are in a good position to mock "them," the risk-averse, self-conscious but unreflexive modernizers (Neal and Davies 1998: 44) who incompetently rule over "us." Those at the edge are in the best position to create jokes and humor at the expense of the idiocy of urban life promoted by the center. There is an opportunity here for Newfoundlanders to exercise their traditional skill in making humor about stupidity.

When they do so, then at that point there will exist truly *opposed* forms of humor, based on an opposition of content as well as merely style, but at present no such dichotomy exists. Traditional Newfoundland humor is merely a longer-winded, more personalized, skilfully told narrative version of the snappier, often riddle-like, well-made jokes about "Newfies" told in mainland Canada. The two sets of jokes differ in form rather than content in the way that contemporary Scottish jokes differ from those collected and published in the late nineteenth and earlier twentieth centuries as discussed in chapter 2. The differences in form reflect also the difference and the shift between rural and urban styles of jokes and anecdotes (Utley 1971: 3) . The new urban style is more efficient and less discursive, gets to the punch-line faster and avoids irrelevant detail. Yet from the point of view of the people of Newfoundland it may well be the detail that locates the joke and establishes their ownership of it. These jokes are still funny to outsiders but the details may be a baffling distraction. It is a matter of taste whether one prefers one or the other of these two styles of humor on aesthetic grounds or because one is found funnier than the other and this will be influenced by the social backgrounds of tellers and listeners, compilers and readers. In this respect it would be interesting to know if the preferences of Newfoundland jokers differ by age or place of residence. The impression given by the files in the Memorial University of Newfoundland Folklore Archive is that the snappy jokes shared with mainland Canada were particularly popular among young people in the capital St. John's who, as shown earlier, revelled in the jokes about dirty and stupid Newfies. They do not seem to have been concerned about the ownership of the jokes in the broader sense; they were happy to appropriate the newer jokes for their own use. Also the main publishers of the new jokes, at least in English (as distinct from French),

are based in Newfoundland itself. Only a few publishers, mainly in
the other maritime provinces of Canada, compete with them and
only those published in Newfoundland exist in several volumes with
new editions and many re-printings. From a commercial point of
view the Newfoundlanders own the jokes told about them, in contrast to, say Polish Americans. Newfoundlanders use the jokes and
artifacts based on them, such as the Newfie ID card (a badge made
of a mirror fastened to a piece of cardboard) or the Newfie mosquito
trap (like a miniature mouse-trap), as a way of making money from
tourists. Such an option is available to people living in remote, peripheral areas that are for that very reason attractive to holiday-mak-
ers in search of "authentic," unspoiled simplicity.

Newfoundland jokes and jokes about Newfies have effectively
merged into a single common stream of jokes incorporating both
the old anecdotes and the new snappier jokes and they are to a large
extent owned by the Newfoundlanders. The jokes have come to
constitute another example of that self-conscious self-mockery that
is also self-promotional, the promotion of an image of the
Newfoundlanders as an amiable humorous people. There is no reason whatsoever to see Newfoundland self-mockery in any sense as
pathological or indicating self-dislike.

Note

1.   The use of the phrase in this manner and context serves to demonstrate the contra-
      dictions inherent in this concept (see Henri Bergson 1911).

7

American Jokes about Poles

American jokes about Poles are both the newest and the oldest of ethnic jokes about stupidity. They are the newest in that they probably did not exist at all prior to the 1940s, did not become common until the early 1960s, and only appeared in joke books in the 1970s. By the end of the twentieth century they had been in existence for at most sixty years and more probably for only forty years, which is a far shorter period of time than, say, British stupidity jokes about the Irish, which are more than three hundred years old (Davies 1998: 32), or Indian stupidity jokes about Sikhs (Moon 1961: 82), which have also had a long and continuous existence.

Yet the Polish joke cycle in the United States is also the oldest of its kind for it introduced a new style of joking about stupidity and gave a new vigor to the older traditions of ethnic joking about stupidity in other countries, such as Britain, which had languished in the 1950s. The new snappy riddle-type jokes told in Canada about Newfoundlanders which were discussed in chapter 5 are derived from an American model. Sometimes the Canadian jokes are simply copies of American jokes about stupid or dirty Poles and sometimes they have been invented independently in Canada in both English and French, as is particularly clear from those Canadian jokes that incorporate purely local elements. Nonetheless, the basic template is American, a product of a new style of riddle joking developed in the United States and used to produce more direct, blunter, quicker and in appearance more aggressive jokes dealing with death, deformity, and disaster as well as with alleged ethnic traits. American stupidity jokes about Poles spread to many of the countries listed in table 1.1 in chapter 1 where they were accepted and adapted and added to an older local tradition of narrative jokes about ethnic, regional or local stupidity. Danish stupidity jokes about Aarhus in

Jutland, for example, are an amalgam of the new-style American jokes and older nineteenth-century jokes about the people of Mols, a small rural community not far from Aarhus (Holbek 1975; Bason 1977; Jagendorff 1957; Rockwell 1981) or about Jutes in general. The older traditions of ethnic stupidity jokes would probably have boomed anyway during the 1960s and 1970s as ethnic and regional identities underwent a revival, but American cultural dominance meant that the Polish jokes led the way. The patterns that then emerged were universal ones rooted in a common perception of the humorous possibilities of stupidity, particularly in an advanced industrial society and in the universal tendency for those at the geographical, economic or linguistic center of a society or a culture to laugh at those located at its edge (Davies 1990: 40-83). Nonetheless, initially these new cycles of jokes within an older tradition were the product of an awareness of an American innovation.

The very newness of the American stupidity jokes about Poles, however, has set them apart from the older traditions of ethnic joking about stupidity of other countries and, indeed, even of America itself. Although the stock of Polish jokes in America grew through the recycling of older American jokes about Irish stupidity, in the process the jokes lost not only their Irish identity but also a great deal of their narrative richness (which had, of course, given them a distinctive Irish flavor by drawing on the extravagant Irish use of figurative speech). Also the new ethnic jokes did not gain a new and distinctive Polish identity; in the main, American jokes about Poles are generic stupidity jokes that can be transferred unchanged to any other ethnic or social group having an appropriate peripheral or social class location. Thus, Polish jokes in a largely unchanged form are also told locally in the United States about the Italians, the Portuguese, the Aggies of Texas A and M, and many other cognate groups. Indeed, very few of the American jokes about Poles use Polish words, make use of distinctive and authentic Polish ways of speaking English or refer to recognizable Polish institutions. The stupidity jokes about the Irish were and in Britain still are distinctively Irish, but there is very little about Polish jokes that is Polish. Also they have no real geographical location in the sense that Canadian Newfie jokes relate to Newfoundland or Spanish jokes about the Leperos of Lepe in Andalucia or Irish Kerryman jokes to Kerry. They are jokes about a social class, about blue-collar workers in old industries that merely happened to be located in, say, Chicago, Detroit, Milwaukee, Buffalo or Pittsburgh where people of Polish ancestry are concentrated. Stupidity jokes about the Irish in Britain or the Laz in Turkey or the Newfies in Canada are social-class jokes (in particular they often refer to the employment of these groups as laborers in the construction industry or in primary production), but they do also refer to these groups as people from a particular place on the edge of each of these countries and as groups possessing their own ways and traditions.

The collections of Polish jokes in American folklore archives show that the tellers have little awareness of the nature, existence or even location of the country from which the ancestors of the Polish Americans came. By contrast the British know about Ireland and the French know about Belgium, the countries of the butts of their stupidity jokes. For Americans, Poland is simply a small country a long way away that only impinges briefly on the American mind when it is mentioned on television, as when Poland became a significant aspect of America's long confrontation with Soviet Communism or with the election of a Polish Pope who immediately became the butt of American jokes (Dundes 1979; Fish 1980). Having lectured on Irish stupidity jokes in Belfast, Cork and Dublin, on Newfie jokes in St. John's, Newfoundland, and on American jokes about Poles in Kraków, Poland, the author can say that whereas the Irish and the Newfoundlanders know that the jokes are about their own group, Poles in Poland see them as referring purely to Polish Americans. Indeed, recent Polish immigrants to America who are often self-consciously cultured and educated people see the jokes as not referring to their own group at all but purely to the blue-collar class they see as constituting America Polonia.

One consequence of this is that Polish Americans don't have much input into or identification with the jokes told about themselves. Although the jokes about Polish stupidity may have begun as local and social-class jokes within Polish communities, possibly between North side and South side Poles in Milwaukee (Welsch 1967: 184), and although the jokes circulate freely among Polish Americans who can appreciate their humor as well as anyone else (Kusielowicz 1973 [1969]: 100-3), the kind of analysis that was provided in chapter 6 about the two kinds of jokes in Newfoundland has no application to Polish jokes in America. No doubt Polish Americans do invent new jokes about Polish stupidity and put them into circulation, but there is no way in which such jokes can be identified and distinguished or said to be owned by Polish Americans in the sense that the Australians or Jews or Newfoundlanders or Scots can be said to own their own jokes.

In chapter 6 it was noted that traditional Newfoundland humor is merely a longer-winded, more personalized, skillfully told, narrative version of the snappier often riddle-like, well-made jokes about Newfies told in mainland Canada. The purpose of pointing this out was partly to stress the overwhelming importance of the *objective* contrast between center and periphery in determining humor and the shakiness of the distinction between insiders' and outsiders' humorous folklore. We cannot fully define the world to suit ourselves, for there is a material reality out there that overrides as well as shapes subjective perceptions and social constructs. Nonetheless, the *absence* among Polish Americans of any real equivalent of the Newfoundland tall tales, or the wit of Upper Island Cove, is an important phenomenon. Because the Newfoundlanders can own and cherish one aspect of the stupidity humor about themselves and can stamp on it their own skills, language, and particular qualities, they are also able to take charge of the modern Canadian jokes about Newfies even though these do not in any way differ from the jokes told about Poles in America. The Newfoundland folklore archive contains a large number of the modern Canadian jokes that have been told by and about Newfoundlanders, but in a sense they are collected and cherished mainly because they can be placed alongside the distinctive local narrative jokes. Such a possibility is not open to the Polish Americans and so it is easy to see why they were not pleased when the citizens of Longmeadow, Massachusetts, placed a book of stupidity jokes about Poles in a bicentennial time capsule and buried it for posterity (Bukowczyk 1987: 141). Neither the editors nor the publishers of the *main* American joke books about Poles tend to be Polish, whereas many volumes of Irish jokes in Britain have Irish editors, notably Professor Desmond MacHale (1984), the Cork mathematician and biographer of Boole, and most of the English language collections of Newfie jokes in Canada are published in Newfoundland and edited by Newfoundlanders. The comic image of the Newfie is thus an asset to the Newfoundlanders and also, as we have seen, one that can be exploited by the local tourist industry.

The Newfoundlanders have no inhibitions about exploiting the whimsical, self-mockery of Newfoundland humor rather in the way that Hillbillies do in the Appalachians or the Leperos do in Spain, where the people of Lepe who are the butt of Spanish stupidity jokes have made their joke status the basis of a festival and carnival. It is part of the image of a slow-moving, old-fashioned, story-telling, rural periphery that appeals to tourists and is not in any sense demeaning for those who peddle it for they are also seen as good-humored and charming. This option is not open to Polish Americans who are popularly associated only with an industrial working class. Artifacts such as the Polish calculator (a pencil fastened to an electric plug) or the Polish room freshener (a plastic turd) are to be found in American joke shops with no Polish affiliations and manufactured in states such as Oklahoma with no substantial and visible Polish population. Polish jokes do not harm Polish Americans, but neither are they in any sense a source of profit to them. Likewise, there are no prominent Polish comedians who can use Polish jokes to bring together Poles and non-Poles in the United States in the way that Portuguese comedians do in Hawaii (Oshima 2000) or Irish comedians, such as Dave Allen, do in Britain. There are no American programs about Poles comparable to Britain's television comedies about the lovable, foolish Irish, such as *Father Ted*, or *Me Mammy*. Father Dougal, Father Jack, and Mrs. Doyle, the main supporting characters in *Father Ted*, may have been idiots, but they were likeable idiots and both they and the other inhabitants of the remote Craggy Island where Father Ted was the priest are part of a long tradition of affectionate, sentimental, whimsical, cheerfully patronizing British humor about the Irish (Somerville and Ross 1899 and 1908). It is not surprising that *Father Ted* had proportionately as many fans and viewers in Ireland (where British television is popular and easily available) as in Britain itself. There are no equivalent amiable or sentimental situation comedies about Polish Americans on American television, not even bad ones. It is possible for Irish viewers watching British television to feel appreciated as well as mocked, but Polish Americans are and feel (at best) ignored and excluded by the American media (Bukowczyk 1987: 112-6). The Poles in America have no comic voice, no raconteurs, no latter-day equivalent of Finley Peter Dunne's (1942; 1963) Mr. Dooley. Those who control television comedy in America never seek to portray, flatter, court or humor the Poles in the way that they lay it on for other more favored ethnic groups (Andreski 1973: 116).

The mechanical and one-dimensional quality of stupidity humor about Polish Americans relative to that of other groups in America, and the butts of stupidity jokes in other countries has misled many scholars into thinking that Polish-joke-telling Americans are not just hostile but uniquely hostile towards Polish Americans. Sometimes they even mistakenly refer to the jokes as "anti-Polish" jokes. They have then gone on to manufacture explanations for this supposed social fact, rooted in an alleged Polish threat to other ethnic groups, notably to those above them in the hierarchy of social classes. There is no independent evidence for the existence of such hostility and the attempts at explanation are not only baseless but unnecessary.

The mistaken view that the existence and circulation of Polish jokes in America is or was an expression of hostility towards Poles is usually based on the application of unproven and dubious theories about the nature of humor to the particular case of Polish jokes (e.g., Bier 1988), but other versions of this thesis (see McCosh 1976: 120; Schwartz 1973; Welsch 1967) purport to have a comparative dimension, though the comparisons made are in each case shallow and the analyses lacking in rigor. These explanations will be refuted first by an examination of American folklore about the Poles *other* than jokes and humor, secondly, by using a more informed and analytical use of comparisons to undermine the feeble attempts at comparison that have been used to buttress the hostility thesis and, finally, by looking at the history of the Polish joke in America in conjunction with the social history of the Polish Americans and their relationship with other Americans.

If American ethnic jokes about the Poles were an expression of hostility then we would expect there also to exist a significant body of *serious* American folklore about the Poles ascribing negative characteristics to them. After all, *serious* "ethnic slurs" about *other* national, regional and ethnic groups are common in America and so, too, are *serious* "ethnic slurs" about the Poles among their European neighbors. Yet such serious ethnic slurs about Poles are very rare in the United States and the view that blasons populaires about Poles are widespread is based entirely on the *misclassification* of Polish jokes as blasons populaires thus putting them in the same category as serious "ethnic slurs."

Numerically, ethnic jokes about the Poles are probably the most common of all American ethnic jokes, and ethnic jokes are the dominant form of folklore about Polish Americans. Distinguished folklorists who have analyzed this humorous folklore have categorized the jokes about Poles as blasons populaires or ethnic slurs (Dundes 1971) because of the superficial similarity between the jokes and the kind of serious statements made in other kinds of folklore, such as routine abusive epithets, proverbs, similes and metaphors. They are mistaken. Jokes are not like serious folklore, but are part of an entirely different mode of communication: humorous, not bona fide (Raskin 1985). Ethnic jokes about the Poles' stupidity, dirtiness and vulgarity (or the essentially similar jokes told about the Portuguese or Texas A and M) are *not* ethnic slurs nor blasons populaires. They are known by the joke tellers to be fictitious comic scripts and most of the tellers neither link them to any salient and seriously held stereotype nor do they care one way or another about Polish Americans or Poles in general.

The key point that must be stressed is the *absence* of serious ethnic slurs against the Poles in America, or indeed in the English language (Mencken 1977: 611). In Abraham Roback's list of "Ethnopaulisms in English" (ethnic slurs) only two terms for the Poles, Polack and Polander, are listed, both of which he terms "jocose" (Roback 1944: 58-9). It is possible as Roback says, that in American English "Polack" is used in a derogatory way to mean "A Pole, usually of the slow and ungainly type" (Roback 1944: 58). However, Roback's only other reference to the Poles in English is to the Polish disease, *plica Polonica*, a disease of the scalp endemic in Eastern Europe (Roback 1944: 58-9).

Roback (1944: 109-11, 211-15) has thirty-six ethnic slurs about the Poles in German and fifty-eight derogatory proverbs about the Poles from French, German, Latin, Russian, Ruthenian, Ukrainian, Yiddish and even Polish, but he cites *none in English*. Likewise, there are very few similes and metaphors about the Poles in English, and those that do exist are not important. There is no real equivalent in English of *ivre comme un Polonais* (drunk as a Pole) or *Polnische Wirtschaft* (disorder, inefficiency) (Roback 1944: 110; UCBFA, German Blason Populaire Anti-Polish file, n.d.).

After much searching in several folklore archives, the author unearthed only five serious or perhaps merely jocular-serious items of modern American folklore relating to Polish Americans:

1. "Polish bungalows," "typical coarse red-brick houses that sprung up in the 1930s" in Chicago (UCBFA American file P6 Miscellaneous. Blason populaire Anti-Polish general. Collected by Mary Elizabeth Manion in 1979 from an Irish-American informant who heard it in 1956).

2. "Polish Cadillac," a Studebaker "particularly the cheaper Lark models." (UCBFA American P6 Miscellaneous file. Blason populaire Anti-Polish general. Collected by James V. Janowiak, a Polish American from his memory of the 1960s).

3. "Polocky" meaning "garish," "over-dressed," "over-done," in bad taste (UCBFA American file P6 Miscellaneous file. Collected by Phil Peek in 1966 from first- and second-generation Czech-Americans from Chicago). Compare also "Portuguese Pink" meaning "dressed very flamboyantly (in poor taste)" (UCBFA American file P6. Blason Populaire Anglo).

4. "Polish system calculator," a small sophisticated Hewlett-Packard calculator with an "unorthodox method of operation," i.e., the sequencing of numbers and instructions differed from that of regular calculators. The collector, Kathy Orcutt, comments "Even sales representatives of the company call it by its nickname....This method is considered backward and stupid by many who use it." (UCBFA American P6 I5 Miscellaneous file. Blason Populaire. Collected 1974 from a Canadian civil engineer in California). Orcutt's interpretation is probably incorrect. The calculator was cleverly designed using Polish expertise in mathematical logic.

5. "Portugi," "Polish Special" or "tuna job"; "anything done in a sloppy slip-shod manner" (UCBFA American file P65. Blason Populaire Anti-Portuguese. Collected by Jennifer Stevenson from an Irish-American in 1971). Compare also "Proper Penclawdd," a Welsh North Gower term having the same meaning. Penclawdd was a cockle-fishing village, the cocklers and cockle traders being women, on the edge of a coal mining area where men had the employment and made the money.

None of these terms are the stuff of which ethnic hatred is made; rather they are an American way of expressing disdain for blue-collar workers in a class-based society dominated by a national myth and ideology that denies that social classes exist in America. Also such slurs are *few* in number and very similar expressions are used in California and Hawaii about the Portuguese. It is a *world apart from the earlier folklore* of Eastern and Central Europe, which constituted *a veritable system of ethic slurs* expressed about the Poles by several different peoples who had been involved in long-lasting and very violent, national and ethnic conflicts with the Poles. The recent experience of Polish immigrants in America and other English-speaking countries has not been like that. Mild snobbery is quite distinct from real hatred. Germans, Russians, and Ukrainians have a long history of hating and slaughtering Poles. Americans do not.

The *absence of numerous serious ethnic slurs against the Poles* in America despite the prevalence of Polish ethnic jokes is proof that ethnic jokes are a different phenomena from ethnic slurs and blasons populaires, and that these two sets of humorous and serious folklore, respectively, should *not* be classified or analyzed together. There may well be in some cases a relationship or overlap between jokes and slurs, but the nature of this relationship is varied, contingent, differs greatly between one situation and another and should be the subject of careful empirical investigation not crude a priori assumptions.

The inability of American social scientists to come to terms with the importance of this distinction is revealed in Irving Lewis Allen's (1983) *The Language of Ethnic Conflict, Social Organization and Lexical Culture*, whose basic thesis is that the number and nature of nicknames and particularly derogatory nicknames for particular ethnic groups in America is a reflection of the strengths of the ethnic conflicts in which they have been involved and the kinds of ill-feeling that such conflicts generate. Allen is able to record only eleven American nicknames for the Poles, *far less* than for most other ethnic groups, and of these only one refers to their character (Allen 1983: 80). A careful examination of his list of eleven reduces the number even further, since he includes Bohunk and Hunky, which refer to central Europeans in general not Poles as such. (Bohunk = Bohemian/Hungarian and Hunky may be the origin of Honky, i.e., the African American term for European-Americans in general). Polack and Polacker are essentially the same word and Pole is not a nickname, yet Allen cites it as such. He also lists Pscrew and yak, which are merely obscure Chicago dialect words from a single source based on Russian and Polish phrases. That leaves *only five* nicknames for Poles. Whether the true figure is eleven or five it is still remarkably low given the visibility, prominence and importance of the Poles in the United States. The Poles are way behind the African Americans, the Irish, the Jews, the Chinese, the Italians, the Germans, the Mexicans, and even the French-Canadians and Swedes when it comes to being called derogatory nicknames.

Allen comments on his own findings: "The Poles for unclear reasons have collected disproportionately few nicknames, although they are relentlessly derogated by other devices (Welsch 1967; Dundes 1971)" (Allen 1983: 90). By "other devices" Allen means jokes, as is clear from his references to Welsch and Dundes as secondary sources, but he is unwilling directly to use the "J word" and does not study humor himself (it is very odd that he should use such a vague and evasive term as "devices" as if he were speaking of a third-world nuclear bomb). If Allen's thesis is true, it follows logically and inexorably that the paucity of nicknames for the Poles implies that they have been involved in fewer ethnic conflicts than other American minorities. It will not do to try and avoid coming to this conclusion by saying that this is for unclear reasons; it is necessary to provide independent evidence to show why the Poles might be an exception to his general hypothesis. To wheel in the existence of "other devices," by which he presumably means jokes, to plug the gap is quite unsatisfactory. America's Polish jokes are *not* part of the language of ethnic conflict and this is reconfirmed by the relative absence of the language of *serious* conflict in America in relation to the Poles when compared with other ethnic groups. No doubt those who are determined to show that the jokes are a vehicle for conflict and hostility will argue that the absence of negative terms for the Poles is evidence for the Americans' total repression of their intense inner hostility towards them, which then has to emerge in comic form as a means of release. Such an argument would be so contrived and dependent on so many arbitrary assumptions that it could not be taken seriously. Why, for example, should hostility to ethnic groups other than Poles *not* be repressed but expressed openly through serious folklore and derogatory epithets? Why should *other* ethnic minorities such as the African Americans or Italians be the subject *both* of serious negative blasons populaires and negative epithets *and* of ethnic jokes when the Poles are not?

The shift in the style of stupidity jokes that occurred in the 1960s first in America and then internationally has also misled other scholars into thinking that hostility and conflict have increased and have been particularly directed against Polish Americans. Thus, Alvin Schwartz (1973: 109) drew a sharp contrast between the "gentle, good natured" stupidity jokes of the past with the "angry, insulting hate jokes" about ethnic stupidity and Poles that prevailed in America

in the 1960s and 1970s, which he saw as hostile put-downs generated by inter-ethnic competition for jobs and housing (Schwartz 1973:
75). Yet an examination both of older American jokes and of contemporary jokes shows decisively that he is wrong. What occurred
in the 1960s was a change in the *style* of ethnic stupidity joking,
such that the jokes became blunter and more direct, and thus appar-
ently more aggressive in form than, say, American nineteenth-century jokes about Irish stupidity. The older American jokes about the
Irish flourished at a time of very real ethnic conflict and competition
for jobs, housing, and political power between the Irish and other
ethnic groups, not just old-stock Americans but also German, Italian,
Jewish and Chinese immigrants and African Americans; the last of
these originally moved to Harlem to escape from an invasion of
drunken and violent Irish immigrants (Sowell: 1981: 277). The nineteenth-century Irish were perceived as a threat in a way that was not
true of the Poles of the 1960s. If the jokes about the latter seem less
"good-natured" and more angry and insulting it merely shows that
changes in styles of joking are autonomous and that although these
changes in style may be the product of social change they are not
driven by intensified conflict or hatred. The point may be further reinforced by looking at the case of Canada, where the new American-
style stupidity jokes were rapidly pinned on the Newfoundlanders, as
shown in chapter 5, yet coincided and coexisted with the older "gentle,
good-natured" jokes of chapter 6 told by the Newfoundlanders themselves. This was also the case in Britain where old-style and new-style
jokes about the Irish were also blended together. Even in America,
many of the older stupidity jokes about the Irish were recycled as
jokes about the Poles, but Schwartz failed to realize this.

No one has suggested that there is any significant Canadian hostility towards or conflict with the Newfoundlanders, yet as shown in
chapter 5 the jokes about Newfies are more or less identical with
American Polish jokes. In particular, despite attempts at censorship,
the Canadian jokes depict the Newfoundlanders as being dirty as
well as stupid which refutes Sandra McCosh's (1976: 120) suggestion that the attribution of dirtiness to the Poles in American jokes
(which does not occur in British jokes about the Irish) is a special
mark of exclusion and rejection. Given that there has been far more
conflict between the British and the Irish than between Polish Americans and Americans in general, this claim is utterly circular. The

tagging of jokes about dirtiness onto jokes about stupidity was an American innovation of the 1960s, but as the author has shown elsewhere (Davies 1990 and 1995), it was a product of a North American (i.e., Canadian as well as American) obsession with rational hygiene not of a special hostility to Poles or Newfoundlanders. No evidence has ever been forthcoming that modern Americans seriously perceived the Polish Americans in such a strongly negative way.

The view that American-Polish jokes are a response to the threat provided by the arrival, presence, or upward mobility of the Poles is one that has been put forward independently by several American authors (Bier 1988; McCosh 1979: 120; Schwartz 1973: 75; Welsch 1967: 183). None of them provide any empirical evidence to support their claims, but they are presumably drawing on a commonly held, if unsubstantiated, theory. The theory, however, collapses when the actual history of the Poles and of Polish jokes in America is looked at in detail.

Roger Welsch, in his article, "American Numskull Tales: The Polack Joke," wrote that:

> Throughout Europe there are individual communities that enjoy the reputation of being peopled by idiots, Gotham in England, Kampen in Holland, Nol (Mols) in Denmark, Schildau in Germany for example. In the United States the numskull tale has taken on an interesting aberration, perhaps reflecting the geographic, economic, and ethnic mobility of American society...in general numskull tales have been associated with various immigrant groups...(this) probably represents a reaction to the imagined threats posed by a sudden influx of an immigrant group at a particular point in history. Thus Pat and Mike jokes gained particular prominence following the potato famine and Hans and Fritz jokes...reflected the insecurity of the American public in the face of mid-to-late nineteenth century German immigrations. The Polack joke is probably a parallel phenomenon. (Welsch 1967: 183)

Whether Welsch is right about the nineteenth-century ethnic jokes concerning the Irish or the Germans may be doubted, both in regard to the timing and the significance of these jokes. However, he is completely wrong about the Poles. If the Polack jokes were a response by established Americans to a major perceived threat from a new group, then the jokes should have flourished in the period 1880–1920, when there was a huge emigration of poor peasants and landless laborers from the more backward parts of Poland to the United States, creating not only competition for jobs and housing, but also a sense among earlier arrivals in America that their neighborhoods, traditions and culture were being taken over and destroyed.

Although there had been a trickle of Polish immigrants into the United States throughout the nineteenth century, often involving political refugees (Baker 1979; Thomas and Znaniecki 1958: 1486), the really massive influx of over a million Poles into America occurred for economic reasons during the period between the American Civil War and the First World War with a peak of 140,000 Poles emigrating to America in the year 1913 (Thomas and Znaniecki 1958: 1510, 1511). They provided unskilled labor (Morawska 1977: 12, 15; Zurawski 1975: 123-8) for such rapidly growing industrial centers as Pittsburgh, Buffalo, Cleveland, Detroit, Chicago, and Milwaukee (Thomas and Znaniecki 1958: 1511; Lenski 1961: 33), which developed huge Polish colonies from the influx of large numbers of young immigrants with a high birth rate (Thomas and Znaniecki 1958: 1516).

It is clear that the arrival of the Poles led to sudden and at times strongly resented changes in the ethnic composition of particular neighborhoods. In Chicago, for example, which by 1914 was the home of 360,000 Poles and the third largest Polish city in the world, there were "three large Polish neighborhoods, each including several primary parish-communities—located on the north side, around the stockyards, and in South Chicago..." (Thomas and Znaniecki 1958: 1545). To some extent the squeezing out of other ethnic groups was the result of collective, as well as individual, action taken by the Poles at the level of the individual Roman Catholic parish. As William Thomas and Florian Znaniecki (1958: 1545-46) put it:

> This process is consciously fostered by the parish committee and the priests who endeavour to select the location for the church as close as possible to the centers where most of the Poles work and also take care to choose a neighborhood where rent is low and real estate cheap. If the choice has been successful the process of territorial concentration begins at once. The original population of the district is slowly but ceaselessly driven away, for an Irish, German or Italian tenant or house-owner who sees Polish families take the place of his former neighbors and knows that they have come to stay near their parish-center soon moves to a more congenial neighborhood....The very growth of concentration produces new factors of further concentration. Polish shops...attract Polish customers and consciously contribute to the Polonization of the neighborhood.

Social changes of this magnitude were presumably resented by the various ethnic groups who had been driven out. Even in New England where relatively fewer Poles settled, Daniel Brewer (cited in Morawska 1977: 32) could write in 1926 in his significantly titled book *The Conquest of New England by the Immigrant*, "There are (here) plenty of Karolczaks, Olszewskis and Szunskis....Both the ear and tongue stand aghast at the titles which the Polish people...display in (this) tabulation of names which talk of Anglo-Saxon decadence." Likewise, Eva Morawska's (1977: 43) interviews in the 1970s with elderly New England Polish Americans "revealed many bitter memories from this period, when Irish priests in South Boston and Dorchester would recommend that their (Irish) parishioners 'not sell their houses to them Polacks.'"

The earlier days were clearly a time of great ethnic tensions and resentment between the Poles and those whose ancestors had come to America earlier, stemming from sudden changes in the ethnic composition of particular urban areas and the corresponding pressures on the housing market. Indeed, through the new immigration quota acts of 1920-24 the Americans severely restricted immigration into the United States in order to prevent any further influx of new and unfamiliar immigrants from Eastern and Southern Europe.

If ethnic jokes were a simple index of rejection, conflict and hostility, then Polish jokes should have flourished mightily during this early phase of massive Polish settlement when prejudice, conflict, and hostility were at their greatest. They did not.

During the period 1864-1920, the time of the "Polish threat," there were no jokes about Poles. During this period many joke books, collections of humorous recitations and sketches were published about African-Americans, German-Americans, Irish-Americans, Italian-Americans and Jewish-Americans, often with epithets such as Coon, Dago, Dutch, Hebrew, Nigger or Wop in the title or sub-title, but there were none about Poles. American reciters were thus able to give comic recitations supposedly based on the speech patterns of Southern blacks or of relatively recent German, Irish, Italian or Jewish immigrants, but there was no Polish pattern for them to imitate. The Poles were invisible as far as American humor was concerned; they were neither joked about nor imitated. A lengthy perusal of the extensive collection of late nineteenth- and early twentieth-century joke books in the Schmulowitz Collection in San Francisco's public library produced only one joke involving Poles and even in that joke the Poles have only a minor part in a joke that is mainly about Southern blacks.

A family that had lived in the South for some time recently returned North and, on reaching the new home in a big metropolitan city, a nurse was employed for the baby. Hearing the baby crying piteously one day the mother hastened to the nursery to investigate the trouble.

"What in the world is the matter with the baby, Norah?" asked the matron of the new nurse who was an attractive Polish girl. "He has been crying like that for the past three days."

"I don't know ma'am," answered the girl despairingly. "He cries and cries and I can't do a thing to quiet him."

"I know now," calmly rejoined the mother. "His nurse in the South was a colored woman. You will find the stove polish on the top shelf in the kitchen closet."

(*Button Busters. Jolly Jokes no. 49*, 1915: 21)

It is fatal for the proponents of the threat and hostility thesis that there should have been no Polish jokes at this time. Instead, Americans continued to pin stupidity jokes on the Irish as they had done since the beginning of the nineteenth century and went on doing so until the middle of the twentieth (Ford et al. 1947). The first generation of Poles in America were too strange, too alien, and too incomprehensible to be the butt of jokes about stupidity. The familiar Irishman with his brogue spoke a comic version of American English and could be laughed at as being an American seen in a distorting mirror. The first generation Poles who spoke no or very little English were, from the American point of view, simply "dumb Polacks." Also the Poles were not traders forced to communicate in intelligible but broken English with the native speakers as the Germans, Italians, and Jews had to do. The dialect speakers in nineteenth-century American jokes are very often peddlers or merchants, the German storekeeper or beer-seller, the Jewish drummer or clothes-dealer, the Italian fruit or ice-cream vendor. As Aristotle noted in *The Poetics* (1449 a 27, p. 150), for a defect or failure to be funny, it must not be so great as to destroy or depart too far from the original with which the butt of the jokes is implicitly compared; "a foreign accent for example is ludicrous when it does not render the words unintelligible."

The Poles only replaced the Irish in American stupidity jokes after the Second World War when long-residence, assimilation and upward social mobility turned most Irish-Americans into invisible middle-class suburbanites (Sinha 1975) who appeared to be the same as everybody else. The Irish had assimilated and, except in parts of Boston and New York, only became visible during St. Patrick's Day parades with their associated inebriation, a subject which is now the central theme of American jokes about the Irish (Davies 1998: 107-120).

Nonetheless, by the late 1920s a new generation of English-speaking Polish Americans who had been born in America had become sufficiently similar, familiar, and accepted to be the subject of informal teasing and kidding at work about their Polish ancestry and supposed lack of mental capacity. Good examples of this can be found in Fritz Roethlisberger's and William Dixon's (1942) study, *Management and the Worker*, based on research carried out at Western Electric's Hawthorne plant on the border of Chicago and Cicero in the years 1927-1932. A substantial part of the labor force at the plant had been either born in Poland or in America of Polish parents (Roethlisberger and Dixon 1942: 6). In the bank wiring room of the factory where much of the detailed observation of the workers' behavior took place, the wiremen and soldermen were a mixture of Poles, Bohemians, Germans, Irish, and old stock Americans. All the Poles in this group had been born in America and all but three of them had foreign-born parents. There was a good deal of good-natured ethnic humor about Poles in the group as can be seen from the observers' description of the behavior of W1 (wireman 1), who was a Pole born in America:

> With S1 (solderman 1) he was friendly. He traded jobs with him and frequently soldered for him when he was absent without leave. He did not claim daywork for time thus spent. Between W and S a great deal of "kidding" went on, most of which was instigated by S1. In some of their verbal interplay, W's nationality figured prominently. The nature of these arguments which afforded a good deal of amusement to the nonparticipants can best be illustrated by quoting from the observers' record:
> "S's family is going to move. He told W that they're moving to a neighborhood where no Polacks are allowed." (Roethlisberger and Dixon 1942: 460)

Elsewhere as a further expression of a relationship characterized by "kidding, sarcasm and fun-making" (Roethlisberger and Dixon 1942: 480-1) the following exchange occurred:

> At 1.30 the inspection section chief and the operating section chief came in and told the group that they had to take some intelligence tests.
> Wireman 1 (a Pole): "Can I take my chew along. I can't take a test without a chew."
> Solderman 1 (to section chief): "You can't take W over there. They ain't got no tests for Polacks." (Roethlisberger and Dixon 1942: 461)

It is clear from the Roethlisberger and Dixon study that there were ethnic tensions among the workers at a time of growing economic difficulties when the workers were seeking to establish collective control over the level of output of each individual worker; this was bound to cause difficulties within such a heterogeneous group. Nonetheless, the joking and kidding with the Poles occurred not as an aspect of these potential conflicts, but as a mark of acceptance and solidarity.

What we can see here are the prototypes and precursors of the Polish jokes that were to become popular thirty years later. It is probably the case that many well-crafted ethnic jokes began life as spontaneous wise-cracks arising in ordinary social interaction, which the joker or one of his or her audience subsequently shapes and polishes into a set-piece joke fitting a widely known genre that can be deliberately performed and put into general circulation. However, this does not seem to have happened systematically in the period 1930-1960, for although there are occasional reports of "jokes about Polacks" very few fully-finished texts have been recorded.

The Chinese scholar George Yao (1946: xxv) notes having heard a joke about Polacks but does not say what it was, and Roger L. Welsch (1967: 184) quotes a letter written to the local newspaper in Lincoln, Nebraska, which said:

> In Milawaukee for 30 years a feud has been going on between Northside and Southside Polacks. That is where the Polack jokes started. I was raised as a Northside Polack. In 1944 when we visited Milwaukee, Polack jokes were rampant.

Unfortunately, the writer cited by Welsch quotes no examples, so it is difficult to know exactly what kind of jokes flourished in Milwaukee in the 1940s. Also he gives no details of the feud between Northside and Southside Polacks (the Southside Poles were poorer and had inferior housing [Ripley 1985: 150-51]), which might have helped those wedded to conflict theories of humor to construct a more sophisticated model than the defective one they have used. If he is right, then the Polack jokes must have been born within the community of Polish Americans, which also contradicts the dominant version of the conflict and hostility thesis that sees the jokes as imposed from the outside. However, if this had been the case it is difficult to see why there does not exist a residue of stupidity jokes of distinctively Polish flavor and origin similar to those cherished in Newfoundland.

Some of the proponents of the competition, conflict, and hostility theory of the origin of the spontaneous boom in jokes about Polish stupidity in the 1960s were uneasily aware that the Poles as threatening immigrants model did not work at all. Indeed Welsch (1967: 183) rapidly shifted his ground to argue that the "Polish threat" underlying the jokes was really a product of recent social mobility:

As the Polish laborer has gained greater social mobility from increased affluence and the influence of labor in general, he has moved into neighborhoods outside of the Polish ghetto, usually to the less magnificent apartments of the area, for example basements.... As other social and economic strata come into contact with Polacks—American Poles— they learn more about their character, real and supposed and feel more and more threatened by them.

Welsch's account is unsubstantiated, yet Bier (1988: 140) pro-duced essentially the same argument over twenty years later when he asserted that old stock Americans and other established groups in American society felt threatened by "the very rise and success of modern-day Poles." He went on to argue:

The fact is that they (the Poles) *are* distinguishing themselves outside the football arena. They have become true presences in American life, like everybody else. If they won't stay in their gladiatorial or menial place anymore and are acquiring national (and inter-national) prestige in politics and communication, they are threatening to those who have grown used to them as necessary stereotypes. A group of people who have been the standard object of scorn for so long in our country have no right, in the perverse logic of bigoted humor, to rise to any prominence at all.... Now that they are becoming truly integrated into American life, with varied qualities and manifest intelligence of their own, they are all the more feared by those who find it psychically necessary to maintain a dumb underclass beneath them. The durability and increase of the Polish joke is a warrant of the opposite condition, the threatful rise and not comforting lowness of the subject.

Neither Welsch nor Bier, both of whose articles were published in scholarly refereed journals, bother to produce any independent em-pirical evidence whatsoever that other Americans really did feel *threatened* by Polish upward social mobility. Indeed, the author knows of no such evidence. Both Welsch's and Bier's arguments are totally, indeed laughably, circular. The existence of a threat is de-duced from the popularity of the joke cycle and the threat is then used by Welsch to explain why Polish jokes were created in the first place and by Bier to explain why in 1988 they had persisted for nearly thirty years, a much longer life-span than most joke cycles. Neither of these scholars consider what the implications of their theory are for other kinds of ethnic jokes, nor do they refer to any empirical studies of the relative rates of upward social mobility of the Poles and other groups.

Had they bothered themselves with these vulgar empirical con-siderations, they would have noticed, for instance, that the social and geographical mobility of the Irish out of their old visible settle-ment areas into middle-class suburbia in America after World War II was accompanied by the *decline* of stupidity jokes about the Irish.

The last substantial collection of them in the 1940s is that by "Senator" Ed Ford, Harry Hershfield, and Joe Laurie, Jr. (1947), and they were replaced by jokes about those who had remained in substantial numbers in working-class ethnic enclaves, notably the Poles and the Italians. If Lawrence McCaffrey (1976: 158) is right in saying that "the American Irish took their biggest leap forward in social and occupational mobility after World War II, with education providing the springboard," then there should according to the upward-social-mobility-is-threatening-to-others-and-leads-to-ethnic-jokes-thesis have been a boom in stupidity jokes about Irish-Americans. Exactly the opposite happened.

Very rapid rates of upward social mobility *can* be perceived as a threat and lead to resentment among other groups and attempts to block it with discriminatory quotas, as has happened in America in the case of the Jews on the East Coast and of East Asians in California. If jokes are produced in such a situation they are always about canniness, which is the very opposite of jokes about stupidity. The jokes express both the outsiders' and the rapidly mobile insiders' *perception* of the members of the group's disproportionate success in business and the professions.

By contrast although there has obviously been upward mobility among the Poles, there still remain in many American industrial cities large, visible tracts inhabited mainly by Polish American blue-collar workers. As the distinguished Anglo-Polish sociologist Stanislav Andreski noted in 1973 at a time when jokes about Polish Americans were at their peak:

> The Poles...even more seldom than the Italians, were able to rise above the condition of unskilled labor in the second generation and even the third or fourth generation today remains predominantly in the ranks of manual workers...Being of Polish origin is no feather in the cap in the game of status-seeking in America. (Andreski 1973: 83)

The upward mobility of the Poles in America has been steady but *slow* (see Morawska 1974: 18, 41; Wytrwal 1997). In their case, as with upward mobility in industrial societies generally, much of the mobility has been caused by changes in the occupational structure of the society. As industry becomes more automated and sophisticated and the service sector grows relative to manufacturing and agriculture, the number and proportion of professional, managerial, and white-collar positions in the society increases and the number and proportion of blue-collar, semi-skilled and unskilled jobs decline (Saunders 1996). In consequence, there is a great deal of upward mobility that does not displace the sons and daughters of established American middle-class families; Poles coming up in the world do *not* constitute a threat to anyone. Furthermore, it means that the important observation to make when studying ethnic groups such as the Poles is not the mobility of its members per se, but the contrast between those groups whose members experience *very rapid* upward mobility, such as the Jews or the Japanese-Americans, and those whose upward mobility is *slow*, which has been the case for many Roman Catholic ethnic groups in America and especially the Poles. It is also worth noting that whereas the *rapid* upward mobility of the members of a group is *very visible* (and may well be resented and blocked by others), slow mobility is neither visible nor remarked upon.

The Poles have been held back by two cultural factors, which have shaped their work ethic in ways inimical to high levels of individual achievement in a competitive society, namely their Roman Catholicism (Lenski 1961) and their origins as Slavic peasants (Bodnar 1976). Roman Catholics in America have tended to see work in an instrumental way, to value security and to rate family solidarity higher than individual achievement. It is a valid and honorable tradition that has made an important contribution to American society, but it is less conducive to individual success (Lenski 1961: 88, 97, 110) than the classical Protestant ethic view of work as important in and of itself, as a source of accomplishment and an opportunity for advancement (Lenski 1961: 85). It is the relatively inert Roman Catholic view of work that has retarded Catholic mobility and competitiveness and made Roman Catholics the butts of jokes about stupidity, not just in relation to the Poles, but also in the case of the Irish in the past and more locally in regard to the Italians in New Jersey and the Portuguese in San Francisco and in Hawaii. It is *not* the dissolution of a pattern of stable working-class employment that leads to ethnic stupidity jokes but its persistence.

As with other Slavic peasants coming to America, the Poles stressed short-term material *security* with an emphasis on the respectable but restricted goals of home-ownership and advancement within the blue-collar stratum (Bodnar 1976: 53). These traditional Polish values persisted and even in the 1970s the Poles still valued family security, a good reputation with others, and a home in a "nice and decent" Polish neighborhood, rather than an endless striving for economic success. Over time, this has changed and will change even more as it did earlier in the case of the Irish, but the result has already been and will be the decline of the Polish joke, not its revival.

What is, indeed, striking about the Polish Americans of the period 1960-2000 is how very *un*threatening they were. They neither enjoyed great social, economic or political power nor did they seek it or show any chance of gaining it. They were in no position to dominate society, nor did they seek radically to change it.

The question of whether or not the group that is the butt of stupidity jokes poses a threat to or is in a state of conflict with the joke tellers is irrelevant, as may be seen from the cases listed in table 1.1 in chapter 1; sometimes the butts of the jokes constitute a threat to the joke tellers and sometimes they do not. The key to explaining the jokes is the relative social position of the joke tellers and the butts of their stupidity jokes, *not* whether the joke tellers feel threatened by or are hostile to the butts of their jokes.

8

Polish Jokes and Polish Conflicts

Granted that Americans in general do not feel threatened by or hostile towards the Poles who are the butts of their stupidity jokes, it is, however, worth considering a more subtle version of the conflict and hostility thesis, namely that members of other minorities in American society with more reason to dislike the Poles than Americans in general may have been responsible for maliciously initiating or propagating the jokes about Polish stupidity. Two possible candidates will be considered on the grounds that in each case there is some, if slight, evidence to go on; they are the German Americans and the Jewish Americans, both of whom have been involved in conflicts with the Poles in America. In addition, some members of each of these ethnic groups will have come to America as refugees from Poland and others will have memories of their ancestors' conflicts with the Poles in Europe. The third case of a minority to be considered as possible begetters of the Polish joke are an ideological faction that I shall term the "ultra-liberals," using "liberal" in the American, not the European, sense of the word.

Germans and German Americans have in the past often been in conflict with the Poles. Were there any truth in the hostility theory of humor it is just possible that German Americans in states such as Wisconsin where German and Polish communities have long lived alongside one another with something less than complete amity are the original begetters of the Polish joke. Only detailed *local* research into the history of joking, in particular local communities, could throw any light on this. Otherwise it remains mere speculation like the other Wisconsin-based suggestion put forward by Roger Welsch (1967: 184) that Polish jokes emerged from a feud between Northside and Southside "Polacks" in Milwaukee.

It is also possible that some of the earliest American Polack jokes were originally imported from Germany. Jokes about stupid and dirty Poles were told before World War II in border regions such as Silesia at a time when there was and long had been considerable antipathy between the two nations, as can be seen from the following example from the German files in the folklore archive of the University of California, Berkeley. It is a German joke about Poles, collected by an eighteen-year-old student from her forty-seven-year-old German American mother in 1969, following a discussion about American ethnic jokes:

> And then I told the riddle, "How do you catch a Pole?
> By slamming the toilet lid on his head while he's taking a drink of water."
> My mother then said, "Now I want to tell you I don't come from Poland," and proceeded to tell this joke: "There were three men: An Englishman, a German and a Pole. They each order soup in a restaurant. The Englishman gets soup with a fly in it and he says, 'Take it back,'—he doesn't want it. The German throws the fly out, picks it out with his fingers and eats it (the soup) anyway. The Pole eats the fly and the soup."
> I said, "Mother! you never told me that one," and she said, "Ach, of course I did!"
> When I asked what she thought of the joke, what did the joke mean, she replied, "We the school children, were indoctrinated. We were taken on field trips to the Polish border where markers were between the house and the barn of a farmer. The injustice of it, who did it to us? I guess Versailles."
> The informant, my mother, was born in Goerlitz and lived most of her life in Breslau, Silesia, formerly Germany, now Poland. She came to the United States in 1948. The Polish-German dichotomy is very apparent in Breslau because it was formerly only a few miles from the Polish border. Most of the Germans had professional jobs or owned farms; the Poles were the laborers and the tenant farmers." (U.C.B.F.A. German file Blason populaire. Collected 1969)

However, the Silesian joke about the fly in the soup cited by the mother is a well-known international joke in which the somewhat coarse second and third nationalities involved are very easily changed. There are no similar jokes about Poles in the numerous German joke books published between 1900 and 1945 in the extensive Schmulowitz collection of old joke books, but it may be that such jokes were only to be found in compilations brought out by small local publishers in Silesia. Such joke books along with other locally produced German books would have been destroyed in the turbulent period at the end of the Second World War when the German population of Silesia were driven out by force and fear. It is possible, though, that a diligent search in the libraries and archives of Wroclaw (formerly Breslau) or in the repositories of Silesian folklore in Berlin and Düsseldorf may one day uncover a cache of printed jokes told about Poles by the former German population of Silesia.

Stupidity jokes were also told in the then German Silesia about two Polish coal miners called Antek and Franzek. They were both idiots but one was more stupid than the other:

> Antek has six children. He goes to a doctor and he says
> "Doctor you have to help me. I cannot have more children."
> The doctor says, "You have to use a condom."
> Six months later Antek's wife is pregnant again. (Joke teller laughs.) Antek goes back to the doctor and says
> "This condom is no good!"
> The doctor says, "What do you mean?"
> Antek answers, "After a while they got too expensive so my wife crocheted one for me." (UCBFA German File Blason Populaire. Collected in 1969 by Aaron Plant from a German-American housewife who had heard it as a teenager in Lower Silesia during World War II)

> Antek and Franzek fall asleep, drunk in front of a drug store. The next morning, they wake up. Antek says "We have a new government."
> Franzek says, "You are crazy, we have Hitler's government."
> Antek says, "No! Can you not read? Heil Krauter." (The sign actually says Heilkrauter or healing herbs, but Antek reads it as if it said Heil Krauter! as in Heil Hitler!). (UCBFA German File Blason Populaire. Collected by Aaron Plant in 1969 from a German- American housewife who had heard it as a teenager in Lower Silesia during World War II)

The German-American displaced person who told both jokes had brought these jokes with her to America, presumably in the late 1940s, after she had fled westwards from the invading Russian army prior to emigrating to America. Indeed, she suggested to the collector that the jokes, which would originally have been told in broken German, "were probably the first Polish jokes. They made fun of Polacks there (in Germany) too."

If indeed American Polish jokes did originate in the National Socialist era in Germany in this way then they really were born in a time of intense conflict and of hostility to the Poles. During this time, German National Socialist propaganda depicted the Poles as a dirty, stupid, inferior people (Goebbels: 1982 (1939-41): 16, 36-7, 274; Szarota 1978), fit only to serve the German master race in some menial capacity (Bethell 1976: 147-49, 153). Intellectuals, priests and aristocrats were murdered by the Germans and also by the Soviets during World War II to deprive the Poles of any kind of leaders (Bethell 1976: 143-44; Fitzgibbon 1971), and the Poles were the victims of ethnic cleansing in West Prussia by the Nazis and in Eastern Poland by the Soviets who deliberately inflamed the Ukrainian peasants' hatred of the Poles. About six million Poles died violently during the war, half of them Jews, the other half Christians. Nicholas Bethell has written of German official policy that:

> The Nazis' policy was to crush the Poles morally as well as physically. As part of their plan to "behead" the nation, petty rules were introduced to stamp out all vestiges of an intellectual or middle class. For instance, no Pole was allowed to carry a stick or an attaché case, to wear a fur coat or a felt hat, to use a telephone box or make a long distance call, to ride in a taxi, to take part in athletics or to have his teeth filled with gold. (Bethell 1976: 152)

It may well be that from an early date Germans migrating to America had taken with them a negative view of the Poles expressed in the kind of serious ethnic slurs against the Poles noted earlier (see chapter 7; Dundes 1987: 133, 193, 194; Roback 1944) and that this also contributed to the hostility between the two communities in states like Wisconsin, where both settled in large numbers. Also after the Second World War many Germans who had been driven from their homes in East and West Prussia, Pomerania, and Silesia by the Soviet army emigrated to America as displaced persons and refugees. The individuals constituting this group had both been involved in direct conflict with the Poles and subjected to Nazi propaganda about the Poles allegedly filthy habits (Szarota 1978) and may well have brought to America humorous tales about, as well as serious prejudices towards, the "*dreck* Polacks" (dirty/shitty Poles).

If this were the case then American Polish jokes would have a very nasty origin, indeed, and might seem to fit the conflict and hostility thesis. However, there are serious problems with such an argument. First, the link between the American jokes of the early 1960s and the German jokes of the early 1940s is tenuous and unproven. Second, there is no reason to suppose that Americans enjoying the Polish joke cycle, other than possibly a tiny number of disgruntled German-American refugees, saw the jokes as a means of expressing hostility towards the Poles or as an expression of serious sentiments embodying true statements about Poles. Third, the Silesian jokes about Antek and Franzek are no different from the good-natured local dialect jokes told in other regions of Germany about hard-drinking pairs of idiots, such as the Tünnes and Schäll jokes told in the Rhineland (*Tünnes und Schäll Witze* 1976). Tünnes and Schäll are undisputedly German and not a target or vehicle for hostile propaganda. If, indeed, the Nazis' strongly expressed hatred and contempt for the Poles failed to influence Silesian jokes so as to make them *more negative* than the jokes told about Germans in the Rhineland, then jokes are not a suitable vehicle for this kind of propaganda. If you wish to dehumanize an enemy, as the Nazis did in the case of the Poles and the Jews, then spreading Antek and Franzek jokes would be, as Hitler (1974: 287) well knew, counterproductive. In any case the jokes are clearly a spontaneous local phenomenon which are rooted in social class differences reaching back to the nineteenth century rather than a product of Nazi propaganda. One of the jokes even makes fun of Hitler, who becomes Herr Kraute, the Kraut. What is more, as the author discovered during a visit to Opole and Kamien Slaski in the now Polish Silesia in 1999, the Antek and Franzek jokes are still being told in Polish in that part of Poland. They are clearly regional and social-class jokes that in the past were shared by both Poles and Germans and which survive today precisely because they are still seen as funny by the Poles.

American Polish jokes then cannot really be traced back to, nor do they in any sense express the historic Old World hatreds of the Germans for the Poles. A diligent search by the author has been able to trace no more than the faintest of connections and further searching is unlikely to produce anything more significant. American Polish jokes are an American phenomenon.

It can be hypothesized that another set of individuals likely to depart from the benign attitude taken towards Polish jokes, exhibited by most Americans, who see them and use them as mere fun and not a means of expressing hostility or aggression, might well be American Jews of Polish descent who constitute a high proportion of America's Jews. Both historic and continuing anti-Semitism in Poland itself and in America on the part of Polish immigrants and their children (Helmreich 1982: 178; Lopata 1976: 179) have understandably biased Jewish Americans against Polish Americans.

Jewish Americans, like the Jews in other Western countries, are well aware not only of past anti-Semitism in Poland, but of its *continued* existence after 1945 (Baron 1946: vii; Mahler 1946: 171; Scharf 1996: 222-24, 253) despite the death of nearly all (three million were murdered) the Polish Jews in Hitler's Holocaust. There were even a few Polish pogroms in the period immediately following World War II, notably in Kielce. This Polish anti-Semitism without Jews found strong official expression in the 1960s (Courtois et al. 1991: 386; Scharf 1996: 253) when many of the few remaining

Jews, the "rootless cosmopolitans" among the Polish elite were purged and expelled by the Communist regime and forced to leave for Israel, Britain, and America (Sword 1996: 46). This was a curious twist to events in that some of the Jews who were now expelled had fled to Russia during the Nazi invasion of Poland, had survived Stalin's anti-Semitic paranoia (Tolstoy 1982: 196, 395; Vaksberg 1994: 103-6) and had returned to Poland with the Soviet army that established a puppet government there. In 1968 after Israel's defeat of the Soviet-backed Arabs in the Six Day War such people were caught in a double trap of Polish anti-Semitism, being portrayed as Zionist traitors by the other communists and as Soviet socialist stooges by patriotic Poles, who now spoke of two opposed factions in the Communist Party, the Jews and the Partisans. There was even a rather ambiguous Jewish and Polish joke on the subject told in Poland in the 1970s:

> Two Jews who had not seen each other for a long time met by chance in the streets of Warsaw. One of them asked the other how his three sons were prospering in their chosen careers.
>
> "Well" said the second Jew, "my eldest son, Moishe, has a very well-paid job in Russia helping to build socialism. He's really very successful there. And then there's my second son, Chaim—he's got an equally good job in Prague. He's helping to build socialism, too."
>
> "What about your third son, Isaac?" asked his friend. "He was a very able boy."
>
> "Oh, he's emigrated to Israel," he said. "He's done very well, too. He has an excellent job in Tel Aviv."
>
> "And is he also helping to build socialism?"
>
> "Oh no, he wouldn't do a thing like that; not to his own country."

It is a joke that can be perceived in many different ways, but it *plays with* both of the key anti-Semitic beliefs then current in Poland, namely that the Jews were responsible for inflicting socialism on the country and that their only real national loyalty was to Israel.

American Jewish jokes of the 1930s and 1940s reveal a continued memory and awareness of past anti-Semitism in Poland. The jokes are about old world events but they must have made sense to those who told them in America. The Polish anti-Semites of the jokes are depicted as stupid, but then that is the case with Jewish jokes about anti-Semites in general.

> There is an anecdote current among American Jews of Eastern European origin which illustrates their view of Polish anti-Semitism. The story tells of a Jewish innkeeper who during the Polish insurrection of 1863 risked his own life to save the life of a Polish nobleman who had taken refuge in the Jew's cellar. On bringing down some food to the

cellar the Jew forgetfully failed to uncover his head before the nobleman. The Polish aristocrat flew into a rage, stamped his feet and shouted, "Take off your hat, you dirty Jew!" (Mahler 1946: 145)

IT WORKS BOTH WAYS

Ignace J. Paderewski, post-war premier of Poland, was discussing his country's affairs with the late President Wilson. "If all our demands are not granted at the peace conference," said Mr. Paderewski, "I can foresee serious trouble in my country. Why, my people will be so irritated that many of them will go out and massacre the Jews."
"And what will happen if your demands are granted?" asked Mr Wilson.
"Why, my people will be so happy," replied Mr. Paderewski, "that many of them will get drunk and go out and massacre the Jews." (Mendelsohn 1935: 46)

More recently Rabbi Joseph Telushkin has cited two Jewish jokes of tremendous ingenuity that have even managed to make fun of Polish anti-Semitism through humorous anecdotes about those righteous Poles who saved Jews from the Nazis during the Holocaust:

Two Jews meet in Warsaw in 1968.
"Rosenberg," says the first, "they tell me that you have lost your job, and yet you look well, happy, and prosperous. How is this? What are you living on?"
"I'm living by blackmail," the other replies.
"By blackmail?..."
"It's very simple. There is a Polish family that hid me during the war against the Nazis."
"So?"
"I'm blackmailing them" (with the threat that otherwise I will tell everyone that they had saved a Jew). (Telushkin 1992:113)

Jews from a Polish village have survived Hitler and have established themselves as an egg and poultry co-operative in Israel. They are grateful to their friend, the peasant elder, for helping to save them from the Nazis, and they are proud of having made themselves into productive, progressive agriculturists...So they pool their money and send a ticket to the old peasant, who eventually comes from Poland to visit them. They show him their modern equipment and methods and he is impressed. Then they show him how artificial light twenty-four hours a day keeps the hens laying eggs without interruption. He shakes his head and says "Ah, Zhidy, Zhidy! You have no honest Poles to trick any more, so you trick chickens." (Telushkin 1992: 68)

The circulation of such jokes in America (as well as in other countries) indicates a continuing sense of awareness of the existence of anti-Semitism in Poland by Jews in America. If jokes of this kind about the *stupidity* of Polish anti-Semitism exist in America, then it is possible that members of the Jewish community were also the initiators and main circulators of jokes about Polish stupidity. Such a view would certainly fit well with those theories of humor that see ethnic joking as a way of pursuing ethnic conflicts and resentments by other means.

Furthermore, Polish anti-Semitism in America itself also features in American Jewish humor, notably in Lenny Bruce's sketch, *"One who Killed our Lord"*:

> I am of a Semitic background—I *assume* I'm Jewish. A lot of Jews who think they're Jewish are not—they're switched babies.
> Now, a Jew, in the dictionary, is one who is descended from the ancient tribe of Judea, or one who is regarded as descended from that tribe. That's what it says in the dictionary; but you and I know that a Jew is—*One Who Killed Our Lord*. I don't know if we got much press on that in Illinois—we did this about two thousand years ago—two thousand years of Polack kids whacking the shit out of us coming home from school. Dear, dear. And although there should be a statute of limitations for that crime, it seems that those who neither have the actions nor the gait of the Christians, pagan or not, will bust us out, unrelenting dues, for another deuce.
> And I really searched it out, why we pay the dues. Why do you keep breaking our balls for this crime?
> "Why, Jew, because you skirt the issue. You blame it on Roman soldiers."
> All right. I'll clear the air once and for all, and confess. Yes, we did it. I did it, my family. I found a note in my basement. It said:
> "We killed him."
>
> signed,
"Morty."
>
> And a lot of people say to me, "Why did you kill Christ?"
> "I dunno.... It was one of those parties—got out of hand, you know."
> We killed him because he didn't want to become a doctor, that's why we killed him. (Novak and Waldoks 1981: 219)

It is certainly the case that some of the leaders of the Polish American community see the Jews as the key disseminators of Polish jokes and of serious negative images of the Poles in films and on television in America as a form of revenge for anti-Semitism (Bukowczyk 1987: 111-12, Wytrwal 1997: 498-507).

John Bukowczyk (1987) speaks of the offense given to Poles in Chicago after a local newspaper reported a fashionable and extravagant Jewish birthday party at Mr. H's "spectacular Northbrook summer house," celebrated with a Polish picnic to which guests came in a U-Haul truck, dressed in overalls, undershirts and tennis shoes. Polish presents were distributed from a garbage can.

Polish Americans also point out that the leading commercial compiler and editor of collections of Polish jokes, Larry Wilde, originally called Wildman (Chetkin 1985: 128), was of Polish-Jewish extraction (Bukowczyk 1987: 114). It is striking that Wilde has received many abusive letters from Polish Americans, but not from the subjects of his other ethnic joke books. During the author's interview with Larry Wilde in 1979, Wilde made it clear that his motive was not to abuse the Poles, but to create enjoyment and make money. He was a very successful joke-book editor, a stand-up comedian who understood the craft of joke-book writing and was willing to publish collections of jokes on any subjects, whether ethnic, political, religious or sexual that were going to sell. It was simply that the Polish joke books (Wilde 1973, 1975, 1977, 1983) sold very well indeed. Wilde also brought out very successful collections of ethnic jokes about the Irish (drunk) (1974, 1979, 1983A), the Jews (canny) (1974, 1979, 1980, 1986), and the Italians (stupid, dirty cowardly) (1973, 1975, 1978A), a book of jokes about "White Folks/ Black Folks" (1975A) (it is clear from the oddly apologetic cover that the publishers were nervous about this one), and also a complete book of ethnic jokes (1978) that mocks a very large number of nations. He did not specifically pick on the Poles.

Nor did Wilde invent all the Polish jokes in his books; that would have been impossible. He merely collected and improved and polished jokes invented by the great mass of ordinary anonymous jokers. He followed a fashion; he did not create it. Wilde's first book of Polish jokes was published in 1973 after the Polish joke cycle had already been flourishing for a decade. An earlier collection of Polish jokes had already been published, whose editors ostensibly had Polish names, in particular, E. D. Zewbskewiecz, Jerome Kuligowski, and Harvey Krulka's *It's Fun To Be a Polack* (1965), and Mike Kuwalski brought out *The Polish Joke Book* (1973) in the same year as Wilde's first book. Wilde's work differed from these earlier collections and from Pat Macklin and Manny Erdman's *Polish Jokes* (1976), mainly in being more skillfully put together. Wilde's books were also more successful commercially due to their being produced, distributed, and marketed by larger publishers for whom he compiled and edited some very well thought out series of joke books. Wilde was a good entrepreneur who gave the American public what it wanted to buy. In the absence of successful censorship by pressure groups consumer sovereignty wins.

An empirical examination of comments made by Jewish joke tellers about Polish jokes reveals, as one might expect, a very mixed set of responses from what is, after all, a highly varied group of people. One important factor is that Polish Jews, who might have most reason to relish "hostile" jokes about Poles, are themselves the butts of jokes about Polacks, about *Poylischer gonif* (thief, untrustworthy), about Galitzianers (Mencken 1977: 611; Rosten 1970: 124-5, 214-5; Rosten 1983: 140-1) and *Ostjuden* (Oring 1984: 42-3) that have long been told particularly by German Jews (Rosten 1970: 435-6; Oring 1984: 42-3) and by Lithuanian Jews (Rosten 1970: 214-5; Rosten 1983: 193-4; Olsvanger 1965: 26). A Jewish joke from around 1920 about Polish Jewish immigrant tailors in America makes this point:

> I worked for a man, that was way back, and he used to cut clothes by looking, by eye, he didn't have any system of cutting, he just take a piece of chalk and cut a front, cut a back, cut a sleeve—so naturally they didn't fit. So finally the customer comes in and he puts on the suit, the suit doesn't fit and he says: "Tailor, this suit doesn't fit me at all." So he says in Polish—it's a Polish tailor and a Polish customer—"I don't know," he says, "on the table it fitted (*na stole bylo dobre*) and on you it's like on a pig! (*a na panie jak na swinie*)." (UCBFA American file P6 15 miscellaneous. Blason Populaire. Collected by Neila English from an elderly Russian-Jewish American in 1971)

The tailor and customer are explicitly identified as Polish and though the joke was told in English the punch line was given in Polish as well as in translation, thus emphasizing the national and linguistic origins of the participants in a joke set among Jewish workers in the garment industry.

> *Question*: What is the epitome of conceit?
> *Answer*: A Pole floating down a river on his back and yelling, "Open the drawbridge, open the drawbridge!"
> The collector comments, "The informant first heard this joke in Germany circa 1935. It was told to him by his father who was like himself Jewish and born in Germany...German Jews have an intense dislike for Polish Jews and vice versa.... Among the people who don't like the Poles, one of the main complaints is that they are very conceited. (UCBFA American file P6 miscellaneous. Collected by a relative of the joke teller in Los Angeles in 1968)

This joke could be a German joke about Poles or a German-Jewish joke about Polish Jews. It indicates both that jokes of this kind were in circulation in Germany well before the long American joke cycle of Polish jokes began and that for joke-telling purposes Polish Jews may well be classified as Poles.

This point has been made by a number of Polish-Jewish-Americans when telling Polish ethnic jokes to collectors of folklore.

Thus the joke, "Why is semen white and urine yellow? So a Polak can tell whether he's coming or going," was told on the phone by a Jewish former producer of the American television series *All in the Family* to the collector, a female member of his family. She commented that he "enjoys telling jokes such as this one, but he tells them as an 'insider.'" The joke-teller's parents seem to have emigrated to America from the then Russian-ruled Poland at the turn of the century (see UCBFA file P6 F4. Blason Populaire. Anti-Polish Sexuality. Collected 1977 by a student from Los Angeles identifying herself as Jewish).

In the files of the folklore archives studied by the author there are a few (but only a few) comments from Jewish respondents who say either that they enjoy jokes about Poles because they are hostile to Poles or that they know other Jews who enjoy Polish jokes for this reason. The existence of such comments would be an unimportant phenomenon that could be safely ignored, but for the fact that those Americans providing jokes for folklore collectors whose recorded ethnic background does not imply any kind of present or ancestral conflict with the Poles never make comments of this kind. Indeed, they rarely present any evaluations of the Poles at all, neither negative nor positive.

> In a comment on the joke, "What's the Polish National bird? A fly," the Jewish student telling the joke said that he had learned it in a mostly Jewish high school where there was "a disdain for Poles." (UCBFA American file P6 N3 Blason Populaire. Anti-Polish. Collected by Patricia Slater)

In another instance a Jewish respondent told the collector the joke, "What's a group of Polaks standing in a circle? A dope ring," and his comments on it led the collector to note: "My informant thinks the joke is funny because he feels a bitterness against the Poles for their treatment of the Jews during World War II. He doesn't like the Polish government and thinks that Poland is a 'diddly-shit country'. He likes the joke because it stereotypes the Poles as being extremely stupid" (UCBFA American file P6 I5 miscellaneous Blason Populaire. Collected by Gregory C. Humpal in 1969 from a Jewish student in Berkeley).

A similar comment was recorded in 1994 by another folklore collector:

> I was told by a Jewish friend that Polish jokes were actually started by Jews because the Poles were extremely anti-Semitic. This seems to be a form of retaliation against the Poles because during World War II they had supported the Nazi persecution of the Jews....This may be true or just a legend within the Jewish community. (UCBFA American file P6 I5. A comment made by Debbie N. Tran on a Polish joke collected from an American with a Scottish surname)

This is almost certainly just a Jewish legend and nothing more and merely reflects the Jews' greater knowledge of and possible tendency to believe the theories circulating among liberal intellectuals that ethnic jokes are a kind of aggression consciously directed against groups one dislikes. No doubt *some* American Jews *did* see Polish jokes, as a kind of revenge and put down, but other more politically correct American Jews were reluctant to tell Polish jokes, precisely because they feared that this would involve a sense of retaliation on their own part. One Jewish collector of Polish jokes from a high school in Los Angeles with a large proportion of Jewish students has commented:

> Racial slurs against Polish people are common in many Jewish communities, reflecting a distrust of and dislike for the Poles. This animosity may stem from the Poles' supposed betrayal of the Jews during World Ward II. I myself am hesitant to tell this (Polish) joke because of its racial overtones. (UCBFA American file P6 I5 Miscellaneous Blason Populaire Anti-Polish, 1979)

The view that the Poles (despite their consistent resistance to Hitler's armies during the entire period 1939-1945, in which they fought bravely alongside the Allied armies in North Africa, Italy and France and in the British Royal Air Force [Sword 1996: 22-25]) betrayed the Jews during World War II (Scharf 1996: 250-3) is possibly widespread among American Jews. But why should it have given rise to jokes about Poles rather than about Hitler's allies the Romanians (with their Iron Guard), the Hungarians (with their Arrow Cross), the Slovaks (with their Guardists), the Croatians (with their Ustashi) or the Austrians who produced Hitler, the admirer of Schoenerer, or about the Ukrainians, Lithuanians, Latvians, Byelorussians (Goldhagen 1996: 409) and French (Arendt 1946: 179, Birnbaum 1992: 117-128), many of whom actively helped to promulgate the Holocaust? Likewise, the Jews in America itself suffered anti-Semitic physical assaults as much from Irish working-class gangs, such as the Shamrocks in New York (Bayor 1978: 156-7), as from their Polish equivalents. Why then are the Jews not seen as the authors of American jokes about stupid Irish drunks or dim-witted French-Canadians, given the past behavior of the bigoted anti-Semitic Irish-American and French-Canadian Catholics stirred up by Father Coughlin and the Abbé Groulx, respectively? Besides, Polish jokes are said to have begun in places like Milwaukee, Wisconsin, rather than in major Jewish urban centers. More to the point, Polish jokes were popular with and disseminated by *all* American national and ethnic groups throughout the 1960s and 1970s. To subscribe, as some American Jews and some American Poles seem to do, to the idea that the Jews started the jokes and were able to persuade the great mass of Americans, who have no animosities towards the Poles, to tell them is to subscribe to a version of the myth that the Jews are all powerful and able to arbitrarily manipulate the behavior and preferences of the more numerous guileless gentiles. Nonsense on stilts.

The most that can be said is that at the height of the Polish joke cycle a (probably small) proportion of American Jews obtained extra satisfaction from Polish jokes because their ancestors in Europe had in times past been involved in conflicts with the butts of the jokes. For most Jews living in America who would have had to respond to much more contemporary threats stemming from Palestinian, Arab and Muslim hostility, from official as well as popular anti-Semitism in the Soviet Union and from anti-Semitic African-American leaders such as Louis Farrakhan (Saper 1991: 45) and Leonard Jeffries (Saper 1995: 67), it is doubtful that their quiescent Polish-American neighbors of the 1960s, 1970s, 1980s, and 1990s were a central concern. No doubt someone will eventually produce the absurd thesis that pent-up Jewish aggression from these other conflicts was displaced onto the Poles, but why would it be necessary, given the many Jewish jokes told in America about the conflicts between the Soviet Union and its Jews or the Arabs and the Israelis or about Jewish fears of predatory aggression from African Americans (Mason 1987: 42)? Very few American jokes about the Poles mention Polish-Jewish conflicts, whereas if the jokes were of Jewish origin this theme would figure far more prominently. When Jews do appear in the jokes it is often as the "canny" antithesis of the "stupid" Poles, which invokes a script that might not be entirely welcome to those who perceive jokes as a way of pursuing ethnic conflicts by other means.

What do you get if you cross a Pole and a Jew?
A janitor who owns the building.

How do you conduct a census in a Polish community?
Roll a nickel down the street, count the number of hands that come out of basement windows and subtract one for the Jew who gets it.

American jokes about Poles are an American, not a Jewish phenomenon and Polish-Jewish conflicts whether in Europe or American are not important in explaining them. The suggestion that they could be is one more example of intellectuals arguing backwards, saying in effect, "Ethnic jokes are always about conflict, hostility and aggression. Let us, therefore, look for any conflict we can find to provide an explanation for jokes about the Poles." It is a circular argument and a fatuous one. In this case a joke is a joke is a joke.

American Polish jokes are, as has been shown, *not* a product of hostility towards Polish Americans on the part of old stock Americans who feel threatened by Polish upward mobility *nor* of hostility from other particular ethnic groups such as German Americans or Jewish Americans. However, attempts have been made to keep the hostility thesis alive by means of the bizarre suggestion that the hostility felt by American whites towards African Americans, as part of a racial conflict between the two groups, has been displaced onto white lower-class ethnic groups such as the Poles. Polish jokes are thus a substitute for jokes about African Americans. Versions of this tortuous psychological thesis have been put forward by Dundes (1987: 137) and Helmreich (1982: 169-174).

Alan Dundes has written:

> One possible reason for the popularity of the Polack (or Italian) joke cycle is that it takes the heat off the Negro. Lower-class whites are not militant and do not constitute a threat to middle class white America. White jokes involving stereotypes of Negroes had to become more and more disguised, as overt "Rasta and Liza" jokes yielded to elephant jokes and "coloured" riddles involving (g)rapes. With the Polack cycle it is the lower class, not Negroes, which provides the outlet for aggression and the means for feeling superior. (1987: 137)

William Helmreich similarly argues:

> It is well known that when people cannot take out their frustrations on that which is bothering them, they will focus on something else. This is sometimes referred to by psychologists as displaced aggression.... Many (whites) felt both guilty about their own prejudices and hostile at having to face up to them. Unable to openly express their racism they returned to more acceptable forms of prejudice. The seemingly innocuous Poles...seemed a perfect group on which to focus. (1982: 169)

However, there is no evidence that the masses of Americans who invented, told and circulated Polish jokes had the slightest interest in "taking the heat off the Negro"; rather they told and tell ethnic jokes about the deviant behavior of underclass blacks *in addition to* stupidity jokes about the familistic blue-collar Poles. Rastus and Liza are alive and well in the jokes told by good old boys throughout the

United States. There are numerous jokes about African Americans in folklore archives in the United States and there is no sign that the tellers of the jokes felt guilty at telling them or ill at ease with themselves. The tellers of such jokes, however, are wary, and when the author was collecting ethnic jokes in the United States in the 1980s, it was always necessary to obtain carefully the trust of his informants. Ordinary working-class and lower-middle-class Americans were sometimes at first inclined to suspect that he might be an agent of the liberal thought police trying to tempt them into humorous indiscretion in order to be able to berate them or to lay a complaint against them to someone in authority. It was exactly the same kind of initial suspicion that the author had to overcome when collecting political jokes in Bulgaria and Czechoslovakia during the same decade (Davies 1990: ix). Once reassured, the American masses provided, as the East European joke tellers had, a wealth of politically incorrect jokes without any signs of guilt or shame whatsoever. In both cases the jokes were especially relished because they were known to be forbidden by outsiders in a position of power. It was not African Americans whom the joke tellers were concerned about (indeed they had often been the original source of the jokes that were told) but the powerful ultra-liberal section of the American upper middle class.

Like the jokes about Poles, jokes about African Americans are to a substantial extent linked to social class, but it is a different class. The Poles are depicted in American stupidity jokes (as the Irish are in England) as regular blue-collar workers with families, that is, they are at the hard-hatted (or in Britain welly-wearing) end of that normal society in which work, family, and law and order are the central institutions. The Poles (like the Irish in Britain) are portrayed as almost like us, as a mildly distorted version of us who are stupidly funny for this reason. These jokes are not a substitute for jokes about African Americans but coexist with jokes about the latter, jokes that have a quite different set of themes. American jokes about African Americans locate them in an underclass, outside and beyond society, characterized by crime, violence, illegitimacy, promiscuity and an aversion to the demands of work, family and legality. These jokes are *very* different from the stupidity jokes told about Poles and are not switchable, that is, they are rarely told about other groups in American society and never about Poles.

A black guy found a bottle, and when he rubbed it a genie appeared and offered him three wishes. "First," he says, "I wanna be white," and poof, he was white. "Second, I wanna a beautiful woman," and poof, there was a beautiful woman. "And last, I don't wanna have to work no more," and poof, he was black. (UCBFA American file. Jokes 3. Negro N4. Collected by Wendy Gardner 1974)

Hanna had been seeing Cazzy on and off for many years. Time passed and she had a child out of their union. One day Hannah met Cazzy by chance and told him she had named the baby Asphalt.
"Why'd you name him that? " he asked.
"Because," said Hannah, "It was my ass an' your fault." (Wilde 1978:50)

A social worker visited a black woman with 12 sons. "What is this one called?" she asked.
"John," came the reply.
"And that one?"
"Also John, they are all called John. When I call them for dinner, I just shout John and they all come running."
"But," said the social worker, What do you do when you just want to call one of them?"
"Oh, then I use his surname." (American Chicago 2000)

On learning that New Jersey had admitted that some state troopers used race as a factor in pulling over motorists, the comedian Al Franken commented: "The only solution I can see is for white people to start committing more crimes." (*Time* 10 May 1999: 22)

What's the definition of confusion?
Father's day in Harlem. (American 1980s)

What's black foreplay?
If you scream, I'll kill you. (American 1980s)

Have you heard about the new black "Welfare Doll?"
You wind it up and it doesn't work. (Wilde 1978: 33)

How do you get sickle-cell anemia?
From licking food stamps. (American 1980s)

Why do blacks hate aspirin?
Coz it's white, it works and they hate picking the cotton out the bottle. (Jake's Jokes 1999; angelfire.com/ok/aavokart/)

Did you hear of the new Black Barbie?
It comes with 12 kids, AIDS and a welfare check. (Jake's Jokes 1999; angelfire.com/ok/aavokart/)

Not only are these jokes widespread in the United States but they have been exported to other countries such as Sweden (af Klintberg 1983) which has no local black population or France where they are specifically told about African Americans as *Histoires noires des U.S.A.* (Climent-Galant 1979: 73-9) and differ from the jokes told about the blacks from *Afrique noir* (Climent-Galant 1979: 65-71). Whereas when American stupidity jokes such as those about Poles are exported to other countries they get adapted to fit some local group such as the Newfies in Canada or the Irish in Britain and Australia, when jokes about African Americans are exported they often continue to be told in the new country as American jokes about an American minority. The jokes are seen as quintessentially American and their international popularity is an index of American cultural dominance as can be seen from the following examples told as American jokes in other English-speaking countries:

What did the little black boy get for Christmas?
My bike. (Canada FAYO. Collected by Mike Koe 1990)

What do you say to a black man in a three-piece suit?
Will the defendant please rise. (Canada FAYO 1990)

An ineffective golfer asked the coach at his local golf club for some tuition. The coach said he was booked up for months ahead but that the club had just bought a robot coach who was supposed to be very good and maybe the golfer would like to try him for a week. At the end of the week the golfer told the coach: " That robot of yours is terrific. I've learned more in the past week than in the whole of last year. I'm away on business for a month but when I come back I want another lesson from him."
A month later he came back and asked for the robot. "I'm sorry," said the coach, "but he's not here anymore. After you left there was a championship match and the local hero only needed to sink a putt on the last green to win. Just as he played, the sun was reflected off the metal of the robot and blinded him and he missed it."
"You didn't get rid of him just for that?" said the golfer. "No," said the coach, "We had him painted black so he couldn't do it again."
"Well then, "said the golfer, "Why did you get rid of him?" The coach shrugged. "Well, he started coming in late to work, he was rude to customers…" (Told by an Englishman in 1992 as an American joke)

Liza: "Rastus, you come away from de edge of dat platform or de train's goin' to come along and suck you off."
Rastus: "Come awwwwn train!" (Canada FAYO 1988)

Why did crimestoppers give the black lady $50?
She had an abortion. (Canada FAYO 1989)

Q.   Why do niggers like fingerbowls in restaurants?
A.   So they can wash the silverware before they steal it. (Australian site 1998; jeack.com.au/~jed/woodpile/htm)

Q.   What's the difference between good nigger kids and bad nigger kids?
A.   Good nigger kids are in medium security prisons (Australian site 1998; jeack.com.au/~jed/woodpile/htm)

Q.   What is the most common form of transportation in Harlem?
A.   Ambulance (Australian site 1998; jeack.com.au/~jed/woodpile/htm)

Q.   Why are so many niggers moving to Detroit?
A.   They heard there were no jobs there. (Australian site 1998; jeack.com.au/~jed/woodpile/htm)

The existence of such a very extensive, long-lasting and widely exported cycle of jokes about African Americans is in and of itself a total refutation of Dundes's and Helmreich's theory that Polish stupidity joke cycles were the product of an unwillingness to joke about African Americans. The very fact that it is forbidden to make openly critical statements about blacks in countries with a single dominant ultra-liberal ideology, such as Sweden or Anglophone Canada, leads to the circulation in those countries, particularly among young people, of jokes of American origin that allow them to play with the forbidden and defy authority (af Klintberg 1983). Why should it have been any different in America?

It is possible to make some kind of sense of Dundes's and Helmreich's arguments if they are viewed in terms of power rather than a set of mythical, shared American values. It would seem that a section of the American upper middle class, enjoying a nearly hegemonic control over the mass-media and education, combined with a disproportionate political influence, was able to ban jokes about African Americans from substantial areas of American public life, much as has happened in the Netherlands (Kuipers 2000: 157-8) with jokes about Moroccans. Politicians or government employees could find their careers ruined merely because an informer reported their telling even one such joke in the course of a private conversation. Likewise, students and staff in educational institutions are often harassed by trivial and vexatious complaints about the jokes that they have told (for examples see Nilsen and Nilsen 2000: 189-90, 198, 229). In the late nineteenth and early twentieth centuries joke books often routinely contained a section of jokes about African Americans being idle, violent, thieving and promiscuous and entire joke books were devoted to these themes. Today such jokes are best sought on the Internet, for almost everything else is censored. As noted earlier, Larry Wilde edited many immensely successful collections of ethnic jokes about the Poles and the Italians and about the Jews and the Irish but only one half of one of his books was about "black folks" (Wilde 1975A). The disparity was not caused by any lack of jokes on the latter subject nor by an unwillingness of the American public to buy such a book. Rather the non-publication of books of jokes specifically or mainly (as distinct from being tucked away quietly within an array of "tasteless jokes" by an anonymous female editor [Knott 1982: 31-44]) about African Americans reflects the coercive pressure exerted on publishers and booksellers to prevent such books being issued and distributed.

Polish Americans have not received the same degree of protective and indignant censorship because the ultra-liberals did and do not feel the same guilt, concern, and anger on their behalf. This is hardly surprising, given the different histories of the two groups in America and the distressful situation of that section of the African-American population stuck at the very bottom of the social and economic order in America, a situation that has not responded to liberal remedies. For the ultra-liberals the jokes about African Americans seem to add insult to injury and to undermine their own efforts.

However, that is another story and not one easily amenable to comparative analysis. Stupidity jokes and canny jokes exist independently in a very large number of countries. It is much more difficult to find a sufficient number of jokes outside America comparable to those told about African Americans, and American exports dominate the market. In any case our central concern here is with jokes about the Poles.

It is certainly the case that Polish Americans (Bukowczyk 1987: 111-3) feel discriminated against by the ultra-liberals' relative lack of concern for their feelings and suspect that this may be due to political hostility. Thus, no one other than the Poles themselves felt offended when the good citizens of Longmeadow, Massachusetts, placed a book of Polish jokes in a time capsule buried as part of the bicentennial celebration of America's independence. Polish Americans were very angry (Bukowczyk 1987: 141), but there was no nation-wide outburst of ultra-liberal indignation nor had local ultra-liberals done anything to prevent it happening. Also, there was no subsequent witch-hunt to find a scapegoat for this defilement of the bicentennial spirit.

Polish-American suspicions, though, are almost certainly unjustified. Ultra-liberals are less concerned about jokes about Poles than about African Americans, but they have tried to suppress jokes about Poles to some extent.

Ronald Reagan got into duck soup, if not hot water (Schutz 1989: 166-7), over his involvement in the telling of the joke:

> How do you tell the Pole at a cock-fight?
> He's the one with the duck. (Reagan quoted in Bukowczyk 1987: 112)

Carl Oldenburg's tale of the fate of the Japanese poet Klutzi is a comic parable about ultra-liberal disapproval of Polish stupidity jokes:

> Klutzi's verse, "The Polish night owl puts its beak under its wing and falls from the limb," written in 1971, has since been banned in Japan. Klutzi went on permanent leave of absence from his status as a freshman in one of the regional schools of Haiku a year after it appeared in print. His studies were not going well and he foresaw his premature departure from the school. Out of spite (one can only surmise) he cast a worthless Polish joke into Haiku form and got it published in the local journal of verse. When the editors learned what had happened they were at first chagrined and then unemployed. The Haiku was banned. Klutzi fell into the habit of loitering in the barrooms of Sapporo telling the story of his infamous "Polish Haiku" to anyone willing to buy him a drink. Doomed to permanent and everlasting dishonor, he may well go down in history as the Archangel of Haiku. (Oldenburg 1975: 48)

Thus, the question that ought to be asked is why have Polish Americans and particularly their community leaders and intellectuals held these unjustified suspicions of the politically correct? Empirical studies have shown that Polish Americans in general were not greatly bothered by the jokes (Sandberg 1974: 61), but those who had taken it upon themselves to act as spokesmen and women for the Poles chose to be more vociferous (Sandberg 1974: 74) about ethnic jokes than the leaders of other white ethnic groups in America who were the butt of such jokes. As noted earlier, the author was able to interview Larry Wilde, America's leading compiler of ethnic joke books in 1979, when the sales of his ethnic joke-books were at their peak, and Wilde kindly showed the author the file of indignant protest letters that he had received. Although Wilde (1973, 1975) had published books combining Polish and Italian jokes in a *single* volume, he had received no angry letters from Italians, but many from Polish Americans, including a senior university professor in Michigan, despite the fact that many of the Polish and Italian jokes were identical in theme, for the Italians were also depicted as stupid and dirty in the jokes. Likewise, Wilde's collections of jokes about canny Jews (Wilde 1974, 1979, 1980, 1986) and about Irish drunks (Wilde 1974, 1979, 1983) produced no hostile response. Why should this difference exist?

Polish Americans seem to feel powerless and disesteemed in America in a way that is not true of most other sizeable white ethnic minorities. They lack the political clout of, say, the Jews or the Irish, both of which have been able to influence American foreign as well as domestic policy, whereas Poland was never anything more than a pawn in America's Cold War with the former Soviet Union. When Jimmy Carter went to Poland and told the Poles through an interpreter's error that he wanted to screw them, he spoke more truly than he knew. Likewise, American Presidents such as Reagan and Clinton have exaggerated their Irish ancestry to obtain votes (even though it was not part of their social identity earlier in life), but no one has ever seriously courted the Poles in this kind of way (Andreski 1973: 116). No one has been willing seriously to denigrate the Irish in the media in late twentieth-century America, whereas American journalists, whether in print or on television, have shown little respect for the Poles. This can be seen from the singularly unpleasant way in which the journalists treated Paul Wrobel's (1979) study *Our Way: Family Parish and Neighborhood in a Polish-American Community*, a sympathetic study of blue-collar workers with very little power in the labor and housing markets, conscious of their low status as manual workers in America, suffering the "hidden injuries of class" (Wrobel 1979: 156) in a society obsessed with economic competition and trying to maintain and retain work, home, family and community under difficult circumstances. When Wrobel gave a paper on his study at the conference of the American Association for the Advancement of Science the press turned up in force and a number of leading American newspapers produced distorted accounts of his study in a way that was seriously defamatory of the Poles (Wrobel 1979: 156-6). NBC set up and filmed a scene of supposedly beer-sodden Poles singing in a bar in Hamtramck in order to confirm this unfair image (Wrobel 1979: 165-6). There had been a similar malicious twisting of an earlier study of Polish Americans in Boston by the American magazines (Wrobel 1979: 156). Polish Americans were deeply upset and Wrobel received in Michael Novak's words "a most touching deluge of letters from sad and hurt Polish-Americans" (Wrobel 1979: 170). Other ethnic groups would not have been treated in this way; it wasn't right and it wasn't fair. Andrew Greeley commented that the "self-proclaimed liberals," the "better people" were to blame for this outburst of denigration (cited in Wrobel 1979: 169), and suggested that it was part of a general modern American contempt for the hard work and self-sacrifice of blue-collar workers.

In late twentieth-century America many ultra-liberals abandoned the cause of the socially conservative blue-collar workers, whom they saw as hostile to their intellectual radicalism. This manifest lack of sympathy and worse with the situation of the ordinary working-class people who constituted "the ethnics" on the part of many American intellectuals (Wrobel 1979: 169), was hardly likely to commend itself to the Poles. Under the circumstances it is easy to see why the leaders of Polish America should be sensitive about Polish jokes and suspect that the leftist liberals might be responsible for them. Their concerns and suspicions might be unjustified, misplaced and unsupportable, but are entirely understandable, given their sense of rejection by the ultra-liberal elite.

There is a complete lack of sentimental regard and affection for the Poles in America or of any positive appreciation of Polish history, culture and achievements. In England jokes about Irish stupidity (often told by Irish comedians) have always coexisted with popular comedies with Irish actors that mock the Irish sympathetically. Indeed, there is a strong and saccharined representation of the Irish in all aspects of popular entertainment in Britain, much as is the case in America. Polish Americans do not enjoy anything like this kind of sentimental celebration and media popularity.

Likewise, whereas an educated English person knows of the contributions to modern literature of, say, James Joyce, Sean O'Casey, Wiliam Butler Yeats, Brian Moore, and Frank O'Connor and of the significance of Boolean algebra and the Fitzgerald contraction named after Irish mathematicians, Americans seem totally unaware of how truly important the Polish contribution to world culture has been. Jesse Bier reveals this when he expresses puzzlement at the sheer length and persistence of the Polish joke cycle in the face of the Poles' rise "to visible prominence with a Polish Pope, a world famous labor leader Lech Walesa, a Nobel Prize-winning poet, Czeslaw Milosz, and Polish Americans like Dan Rostenkowski in the U.S. Congress and Jim Miklawzewski in television journalism" (Bier 1988: 139).

But there was not and has *not been any such rise* in the levels of Polish acheivement except in the perception of those with a very short historical attention span. There have *always* been prominent Poles and it is curious that Americans, including Bier, the Polish

Americans' champion, seem unaware either of the fame or of the Polishness of Copernicus (Kopernik), Marie Skladowska Curie , Leszek Kolakowski, Joseph Conrad (Konrad Korzeniowski), Bronislaw Malinowski, Ignace Paderewski, Frederick Chopin, Zygmunt Wroblewski and Karol Olszewski, or Ignacy Lukasiewic.

Even the ethnic slur cited earlier about the dumb Hewlett-Packard Polack calculator is an expression of popular ignorance about the importance of Polish culture. The Hewlett-Packard calculator was, in fact, based on a clever attempt to keep down the price of what in the 1970s was an expensive item by making best use of the limited memory available through using fewer steps to perform a particular calculation. It was called Polish, not because it was stupid but because it drew on the highly sophisticated work of Polish mathematical logicians, notably the group led by Jan Lukasiewicz. Polish skills in such abstract and difficult branches of mathematics likewise played a major part in the British cracking of the German enigma ciphers in World War II (R. V. Jones 1990; Sebag-Montefiore 2001: 34-48) and in the work of the Polish mathematician Dr. Stanislaw Ulam (Wytrwal 1977: 387-8) on the building of the H-bomb in the United States in 1954. The defeat of the successive totalitarianisms of the Nazis and the Soviets owed much to Polish brain-power as well as courage.

The genius of the Poles is unknown in America because the Poles lack political power. The recognition and celebration of the achievements of members of particular ethnic groups in America has little to do with truth or objectivity or importance. What gets into the curriculum and the text books is a product of who has power in the educational system to decide the matter. Politically influential groups and groups with sponsorship from the politically correct get their heroes and their cultures listed in American textbooks and the syllabus biased towards their achievements even when these are meager. The Poles have no political clout of any kind and always get left out so that yet another generation grows up believing the Poles have never had anything to offer.

In this way the Poles have been trapped in a situation where their lack of political influence, their lack of an ultra-liberal sponsor, and their lack of any influence on the media have excluded them from the proper and deserved recognition of their culture, and elevated other, sometimes less worthy, groups above them in the pecking order.

It is no wonder that Poles wrote indignant letters to Larry Wilde about his books of jokes about their stupidity, whereas Italian and Irish Americans could shrug off their own joke books because the latter groups have been able to force others to recognize the significance of their cultural heritage, whereas the Poles have not had the power to do so. However, even if the Poles had, the joke tellers would simply have incorporated Polish achievements into their jokes much as they did in the case of Italian monuments, Polish resistance to Nazi aggression or the election of a Polish Pope.

Why is the Colosseum round?
To stop the Italians pissing in the corners. (UCBFA Italian file. Collected by Paul Fame (1969)

What did Hitler say to his men before they invaded Poland?
Don't shit in the streets, we're trying to starve them out. (Clements 1973: 15)

What was Pope John-Paul II's first miracle?
He made a blind man lame.
He turned wine into water. (See Fish 1980: 451)

Why did the Pope order all the urinals in the Vatican to be raised six inches?
He wanted to keep the Italians on their toes. (Fish 1980: 453)

Hail Mary Full of Grace.
The Wops are now in second place. (Fish 1980: 453)

Senator Henry Jackson was reported as saying that the Catholic church should substitute vodka for wine to increase church attendance now that it had a Polish pope. (Helmreich 1982: 170)

Established ethnic jokes are thus quite impervious to the fame of individuals and the deeds of nations, and are *not* the result of the blocking by the liberal elite of a fair recognition of Polish cultural achievements in America. Italian cultural achievements are widely, if shallowly, appreciated in America, but this did not prevent the development of essentially similar stupidity jokes about Italians in the United States. The key to the jokes is simply the continued existence of *large visible seemingly static blue-collar* Roman Catholic ethnic enclaves in a society largely dominated by competitive individualism.

Since American leftists are often themselves virulent critics of this same competitive individualism and have a strong belief in state intervention and quotas, they are hardly likely to be the key propagators of the jokes. Leftists are *not* a homogeneous group, but like most ideologically defined entities are divided into squabbling factions and the criticisms of liberals in general by Greeley (Wrobel 1979: 169) and Novak (1973: 8, 40, 63, 69) for being anti-Polish were misplaced. Most liberals, like the vast majority of Americans, were and are quite indifferent to the Poles—the Poles simply were and are not important to them, neither as a group to be criticized, nor as one to be protected and sympathized with. It is easy to see why Polish-American intellectuals are suspicious of liberals, but in fairness the leftist liberals tried to suppress *all* ethnic jokes even if they did so more vigorously with some jokes than others. The leftist liberals failed to stop the continued invention and circulation of jokes about African Americans among the broad masses of the American people, even though these jokes were anathema to them. The source of the Polish jokes is exactly the same, the great mass of ordinary Americans.

There is no reason whatsoever to suppose that the invention, circulation, and immense popularity and persistence of Polish stupidity jokes in America for over forty years was in any way a response by the ordinary Americans who invented and told the jokes to some kind of threat or anxiety, nor are the jokes an expression of hostility. The jokes are identical to those told about Newfoundlanders in Canada, where there are no social circumstances that would make such a hypothesis even plausible. In America the *timing* of the initiation and popularity of the jokes totally contradicts any such theory.

German Americans and Jewish Americans may have reasons rooted in past conflicts to resent the Poles, but there is no real evidence that this played any significant part in the generation of the joke cycle. The same jokes have been pinned on Italian Americans who have not been involved in deep-rooted and much-resented conflicts with Germans or with Jews either in Europe or in America. The idea that leftist liberals were able successfully to persuade or coerce the mass of ordinary American people to tell jokes about Polish Americans rather than African Americans is absurd; it is overturned by the existence of a vast number of jokes about African Americans with a far more negative content. The leftist liberals' ignorance about and indifference towards the Poles and their culture may have set a bad example for the media and greatly irritated Polish Americans, but it is irrelevant to any discussion of Polish jokes.

The entire argument that American jokes about Poles are hostile is based on a simple fallacy. First proposition: ethnic conflicts are exacerbated by competition for jobs and housing; true. Second proposition: ethnic jokes pin negative attributes on particular groups; true. Third proposition: if *serious* accusations of stupidity and dirtiness were made against the Poles in America it might well indicate dislike and hostility and might well be a form of verbal aggression; true. Final deduction: therefore jokes about stupid and dirty Poles are a disguised form of such aggression rooted in an ethnic conflict fueled by economic competition. Nonsense!

Jokes are not disguised expressions of aggression against particular groups (though they *can* be *used* in this way), but rather a form of playing with the forbidden, in this case of playing with inter-ethnic verbal aggression much as other jokes play with forbidden statements about sex, disasters, and politics. There may or may not exist a corresponding serious stereotype for the targeted group, the joke tellers may or may not subscribe to it, and it may or may not bear some relation to the jokes. In the case of the jokes about the Poles, the absence of serious ethnic slurs about Poles in American English would seem to be of some significance, but more to the point the entire attempt to link together humorous and serious forms of communication is profoundly mistaken. They are different phenomena, with different purposes and conducted according to different rules.

It is quite possible that some of the individuals enjoying Polish jokes find them especially enjoyable because they hate Poles with every fiber of their being and that others, though having no feelings about the Poles one way or another, would experience an exultant sense of schadenfreude if a Pole in the audience were to be annoyed at such jokes. But we have no evidence that this is the case for the great mass of Americans who tell and enjoy jokes about Polish stupidity. To assume that it is so on the basis of some speculative view about human nature is absurd. When the joke tellers say "it is just a joke," we should believe them unless we have good direct evidence to the contrary. Neither self-reports nor direct observations of people telling Polish jokes provide any such evidence. The fact that a very few individuals *do* admit to such feelings or that observers have detected the malice of a few more only confirms the reliability of the far greater number of testimonies and observations to be found in archives indicating the benign quality of these jokes. Yet even if these joke tellers revelling in malice were common it would not help to explain why the jokes exist. Many a population convulsed with malice against some group of outsiders lacks any jokes about them whatsoever.

The peculiarly vacuous nature of the various speculative theses about Polish jokes that have been propounded can be seen in a statement Jesse Bier (1988: 139-40) makes about the very basis of his argument when he writes:

> Even adherents of the superiority theory, anchored in a philosophical view of irreducible human orneriness and sadism, have a problem in accounting for the persistence of the Polish joke when other new targets are offered. And people, like myself, who believe that the basic human attitudes, especially in a pluralistic society, arise from profound uncertainty and unease and from various degrees of anxiety, and that people are more truly activated by mutual covert fear than by sheer egotism and aggrandizement have an equal problem.

To start from any general unproven and indeed untestable a priori view of human nature whether one rooted in unease and anxiety or one derived from the superiority theory of humor, and to try and explain a particular social phenomenon on this basis, is in itself unreasonable. Furthermore, if the persistence of Polish jokes does create a problem for hypotheses grounded in these two quite different philosophical premises, then both sets of hypotheses are clearly false and no amount of special pleading should divert us from this conclusion. The comparative and historical analyses employed here demonstrates their falseness. It also should lead us to understand the uselessness of such starting points. Bier had the commendable honesty to make a prediction and to realize that there was a problem, but notions such as "the superiority theory" or "profound anxiety and unease" are made of rubber and could, with due stretching, be made to fit anything and in consequence to explain nothing. They are not true theories and should be discarded. The existence and persistence of the Polish joke cycle is an interesting and significant social fact, but it can only be explained in terms of other comparable social facts—such as the social location of the Poles in American society—and these can only be deduced by comparing these jokes and the circumstances in which they arose with similar joke cycles in other societies, and with both similar and differing joke cycles in the same society. We can only begin to understand and explain the social world if we see it as to some extent consisting of objective, knowable, and discrete social facts, and not as a mere projection of debatable philosophical speculations about human nature.

9

Conclusion

It is appropriate that the last of the series of cases studied should be that of American stupidity jokes about Poles, since it is a striking disproof of the thesis that jokes about a particular national or ethnic group pinning an undesirable trait upon that group are necessarily or even likely to be a response to a threatening situation and an expression of hostility and aggression. As a *general* theory it is falsified by the existence of such a major and glaring exception. Jesse Bier's (1988) attempt to use the case of jokes about Poles to illustrate and support the threat, aggression, and hostility thesis has quite clearly failed. It is refuted by the absence of any independent evidence showing general hostility towards the Poles in America in the *last half* of the twentieth century when the jokes flourished, and by the *absence* of the jokes in the late nineteenth and early twentieth centuries, when there was much more tension between Poles and other Americans. Likewise, it has not proved possible to demonstrate a link between the origin and popularity of American stupidity jokes about Poles and those particular groups of Americans who might for reasons rooted in Europe, as well as in America or in radical ideology, be expected to hold resentful feelings against the Poles. Furthermore, identical stupidity jokes, though with local additions and adaptations, have flourished in Canada, although it has never even been suggested that *any* group of Canadians are hostile to Newfoundlanders or that there has been any serious recent conflict between them. Thus, conflict and hostility are neither a necessary nor a sufficient condition for the emergence of ethnic jokes about stupidity.

Where does Bier's now clearly falsified hypothesis come from? Why should he have put forward a proposition about Polish jokes without any supporting empirical evidence that was so easily overturned? It is because the proposition fitted the then dominant way of looking at ethnic jokes of this type, and because it incorporated taken-for-granted assumptions and confusions that no one had ever questioned.

Lurking in the background is the widespread tendency to confuse serious and humorous statements and to confuse playing with aggression in jokes (Feinburg 1978) with real aggression. As Raskin (1985: 100-4) has shown, joke telling differs fundamentally from other forms of communication, such as bona fide communication or lying. You cannot reduce a joke to a serious statement or treat it as such. The specific ethnic scripts used in jokes such as Polish or Newfoundland stupidity are conventional, fictional, and mythological. They are not intended to be believed but merely to be assumed for the duration of the joke. Now it is *possible* that there also exists a widely held stereotype that Poles and Newfoundlanders really are stupid and dirty but this can *not* be deduced from the mere existence of the jokes. It would have to be demonstrated on the basis of independent evidence that Americans and Canadians, respectively, seriously believed this to be the case to the point where they were willing to act on it. If it could be *shown* that late-twentieth-century employers were regularly unwilling to engage Polish Americans because they were perceived as generally unable to perform complex and difficult tasks or if mainland Canadians declined to take vacations in leading hotels in St. John's, Newfoundland, because they thought that the hotels were bound to be unspeakably filthy then it would be a different matter. But no such evidence has ever been forthcoming. If serious stereotypes of Poles and Newfoundlanders do exist, they are faint and unimportant. The whole issue of stereotypes is an irrelevance and a distraction when analyzing this kind of joke. For the same reason it is absurd to argue in this case that the telling of these particular jokes perpetuates negative stereotypes for there are no stereotypes to perpetuate. The joke is a joke.

This argument is rendered even more powerful by another form of comparative analysis employed here. It has been shown quite clearly that there is to all intents and purposes an absence in America of serious folklore such as proverbs or similes or epithets expressing negative views about the Poles, even though they are present in abundance in relation to other American ethnic groups and are regarded as an index of negative attitudes to and conflicts with them. It is quite unacceptable to try to get round this problem by adding in the jokes to the serious folklore to form a composite category. Folklorists tend to do this routinely and without thought, so that in folklore archives jokes about a group often end up being placed in the same file as seriously held proverbs or superstitions or sayings about the same group, and the file is then labeled *blasons populaires* (see also Gaidoz and Sébillot 1884), presumably on the grounds that both types of folklore involve mockery. Yet as has been clearly shown earlier, serious and humorous forms of disparagement are *quite different* and it is obvious that these files should be disaggregated and the jokes separated from the slurs. Lumping the two together under a French heading is seriously misleading.

It is a matter of debate *how much* impact *serious* folklore has. It is certainly not as influential as political and religious ideology and does not usually have the backing of the state or other powerful institutions, though it could, of course, be co-opted by and into these as a minor auxiliary force. It is easy to imagine a gauleiter or a commissar citing familiar proverbs, slurs, or pieces of folk-unwisdom to support a political decree. Even in unpoliticized everyday life the unsophisticated may be guided in their conduct by proverbs or superstitions though not by set-piece jokes. Jokes can be used to illustrate a point but the point has to be already clearly in place in the audience's minds, for a joke is too ambiguous to be a sure way of putting it there. Jokes are simply a bonus. If no joke is available to a persuasive speaker, it will not significantly reduce his or her persuasiveness.

Jokes are a good method of getting an audience to enjoy itself and to identify with someone speaking on a serious topic and in that sense help persuasion. Jokes are not a good method of inciting hatred or moral indignation, since they divert the audience's feelings away from strong feelings of this kind. Those who listen to jokes are incapacitated by laughter except for those who do not laugh and are offended. Indeed, they may be moved to indignation or retaliation. A speaker skilled in rhetoric will often use humor, but it is striking how unlike set-piece jokes such usages are and how difficult it is to keep them alive and funny when they are taken out of their original context The set-piece jokes with scripts and a punch line that are the subject of this book are nothing beyond being a mere laughing matter for by definition they are canned, they have no context, and are transportable in preserved form. The very factors that differentiate them from their cousins and ancestors, namely wit and anecdotes, render them far less useful for the furtherance of serious purposes. The use of humor as a technique adds pleasure to communication but it may or may not add effectiveness even when it is tailored to a particular purpose and context and used with skill. Jokes are the least likely form of humor to be useful for this purpose since they are repeatable performances whose very structure makes them funny rather than persuasive or an efficient means of incitement. They are the worst possible humorous tool for the persuader or inciter, the least suitable adjunct for real aggression.

Those who dislike set-piece jokes (which often play with aggression) because they are performed rather than spontaneous and part of the sociability (Schutz 1989) of boisterous groups, might also do well to reflect that their own preference for a more individual humor of wit and anecdote brings them closer to the border with the kind of real verbal aggression involved in insults and gossip than the jokers ever get. Those who are genuinely in a position to complain about being persecuted by humorous means within a work group or institution will have been subjected to an individual humor tailored to their own discomfiture. Set-piece jokes would be an inefficient way of doing this. By contrast, skillful and spontaneous witty put-downs can be used to ridicule, control and even express moral criticisms of human weaknesses otherwise best left unadmonished. They are nastier because they are more personal and therefore potentially also catty and spiteful, as are discursive humorous anecdotes which can be used as malicious gossip.

The opposite of the American situation in relation to the Poles has been true, historically, in Central and Eastern Europe where there have been few jokes about Poles but a wealth of ethnic slurs. What is more, the idea that the Poles *really were* stupid and dirty was part of the ideology of the German National Socialist invaders of Poland during World War II and was associated with savage persecution of the Poles. The two situations of humorous America and vicious Eastern Europe could not be more different, and it is both absurd and dangerous to confuse them. Likewise, German aggression against the Poles at that time was real; millions of Poles died. This is not something that Polish Americans have ever had to fear. The stupidity jokes in America about Poles or in Canada about Newfoundlanders merely play with aggression (Gruner 1997: 80).

It is particularly important to make this distinction between aggression and playing with aggression in the case of jokes depicting a group as dirty, since the language of dirt is the language of rejection and potentially of persecution, as Alan Dundes (1997: 92) stresses in his noted essay on anti-Semitic folklore, "Why is the Jew dirty?" "Dirty Jew" was a favored term of abuse by anti-Semites in Eastern and Central Europe and implied both that the Jews were literally matter out of place who ought not to be there and should be cleaned away and that they were physically dirty. Likewise, the Nazis used the same accusation in regard to the Poles at the time when they invaded Poland. But this has got nothing whatsoever to do with jokes about dirty Poles in America. Joel Kovel (cited by Dundes 1997: 107) has confused these two situations by writing:

> Every group which has been the object of prejudice has at some time been designated by the prejudiced group as dirty or smelly or both; thus have the Irish been regarded by the English, the Jews by the Poles, the Poles by the Anglo-Saxon Americans (consider the rash of Polish jokes popular in Chicago and elsewhere).

It is the usual circular argument. Kovel asserts that the Americans who told jokes about dirty Poles really believed that the Poles were dirty and that this was an expression of prejudice. That he has not given the matter much thought is shown by his referring to the joke tellers as Anglo-Saxons when they were just as likely to be Irish, Greek, Jewish, German or African American. For Kovel the joke tellers *must* be Anglo-Saxon to fit his assumption of prejudice and exclusion, even when they are not. Equally, it is difficult to see how he would be able to account for the Anglophone Canadians jokes about dirty Anglophone Newfoundlanders or the *absence* of dirtiness in English ethnic jokes about the "stupid" Irish. He is unable to see that jokes about a group being dirty *may or may not* have a corresponding serious stereotype and *may or may not* be linked to prejudice and rejection. Kovel is truly prejudiced for he has pre-judged a situation and declined to test his assumptions against reality.

A serious meaning can be deduced from North American jokes about dirty Poles and Newfoundlanders, but it refers to the peculiarities of North Americans not Poles or Newfoundlanders in that from the 1960s the jokes fused together stupidity and dirtiness into a single joke in a way that is not usual in Europe. Being "stupid-dirty" is the antithesis of North American rational hygiene (Davies 1990: 94-101; 1995), but this cannot be deduced from the jokes alone, only from a study of the way in which serious American practices in relation to deodorants or the disposal of the dead differ from those of other industrial countries. However, once again the serious has determined the comic, not the other way round, and the importance of studying these jokes lay in their providing not a full explanation of but a starting point for investigating the serious.

Charles Gruner (1997: 147-77) has claimed that there is no such thing as a humor devoid of some degree of playful aggression. If he is right then it makes no sense to single out jokes of the kind discussed in this study as peculiar. Rather we might ask what it is that such jokes have in common with other popular genres of jokes, such as jokes about sex, jokes about well-publicized disasters, or the death of celebrities, or jokes about political leaders and the political system in societies where open political discussion is not allowed. In each case the jokes involve playing with the forbidden and evading a set of rules about the use of language. There are restrictions even in open societies on the ways and contexts in which sex, death, and disasters are discussed, and on serious disparagement of others and in authoritarian societies restrictions on political criticism also. As a simple matter of observation it is clear that human beings enjoy the time off from these restrictions that is provided by jokes, which sneak round them indirectly. The relationship between the existence of the restrictions and the enjoyment of the jokes, however, is not a direct and simple one. It can not be shown, for example, that the number of political jokes is greatest under the *most* repressive regimes nor that jokes about sex flourish best in a very puritanical society. There *could* be a curvilinear relationship with moderate repression producing the most jokes. Likewise, it can not be conclusively demonstrated that it is those who are most inhibited about sex and aggression who most enjoy jokes playing with these themes. It is quite possible that the opposite is true. Nor can it be safely asserted that the jokers secretly rejoice in events such as the space shuttle explosion or the death of Diana, Princess of Wales (Davies 1999) and are using the jokes as a covert way of expressing this. There is no convincing evidence to this effect, as distinct from inferences from so-called "theory" or appeals to the authority of some guru. This study makes only the more modest claim that people enjoy humorous statements whose nearest serious counterparts would shock others and quite possibly themselves. If the jokes themselves are shocking to others then that is in itself a bonus for those among whom the jokes are told. Humor is about mock shocks, mock frights and mock aggression and mock rule-breaking. The rules broken may even be those of language and logic itself as when enjoyment is taken in the exploiting of ambiguity and incongruity, in puns and wordplay or in the creation of nonsense and absurdity. Humor is time off from serious life.

These simple descriptive points do not make any obscure and untestable claims about the nature of the inner satisfactions derived from particular kinds of humor. Also it is necessary utterly to reject all use of the misleading term tendentious (Freud 1960: 90), meaning having or serving a *purpose*. If all that is meant by this is that a particular joke is a way of evading a restriction on our patterns of speech, then it is not problematic, though the use of such terminology adds nothing to our understanding. If, however, the term is interpreted to mean that that joke is a means of either overthrowing the restrictions altogether (in which case there would be no more jokes) or of covertly making a serious statement, then the description is false since such purposes are not properties of the text of a joke and cannot be derived from a text which is of its very nature ambiguous.

Now it is perfectly possible for a Canadian or anyone else to use a joke about stupid Newfies as part of a disguised, or come to that overt, act of serious disparagement of Newfoundlanders either because the joke teller seriously dislikes them, or even if or he or she is indifferent to them and a Newfoundlander is present from schadenfreude. The jokes *can* be used in that way or perceived as such even if no such intention is present. It is *easy* to cite instances of joke telling of this kind, occasions characterized either by gleefully shared malice and hostility against the butts of a particular kind of joke or ending in the angering of and serious verbal or other counter-aggression by a member or affiliate of the butts of the jokes. It is entirely a question of the nature of the frame into which the text is placed, a question of context and tone.

Yet as soon as this is recognized it is clear that tendentiousness is not a property of a joke but of its frame. Even in the examples given by Freud, it is problematic and indicates a total failure on his part to distinguish between jokes and their frames and between witticisms that are tied to context and jokes which are not. It is time to take the Freud out of schadenfreude.

Freud tells a joke about Serenissimus, the conventional name in jokes for a royal personage in Germany at that time:

> Serenissimus was making a tour through his provinces and noticed a man in the crowd who bore a striking resemblance to his own exalted person. He beckoned to him and asked: "Was your mother at one time in service in the Palace?" "No, your Highness," was the reply, "but my father was." (Freud 1960 (1905): 68-9)

Freud comments on the joke:

> The person to whom the question was put would no doubt have liked to knock down the impertinent individual who dared by such an allusion to cast a slur on his mother's memory. But the important individual was Serenissimus whom one may not knock down or even insult unless one is prepared to purchase that revenge at the price of one's whole existence. The insult must therefore, it would seem, be swallowed in silence. But fortunately a joke shows the way in which the insult may be safely avenged.

It shows nothing of the sort. If Serenissimus had the power to exact "the price of one's whole existence" then such a retort could have led to the wit's end anyway. What saved the situation was either that Serenissimus had a good sense of humor and saw that it was just a joke or that social convention in Germany required that kings though powerful enough to be protected from insult were required to restrain themselves in the face of a witty riposte. Besides the analysis confuses jokes and witticism. The tale is told in a *joke* about Serenissimus (his most serene highness), a generic royal person, and we can have no idea whether or not the imaginary man in the crowd felt as Freud suggested or sought a hidden verbal revenge against the monarch. Such a construction is *unnecessary* for our understanding of the joke. All that can be said is that the joke plays with aggression—that is part of its structure. To speculate further about motives and feelings is pointless. It is equally pointless to speculate about the motives of feelings of those who told and listened to (or read) this funny story within a joke frame or whether or not they liked the real-life mockery of kings.

Behind the joke may lie an original anecdote about specified individuals or an actual witticism which might, albeit clumsily and speculatively, be analyzed in its specific original context and a tentative view reached about how humor was actually used on that occasion. Jokes often have their origins in anecdotes about individuals or particular witty exchanges which are then detached from that context and shaped and polished so that they can stand alone and last. Freud's example is just such a "canned" (i.e., treated, preserved, and enclosed in a frame) joke. It can no longer be analyzed as if it were a real event. Cans are not transparent.

How kings respond to a particular joke at their expense depends on which king it is, how unrestricted his power is and the context in which the joke is made. How this response is subsequently reported, recorded and interpreted depends on the images held at the time or later of how kings in general or this king in particular would have reacted to such a joke. These images are important in and of themselves, however insecurely they may be linked to the incident they purport to describe. When William the Conqueror, known in France as *Guillaume le Bâtard* (William the bastard), was besieging the town of Alençon in 1051, the townspeople were said to have placed beaten pelts and skins on the walls of their town and to have shouted "pelterer" at him, thus indirectly mocking his base birth and the social position of his mother, for he was the illegitimate son of the Duke of Normandy. His mother was alleged to be the daughter of a man who either prepared human bodies for burial or else was a tanner (*Gesta Normannorum*, vol. 2, Book 7, 8(18), Douglas 1964: 15, 379-81; van Hout 1995: 125). William was so angry at this joke that on capturing the town he mutilated the citizens who had ridiculed him by cutting off their hands and feet. Sir Frank Stenton (1908 : 94) says that William swore that he would "prune those men as it were with a pollarding knife" in revenge for their joke about his mother, even though no one was implying humorously or otherwise that his father was anyone other than the Duke of Normandy (an implication that *was* jokingly directed against Serenissimus and his putatively adulterous mother). William treated the jokers as one would a plant, as things with no moral claim on our concern or charity. David Bates (1989: 34) comments that "unsurprisingly this is the last reference in the sources to anyone making jokes about his illegitimate birth." Impertinent individuals may well not be able safely to make jokes about the powerful, for the latter are not obliged to behave like Serenissimus.

The joke about William the Conqueror's mother's social standing resurfaced in the reign of his great grandson, King Henry II of England. At a time when Henry was extremely angry with Bishop Hugh of Lincoln he summoned the bishop to his presence, having told his courtiers to snub and ignore him:

No one rose to greet the bishop or said a word to him.... There was a long brooding silence, broken finally by Henry, who, unable to do nothing, called for a needle and thread and began to stitch up a leather bandage on an injured finger. Again there was a heavy silence until Bishop Hugh, contemplating the king at his stitching, casually remarked, "How, like your cousin of Falaise you look." At this the king's anger fled from him, and he burst into laughter which sent him rolling on the ground. Many were amazed at the bishop's temerity, others puzzled at the point of the remark, until the king, recovering his composure explained the gibe to them: William the Conqueror was a bastard and his mother was reputedly the daughter of one of the leather-workers for which the Norman town of Falaise was famous. (Warren 1973: 629-30)

Given that Henry (the same Henry who quarreled fatally with Thomas à Becket) was easily angered and not known for his gentle treatment of bishops, Bishop Hugh's playful insult could have produced a very different and savage response. Henry II's biographer W. L. Warren is able to reassure us that Bishop Hugh knew and understood him well enough to know that Henry would laugh "when his dignity was gently mocked," (Warren 1973: 630), but Warren is only able to do this because the witticism is recorded in context in the chronicles as a real event and not simply as a joke. Even then Warren can only do so because of the detailed scholarship he was able to bring to bear on the character of the two individuals, the nature of their relationship (Warren 1973: 214) and the patterns of behavior expected of the exalted in that society at that time. Warren provides an analysis of a witticism in context, not a speculation about a joke, an analysis of a situation, not of the mere text of a joke. Yet for all their detail, the value of studying such context-bound witticisms is limited. The problem with trying to base an analysis on witticisms rather than jokes is precisely that they are so closely tied to particular incidents depending upon the varied and shifting kaleidoscope of human interaction. They cannot be profitably studied in aggregate in the way that the texts of jokes can.

Even though jokes can be used as serious disparagement this does not explain *why* the jokes *exist* in the first place. It is perhaps easiest to make this point in the case of the jokes about the Newfoundlanders where the use of the jokes in a hostile way is uncommon and thus demonstrably irrelevant to an explanation of the jokes, but even if such usage were common, the point would remain valid. Jokes may well be used to express hostility or in furtherance of a conflict, but this fact is of no assistance to us in tackling the central question asked in this study—why do certain patterns of jokes about particular groups at particular times exist at all? You can not infer tendentiousness from a text. The point is reinforced by the fact that identical or very similar patterns of jokes often exist in circumstances of obvious conflict and of reasonable equanimity. To try to avoid this point by speaking of the latter case in terms of latent conflicts or unconscious hostility is grossly dishonest. It is a way of continuing to uphold a failed argument in the absence of evidence or of dishonestly asserting the validity of one's own intuitions or those of one's guru or ideological associates against those of one's opponents. It also trivializes hostility and conflict and the sufferings of those who have been the victims of the real thing.

There are many cases of national, ethnic, and religious conflict involving strongly held stereotypes that do not give rise to jokes. During the Second World War the Japanese were widely seen in Britain and America as treacherous, fiendish, fanatical, and cruel, and Japanese Americans in the mainland United States were quite unjustly detained in internment camps far from their homes (Helmreich 1982: 94-6). Even before that time the Japanese had been regarded with suspicion and hostility and prevented from entering America as immigrants (Helmreich 1982: 92-3). Yet there were hardly any jokes about the Japanese during that war. There were only overtly didactic hostile political cartoons which have little humorous impact. They merely use a degree of mocking caricature to illustrate an obvious political message (Low 1949; *New Yorker War Album*, 1942). Likewise, there is an absence of jokes about Turks in Ethelyn G. Orso's (1979) collection of modern Greek jokes, despite the bitter enmity that the Greeks have for their neighbor.

In experimental circumstances when students are asked to rank jokes, other things equal, they may tend to express a preference for jokes about members of groups with whom they are in conflict or dislike over jokes about members of groups with whom they identify or feel a sense of affiliation (Weise 1996). However, in practice other things are *not* equal. The largest joke cycle in North America, the stupidity jokes, ended up being pinned on two groups who were not widely or intensely disliked or rejected or in serious conflict with anyone. In other words, theories of humor that explain playful aggression in terms of real aggression have very little predictive power and are of little use for explaining aggregate patterns of national and ethnic jokes.

Indeed, the weakness of theories rooted in real aggression or tendentiousness as a means of accounting for the existence of an aggregate pattern of jokes is shown by the need for evasive measures to be taken to protect them from falsification outlined earlier, when it was asserted that jokes about stupid and dirty Poles exist because guilt-stricken European-Americans would feel bad telling these jokes about African Americans. In consequence it was argued that the jokes about Poles express displaced aggression. No independent evidence was produced to show that any such connection exists and it is anyway undermined by the popularity of another genre of jokes about African Americans involving even more negative characteristics than those pinned on the Poles.

The central fallacy underlying the displaced aggression thesis is that it is once again an attempt to explain the existence of an aggregate of jokes in terms of speculation about the feelings and impulses of individuals and by treating the social order as if it were like an individual. Furthermore, the displaced aggression thesis is an inferior kind of explanation concocted to explain and explain away a single particular case. It can *not* be applied to the telling of identical jokes about the Newfoundlanders in Canada unless it were supposed that the chronic political disputes between Quebec and the rest of Canada are also a source of displaced aggression, even though the conflict is of a totally different nature and one that Canadians are able to discuss freely and honestly. It would indeed be strange, if such were the case, that English and French speakers in Canada should have ended up telling the same jokes about the same displaced target, the Newfoundlanders. It is unlikely that they are both still angry about the original reluctance of the Newfoundlanders to join Canada. The Newfoundlanders remember the controversy, the Canadians do not. The displaced aggression thesis is also inferior in another sense to that provided here in that it is inelegant and requires more factors to produce an explanation of the same phenomenon than the explanation of stupidity jokes provided in chapter 1; what is worse is that the extra factor used has been introduced on an arbitrary *ad hoc* basis.

Ironically, analyses in terms of aggression or displaced aggression might be more appropriately applied to those who respond inappropriately to jokes and reply with disproportionate aggression to them. Jokes do not have consequences when they make people laugh. People laugh and that is the end of it. They only have adverse consequences when someone responds with violence or verbal aggression but the joke is not the cause of this aggression. Those who respond in this way choose to do so and are to blame. At the risk of anachronism it can be pointed out that William the Conqueror did not have to respond to his derisive trip down tannery-mammary lane by mutilating the jokers. What does call for investigation (but is not a concern of this study) are aggressive responses to mere canned jokes that are not directed at a particular individual.

In general, members of an audience do not attack comedians because they know perfectly well that a joke is just a joke, but Littlewood and Pickering (1998: 298) record that the British comedian "Keith Allen was once knocked out by an angry soldier for a joke about the Hyde Park IRA bomb which blew up an RAF band (the reason for this being according to Allen because they were playing out of tune)."

Allen's joke in and of itself merely plays with aggression and is of no significance. It is the soldier's real aggression in reply not to direct personal ridicule but to a joke that has to be explained. Because the soldier was a real individual and not a mere text, it is appropriate, although probably futile, to attempt some kind of interpretive understanding of why he acted as he did. It is easy to see that a man who might well have had the stress of risking his life day after day in ambushes and bombings to save people like Allen from terrorism might have been angry at a sick joke that seemed to make light of this experience and belittle the dead, a joke that blamed the victims, albeit for their lack of musicianship. Can we perhaps say that his anger at his own situation in the most difficult and frustrating of conflicts to fight was displaced onto the wretched comic on stage? Such speculation may or may not be correct but it is at least reasonable; however those who respond like the soldier are rarely subjected to this kind of reductionism. Yet it is acts of individual aggression, not texts that merely play with aggression, that are potentially amenable to psychological analysis.

The same point may be made more strongly in relation to the angry responses made to jokes in joke books or on the Internet where there is no contact between jokers and audiences, no possibility of construing a humorous item as a disguised personal insult, no gloss indicating a political attack (see Nilsen and Nilsen 2000: 19-20, 65, 97, 198, 229 for cases of disproportionately angry responses to humor generally) . Such responses are even more difficult to explain in terms of the content of the joke. An example would be the angry response to a series of jokes called "75 Reasons Why Women Should Not Have Freedom of Speech," placed on the Internet by a group of college freshmen in 1995. Death threats were sent to the jokers and one punitive and vindictive individual declared publicly, "We want them to pay for what they did" (*Debate* 1997: 493, 496). Those who put the jokes on the Internet were merely playing with the shocking and the forbidden and no evidence has been produced that they had any covert motive in doing so. Yet comments are made only about the aggressive nature of jokes, an assumption falsely based on mere content and not about the overt and obvious aggression of those who explode with rage in response to the jokes. Is it normal to send death threats to a group of freshmen? How should we perceive those who scream for revenge and retribution against mere purveyors of jokes? Here is real aggression by particular persons directed against other individuals that *is* a candidate for investigation, perhaps in terms of displaced aggression. Is it the case that for the objectors to these jokes the terrorists and the sexually violent are out of reach, so they attack the jokers instead? Why then do those with a genuine interest in the nature of interpersonal aggression not study the individuals who respond pathologically and aggressively to jokes that annoy them and who can be studied directly and profitably rather than the texts of jokes which lie well outside their area of expertise?

The answer probably lies in the peculiar way in which concepts of causality and blame have fragmented and been politicized in an arbitrary and irrational way during the last half-century (Neal and Davies 1998). This can be illustrated in relation to an argument about J.A.P. jokes. Shirley Frondorf (1990 (1988)) has alleged that a Jewish restaurant owner who killed his wife was falsely acquitted of murder on the grounds of temporary insanity after his lawyers persuaded the jury that the wife had been a real J.A.P. and had nagged and credit-carded him into homicide. In a rational world he would, as a person with no history of mental illness, have been held entirely to blame for killing his spouse. In the criminal justice system it is possible, for ultimately political reasons, to shift the blame onto the victim of a "romantic homicide" who then, of course, ceases to be a victim. Some of Frondorf's readers (see Alperin 1988) blamed the very existence of the J.A.P. jokes for providing the killer and his adviser with such a bizarre defense, yet people holding such views are quite happy to connive at other ways of allowing individuals to evade direct responsibility for their use of lethal personal violence. Jokes do not and cannot blame victims or seek scapegoats, though they may play with these ideas, yet jokes are made scapegoats for social ills whose causes are known but which have proved intractable. Rapists are to blame for rape and terrorists are to blame for terror. Jokes and jokers are to blame for neither. Likewise, those who are clearly guilty of acts of physical or verbal aggression against the purveyors of jokes are likely to try and evade responsibility by blaming the jokes. In neither case is it valid to blame the humorous for the serious.

The error of confusing the serious and the joking and of overestimating the impact of jokes, which has been consistently refuted in the earlier chapters of this book, is to be found in a particularly glaring form among broadcasters. This point can be particularly well illustrated from the war-time archives of the British Broadcasting Corporation, which reveal its most senior officials wrangling foolishly and sometimes acrimoniously about the propriety of an individual joke and drawing up an elaborate rule book ruling out jokes on a very large number of subjects and issues. Because the issues are old ones they are more easily discussed than contemporary controversies that arouse partisan feelings. Also the archives are open for inspection and the reasoning of the censors is exposed to view.

After the Italians entered World War II, jokes about their unsoldierly qualities were banned by the B.B.C.'s Controller of Programmes on 17 June 1940 as part of a policy decision that "The Italian army was pretty bad in the last war but must not now be decried too much as it is likely to be much better under German control and German officers" (B.B.C.W.A.C; R34/275/1). Although the controller does not use the jargon about stereotypes developed later, what he meant is that listeners might believe the jokes, and that the jokes would convey a stereotype of the Italians as cowardly and ineffective to the listeners who might then have falsely optimistic expectations of the outcome of the coming conflicts with Italy. It is an early expression of a fallacy that underpins much work on humor and stereotypes. In a recent study James Olson, Gregory Maio, and Karen Hobden (1999: 214) "found no evidence that disparaging humor had any reliable effects," that is, humor did not have any influence on stereotypes and attitudes. Yet what is curious is that the experimenters should have accepted the intuitive prejudice widely held in their own group that such jokes do have an effect (Olson et al. 1999: 196, 216) to the point where for ethical reasons they only used jokes that targeted advantaged groups such as lawyers "because we expected exposure to have negative effects on stereotypes and attitudes" (Olson et al. 1999: 198). The very expectation that telling jokes to a hundred students in an experiment could have an effect serious enough to raise doubts about the ethics of the experiment is itself laughable. What would they have said to the ethics committee if their subjects had subsequently lynched a lawyer? (Nilsen and Nilsen 2000:187). The fact that the experimenters found that their innovative experiment did not produce the expected results is commendable to them (for recording a disconfirmation of what they expected) and believable precisely because it demonstrated the opposite of what they had so strongly predicted. Yet even if they had discovered an effect, how big would it have been compared with the other real world forces that shape our perceptions of and behavior towards lawyers? It would have been trivial.

These results were in any case not available to the BBC Controller in 1940 whose implicit belief in the power of ethnic jokes led to the ban on jokes about cowardly Italians. Given that during the week prior to the ban the Italians' attempt to invade the south of France had proved a miserable, incompetent and, in the eyes of the French, contemptible failure, despite the exiguous size of the French forces opposing them it is difficult to see why the Controller thought the jokes would have more effect on attitudes than the BBC's own news programs. Jokes can hardly be expected to compete with the impact of the real, serious, and material world. When the Italians were easily defeated in Greece and North Africa (Davies 1990:178-83) and new jokes flourished, the ban was allowed to collapse since it had been overtaken by reality.

A very different kind of confusing the joking and the serious with an over-estimating (this time of the ethical significance) of jokes occurred in May 1944 when William J. Haley, the new Director-General of the BBC, complained to the Controller of Programmes, Basil Nicolls, about a joke that had been told by the British Yorkshire comedian Wilfred Pickles on the radio program *Monday Night at Eight*. The joke consisted of a mock German news bulletin about the war that concluded, "Three of our night-fighters and two of our cities are missing." The Director-General seized on this joke and denounced it as contrary to BBC official policy, that the bombing of German cities be portrayed as a "military necessity performed as coldly and scientifically as a surgical operation." "It is not," he added, "a matter to gloat over or to make jokes about" (B.B.C.W.A.C; R34/275/2, 9 May 1944). The Controller of Programmes in turn interrogated the Director of Variety, John Watt, who apologized and claimed that it had "slipped in." Watt added with a hint of subversive humor, "although I do not feel it to be a very serious gloat, it should have come out" (B.B.C.W.A.C; R34/275/2, 10 May 1944). It was of course absurd and pedantic for the Director-General, who had more important tasks to see to, to intervene *personally* over the matter of the Pickles joke. It demonstrates once again the obsessive nature of political correctness and also its moral shallowness. Between 1942 and 1945 the RAF was destroying entire historic German cities and deliberately creating urban firestorms in which as many as 100,000 civilians might be killed in the course of a single night's raid.

As a member of a small establishment elite, Haley would have known that the leading British politicians and their scientific advisers had had doubts about the efficacy of this kind of carpet-bombing either in undermining German war production (it actually boosted it) or in destroying civilian morale. It was not a scientific surgical operation but a dirty war targeting women and children. Freeman Dyson, who was a scientific analyst for Bomber Command and understood the full nature of the strategy, wrote after the war:

> I felt sickened by what I knew. Many times I decided I had a moral obligation to run out into the streets and tell the British people what stupidities they were doing in their name. But I never had the courage to do so. I sat in my office until the end, carefully calculating how to murder most economically another hundred thousand people. (Quoted in Garrett 1996: 16-17)

Haley would likewise have known of the speeches of Bell, the Bishop of Chichester in the House of Lords, criticizing the morality of this kind of indiscriminate bombing deliberately aimed at destroying ordinary people in their own homes. In the face of this truly horrible reality what was most important to Haley was to ensure that the bombing was only spoken about through emotionally flat, evasive and misleading scientific and medical metaphors and that Wilfred Pickles be prevented from telling jokes about it in what Haley would have seen as a vulgar, common northern accent. Ideology had justified what was being done and had concealed it; the joke had in many senses played with the forbidden and had to be banned. The moral outrage that the real aggression involved in such bombing might have called for was directed at the joke which merely played with aggression. The joke had referred to a subject that those in power did not want mentioned and tweaked a moral issue that disturbed them. For an observer in the twenty-first century, it is possible to see that such jokes would have had no effect on the listeners and they no longer seem to us particularly objectionable, but our contemporaries are unable to see that the objected-to-jokes of their own time are equally trivial in their impact and significance. There continue to be similar controversies about jokes with attempts to censor them and the same kind of humbug and misplaced outrage. The lesson of the archives is that the crucial questions to be asked do not relate to the jokes but to the reactions of those who exercise the power to censor them, whether directly or through their capacity to influence, manipulate and frighten others.

Theories of humor rooted in notions of aggression and superiority run into yet further difficulties when it is clear that the members of a group enjoy or invent and are the prime circulators of the jokes about their own group. The enjoyment of such jokes about one's own group or even an expressed preference for them has often been noted even though it contradicts experimental findings that, other things equal, people prefer jokes about outsiders or their opponents to jokes about their own group, their affiliates, and their allies. But then other things are *not* equal. The much more striking case is where the members of the group are also one of the main *sources* of the jokes about their own group, but an understanding of this phenomenon has been stultified by the fact that *only one* major instance, that of the Jews, has ever been identified as doing so (Freud 1960 (1905); Grotjahn 1970) and studied in detail.

Martin Grotjahn (1970: 135-6) has predictably written:

> The Jewish joke has a special place among witticisms. Like every joke it is a guilt-free expression of aggression, but this aggression is directed against the Jewish person himself. It is aggression turned inward. It is a combination of sadistic attack with masochistic indulgence.

Such an analysis is based on the two fallacies discussed earlier. First, it confuses the expression of aggression with playing with aggression; the dogmatic use of the word "every" and the unjustified assumption that aggression otherwise involves guilt demonstrate this. Underlying Grotjahn's model is a crude theory of human behavior that treats aggression as an animal instinct held in place by guilt. Yet it can be argued that human beings are more likely than other animals to massacre members of their own species because their capacity for creating abstract rules and ideals enables them to override the instinctive restraints that often prevail among more primitive species. Given that ideologies provide ready opportunities for devastatingly guilt-free aggression, who needs jokes? It is not necessary to adjudicate between these two opposed perceptions of the nature of human aggression, merely to accept that Grotjahn's confident dogmatism is totally unjustified. Likewise, when we enjoy jokes that play with the forbidden or break rules, guilt may or may not come into it. Many of those who told political jokes in Eastern Europe under socialism had no sense of loyalty to the regime; joke telling involved playing with aggression in relation to an alien authority that was imposed on the joke tellers and playing with the risk that they might incur official disapprove or worse. The telling of the jokes did not involve any kind of defiance of the joke teller's own conscience. This distinction is one that is blurred over in Freud's analysis of tendentious jokes which muddles together conscience and power and internal and external controls so as to create a useless concept so broad, so ambiguous, and so stretchable that it can not produce worthwhile testable propositions. To try to explain everything is to explain nothing.

The second problem with Grotjahn's proposition is that it again seeks to explain a social phenomenon in terms of the psychological properties of individuals. Grotjahn can not easily explain why, given that there is a pay-off for the individual from this kind of joking, it should be more accessible to and exploitable by the members of some groups than others.

For Grotjahn (1970: 137) the jokes are told by the "persecuted Jew who makes himself the butt of the joke (and) deflects his dangerous hostility away from the persecutors onto himself." Once again a comparative analysis reveals insuperable problems. First, there *are* many Jewish jokes about the enemies and persecutors of the Jews; such jokes are a key aspect of Jewish preeminence in joking and of the balanced and all-embracing Jewish sense of humor. The latter jokes play with aggression against outsiders and play with risk, especially in societies where hostility to the Jews is strong. These jokes are much more clearly a response to a persecuting society than the self-mocking ones, as can be shown by a comparison with the Scottish case where there was no serious persecution of the Scottish people and where jokes about Scots were far more common than jokes about non-Scots. Indeed, it is the flourishing of a very similar genre of self-mocking jokes about canny Scots in Scotland that provides the second and main objection to Grotjahn's thesis. The Scots were not persecuted and had no reason to deflect "dangerous hostility" away from their English neighbors, whom they were free to criticize and to dispute with over everyday political issues without fear of reprisals. The point is not that there was an absence of hostility and tension between the Scots and the English (this would be impossible, for all neighboring and intersecting peoples have conflicts of interest), but simply that the position of the Scots was quite unlike that of the Jews in Continental Europe, where the hatred and hostility of others was a fact of everyday life. Yet despite this difference the Scots developed a remarkably similar self-mocking humor with an emphasis on canny qualities. It is also worth noting that a self-mocking Jewish humor has continued to flourish in Britain and America despite the marked decline in anti-Semitism. Grotjahn's propositions are clearly wrong and once again the theory that the very existence of a specific aggregate set of jokes associated with a particular people can be explained by reference to conflict and hostility has been refuted.

In fairness to Grotjahn (see also Sahl 1976: 64), he does not himself depict Jewish humor as a pathological phenomenon and recognizes that it involves "not defeat or surrender but victory and greatness" (Grotjahn 1970: 137), but in that case why was it necessary for him to use the terminology of masochism at all? Rather the victory and greatness of Jewish jokes, like that of the Scottish jokes, together with other remarkable Jewish and Scottish achievements, are based on a respect for intellect and love of argument, which have been a part of the religious traditions of both peoples, qualities that are indigenous to them, not imposed upon them.

The absence of serious hostility towards the Scots on the part of outsiders has also made it easier to demonstrate that self-mocking jokes can be *used* as a form of self-promotion and self-gratulation. The quality of being canny is a sign of cleverness as well as a failing and so it lends itself to such a use of the joke. That is clearly how the jokes were seen by the compilers of the early Scottish jokebooks. This does not though explain why the jokes exist. Other peoples, who would no doubt like to indulge in self-promotion through jokes in the same way, have not been able to create sufficient jokes and humor about themselves with which to do so. Nor are we forced to accept that self-promotion any more than self-denigration is the predominant motive of the joke tellers. Individuals differ and we neither can nor should try to understand what is distinctive about a nation's cultural traditions by studying the motives of those who seek to promote it.

Furthermore, the very ambiguity of humor means that a joke text used for self-promotion or for Grotjahn's deflection of hostility is always subsequently available to anyone who might wish to use it as a means of hostile denigration. Just as we can not read aggression into a text, so, too, we can not read in benign qualities. It is futile to object to someone else's successful use of a joke to produce laughter in an utterly contrary spirit by claiming "that's not what it really means." If the text works *as a joke* then it has meaning for those using it and they can read into it any implications they like. A particular Scot might well tell a joke about a canny Scotsman in order to promote the Scots and yet find it has had the opposite effect, or tell a joke in order to extol Scotland's canny virtues and yet find that these are despised, or tell a joke in order to ridicule those who really think that the Scots are canny, only to find that those listening see it as confirming their belief in the truth of Scottish canniness. Even if a joke teller is so skilled in his or her presentation of the joke as to exclude these possibilities, once the joke has gone into circulation he or she has no control over its future use. In practice the joke will generally be repeated merely as a joke, that is, as a form of humorous not serious communication, but it does undermine the idea that a successful self-mocking joke always retains the sentiments of its originators. Jokes do not have fixed tendencies.

It is for this reason that the author's attempt (Davies 1986: 75-96) to devise a set of rules for distinguishing between Jewish jokes and anti-Semitic jokes failed since he was unable to prove (see the criticisms made by Telushkin 1992: 198-9) that the anti-Semitic jokes were not of Jewish origin and he later (Davies 1990:121-2) came to the conclusion that no such distinction can be made without reference to the context and tone of the jokes. Indeed, one of Rabbi Joseph Telushkin's chapter headings in *Jewish Humor* (1992) is "So How Do You Make a Hurricane? The Jew in Business, or Jokes that Would Give an Anti-Semite *Nakhas*." It is a point that has been well discussed by Bernard Saper (1993: 84-5) who rightly concludes that Jewish humor should be valued and retained even "if bigots and haters use Jewish humor in order to defame Jews intentionally or unintentionally." Even so Saper had to argue his case in detail; Grotjahn's "victory" is not as easily won as he thinks. It is easy to demonstrate Jewish "ownership" of Jewish jokes but ownership does not guarantee control.

Entire genres of Jewish jokes such as those about Jewish store-keepers who burn down their shops to obtain the insurance money (Geiger 1923) can just as easily be told as "brutal comic stories" by "foreigners" (Freud 1960 [1905]: 111) without even changing the words. Nor can a simple distinction be made between these jokes, as told by Jews and as told by non-Jews, since we cannot crudely as-sume that we know the subjective orientation of individuals simply by knowing to which category those individuals belong. Such an assertion is essentially racist in character and demonstrably false. Jewish jokes about arson can circulate among Jews and non-Jews alike as a form of playing with aggression that is innocent of real aggression. Nonetheless, it is easy to see how and why the arson jokes would be enjoyed by those who perceive them as congruent with their own hostile, ideological perceptions of the Jews (Davies 1986). Once a joke exists people may do what they like with it but that does not explain why it exists.

It is not, though, a cause for great concern, since there is no evi-dence that Jewish jokes, however used, make any significant contri-bution to the kind of anti-Semitism that has led in the past to perse-cution, violence, and genocide. Jokes can have no significant politi-cal impact because there are so many other far more powerful mate-rial and ideological forces shaping the world. Yet such absurd views are held in elevated places, as we can see from the reverberating comments of Umberto Eco in favor of the censoring of jokes (see Draitser 1998: 160). Like a fantasy from his own fiction, Eco says:

> ...jokes of that sort in the end are paving the way for prejudices.... Even if there is a difference between comic racism which evokes a smile and fanatical racism which leads to slaughter, quite often they are interconnected; centuries of satirical depiction of Haims and Izzis preceded Hitler's anti-Semitism. (Eco cited by Draitser 1998: 160)

Shoe repairers! Given that jokes satirically depicting Haims and Izzis are as shown in chapter 3 particularly likely to be of Jewish origin, Eco's argument seems to suggest that Jewish humor, presumably after its annexation by others, has contributed significantly to the growth and savagery of anti-Semitism as indicated by his reference to Hitler. Yet if the question is turned the other way round and a panel of experts were asked to list the main historic causes of anti-Semitism in a rough rank order, humorous tales about Haims and Izzis would not even make the list. The front runners would be (a) the many centuries long (unlike the relatively recent jokes about Haim and Izzi) demonization of the Jews by Christians and especially by the Orthodox, Roman Catholic, and Lutheran churches and their members, (b) the organized politics of envy (Schoeck 1969: 334) directed against trading minorities and employed not only against the Jews but also against the Armenians (Toynbee 1915), East African Asians and overseas Chinese (Davies 1972) who have also suffered serious persecution, and (c) the emergence of ideologically based all powerful states, organized and stratified by party, notably Nazi Germany whose central ideological tenet was the contrast between a master race of Aryan soldiers and state-builders on the one hand and dangerous and subversive Jewish parasites on the other. The frenzy of anti-Semitism was *not* built on imaginative jokes about Haim and Izzi, but on a quite different kind of irrational fantasy—on beliefs in Jews poisoning wells, drinking the blood of Christian children murdered for this purpose, desecrating the Host (Dundes 1991), taking part in the international conspiracy of the learned elders of Zion, causing the First World War and seeking world domination by simultaneously controlling capitalism and communism, and on the perception of the Jews as wreckers, rootless cosmopolitans and Zionist traitors. Jokes about Haim and Izzi do not come into it. Chuck it, Eco! Scholars may differ about the details of the causes of anti-Semitic persecution but all would emphasize religious and political ideologies, economic factors and the question of who has control over the use of force.[1] Men and women will die for an ideology and will kill when driven by ideology and backed by force. Who is going to kill for a joke? Eco's ideas about "inter-connection" and of jokes "preceding" Hitler reveal a serious inability on his part to understand the workings of either history or society.

The very terms and phrases used to assert the consequences of jokes, such as "inter-connections," "reproducing the social order," "perpetuating stereotypes under relaxed conditions," indicate an inability to ask the question "how much?" In consequence massive and important factors are lumped together with trivial ones. Jokes may have had a *tiny* net effect in promoting or in retarding anti-Semitism, depending on where the balance lay between the humanizing impact of Jewish jokes and self-mockery so disliked by anti-Semites (Crosland 1922: 18; Hitler 1974: 287) and the use of jokes in a brutal way by the Jews' enemies, but it would have been far too small to detect or to be concerned about in a world driven by other more powerful forces.

The same question may be posed in relation to the spectacular collapse of the Soviet empire at the end of the 1980s. The collapse had been preceded by decades of the telling of enormously popular and savagely mocking political jokes aimed not just at the individual politicians and their supporters but at the basic institutions of the society and its Marxist-Leninist ideology and sacred icons, including Lenin himself. Yet these jokes are never cited by specialists in the study of the downfall of the Soviet empire as a significant cause of the collapse of a previously powerful regime. It is just as plausible to argue that the jokes were a safety valve and a substitute for political action that delayed the eventual collapse as to see them as a morale booster for an alienated population and a covert means of expressing criticism that undermined the social and political order. It does not matter which it was, for either way the effect would have been miniscule compared with the impact of the inevitable and predictable economic failure of socialism (Hoff 1949; von Mises 1974), nationalist resentments of Russian dominance, and the costs and difficulties of maintaining a coercive system that could no longer be kept isolated from the free societies outside. From the text of the jokes we can infer that the populace had an insightful, even prophetic knowledge of these problems (Davies 1988; 1998: 85-100) but *not* that each joke was a tiny revolution with an aggregate effect rather than a series of tiny substitutes for the planning of a real revolution. The jokes flourished throughout Eastern Europe regardless of the presence or absence of organized political resistance to the *anciens régimes*. They were a way of playing with aggression, not the effective deployment of wit as a weapon. They were even popular with supporters of the regime and those in positions of privilege and influence with a stake in the system (Deriaben and Gibney 1960: 38, 61, 141, 175, 220, 227), for the latter also enjoyed playing with the forbidden and taking time off and time out from the serious political world. The jokes were as usual a thermometer but not a thermostat, a way of gaining insight into the workings of socialist society but not a cause of its demise. The jokes had no effect but then neither did the banning of such political jokes from the media and public occasions have any effect either. The jokes flourished underground among a fearful but in no sense guilt-stricken population.

The tangled way in which social life is constructed means that it is always possible for the amateur to discover "inter-connections" between jokes and conflicts. A leading Belgian academic has assured me that Dutch jokes about stupid Belgians are a product of their resentment of Belgium's secession from the Netherlands in 1830, even though all independent evidence indicates that the Belgian people are viewed favorably by the Dutch who tell jokes about them (Kuipers 2000:163). It is a sad indication of how widely diffused the false theories of humor and aggression are that such an explanation should be entertained. Yet it is the case that the relationship of center and periphery *can* become one of conflict. The contemporary world is full of violent attempts to secede being met by strong repression from the center (as in the Basque country, Biafra, Chechnya, Corsica, Croatia, Eritrea, Jaffna, Kurdistan, Nagaland, Southern Sudan, Tibet, Western Sahara, etc.). Sometimes the seceders and would-be seceders have been the butt of stupidity jokes, more often not. Likewise, the other main social bases of ethnic stupidity jokes, namely class differences and urban/rural contrasts, have led to conflicts, revolutions and the murder of about a hundred million innocent people because of their class origins, ancestry and even level of knowledge (Courtois et al 1999). Yet the blame must lie with those who have been motivated by Marxist-Leninist ideology to use political power to exploit these universal social divisions and deliberately to perpetrate mass murder. It would be quite possible for someone obsessed with the idea that humor expresses real aggression to spell out an entire ecology of stupidity jokes connecting them with these political murderers, but it would be pointless to make such an attempt.

No doubt though someone will try to do so. Within the field of humor scholarship and, indeed, more widely in the humanities and

social sciences there is always a temptation to make one's special-
ism appear far more important than it really is, in order to attract
attention, raise one's status or to help to obtain substantial grants
from those with the power to award them. It *is* important to study
jokes and humor because they employ so much of our time and are
a source of enjoyment and they need both to be explained and used
as a source of insight into other social phenomena, but, fortunately,
the study of humor is not going to provide its sponsors with any new
method either of controlling people or of upsetting the social order.
Jokes matter but *only* as a laughing matter.

The remoteness of the "inter-connection" between stupidity jokes
and political conflict was indicated in chapter 2 in the discussion of
the hate mail and random hate phone calls (Patey 1990) received by
Newfoundlanders from animal activists over the seal hunting controversy (Coish 1979) in which they were called stupid and primitive by their enemies. There was no direct connection between the
Canadian jokes about stupid Newfies and this outburst of viciousness
from people living outside Canada who would not have been aware
of the jokes anyway. Rather both the stupidity jokes and the use of
stupidity as a term of abuse stem *independently* from the geographical and economic position of Newfoundland as a remote peripheral
area in which old activities such as hunting still flourish. The jokes
were and are a harmless (and locally accepted) form of playing with
aggression. The hate messages were quite separate: an expression of
real aggression that achieved its intended effect of hurting the feelings
of and frightening the individual Newfoundlanders who had been targeted and who, with reason, feared that they might be the victims of
lethal violence from animal rights activists. It was ideology not jokes
that provided an opportunity for guilt-free aggression by those with
hard-boiled super-egos. The Newfoundlanders had no reason to fear
the jokers, but idealists can kill. It is quite possible that animal rights
terrorists do laugh and joke as they prepare bombs or send out lethal
parcels or put on their black balaclava helmets but that is irrelevant
to any explanation of their activities.

The main purpose of this study has been to present particular sub-
stantive findings in a coherent way, findings obtained using a particular set of methods. It has to be hoped that other scholars can use
the methods on other data to generate and to test other hypotheses
as to why particular aggregate patterns of jokes exist. In the process

substantial doubt has also been cast on the way in which notions of hostility, aggression, and superiority have been used in the past to explain and analyze jokes.

If there is a further general moral to be drawn, it might well be "only disconnect." Much of the muddle in humor research has arisen because scholars fail to respect boundaries and categories in their thinking. They have confused the serious and the humorous, the levels of analysis appropriate to individuals and to society, texts and facts and the political and the social. There is no reason why one should not consciously move between categories and cross boundaries, but it must be done in a self-aware way, recognizing that this is a phase-change, not by sliding thoughtlessly between them. Likewise, the object of one's study may well not always fit neatly into one category or another, or may move between them but this is a phenomena to be noted in its own right, not one that should be allowed to blur the categories of one's own thinking. The world may be confusing, but that is no excuse for thinking about it in a confused way.

Jokes are ambiguous, do not have clear meanings, break empirical and logical rules and have multiple uses. They are a form of play. Explanations of why patterns of jokes exist by contrast must be serious. They can be playful in style but the core of the argument must as far as is possible be clear and unambiguous and obey the logical and empirical rules that apply to other kinds of explanation (Davies 1998B). All too often humor scholars treat jokes as if they can be reduced to clear, serious objective statements with simple single meanings, and then analyze them in a way that is ambiguous, obscure, untestable and subjective—in a word a joke. It is necessary to keep the serious and the humorous apart not only to achieve any kind of understanding of jokes but also to preserve the integrity of our explanation of jokes. Jokes are based on conventional, fictional, and mythological scripts (Raskin 1985: 55, 100). Explanations should never be. Jokes belong to their own sub-universe, a sub-universe of humor set quite apart from the usual pragmatic world of everyday life and one which has its own province of meaning (Schutz 1962: 207-8, 232, 236). We have to cross the boundary into that world in order to understand humor and while we reside there to clear our minds of cant and fill them with Kant (1951: 37-8), for humor exists in a domain of its own and one which has its own province of meaning. But in order to explain jokes in social and historical terms it is necessary to leave this attractive world of playing with aggression, risk, rules and meanings of all kinds and to return to reality.

Each joke is an ambiguous text that can be both self-promoting and self-mocking, both destructive and sympathetic, both proclaiming and undermining all at the same time, and without further information we cannot know which it is and even when we hear it in context we cannot be sure. Explanations live in the world of facts in which this kind of dialectic is not possible. A and not A can only be true simultaneously in the world of jokes , not in the world of normal explanations.

Jokes are invented and told by individuals. They are usually easy to understand, require skill to tell and are difficult to invent, though the inventing is largely shared as one person produces a proto-joke in the form of a witty comment or a humorous anecdote which is then shaped into a joke as it is relayed from one person to another. It is a game played for enjoyment. Yet observing the game does not help to explain why particular sets of jokes exist and others do not. Rather, we must seek explanations by looking to the social, political, and economic structures within which the jokes emerge, structures on which jokes can have only a negligible impact. Such explanations can *only* be obtained through comparative and historical studies and that has been the task of this book.

Note

1.   The authorities consulted include Arendt 1946; Baron 1946; Bayor 1975; Birnbaum 1992; Carmichael 1993; Cohn 1970; Courtois 1999; Dundes 1991 and 1997; Eban 1976; Friedländer 1976; Goldhagen 1996; Gurian 1946; Holmes 1979; Horowitz 1977; Litvinoff 1974; Mahler 1946; Pinson 1946; Podhoretz 1986; Reitlinger 1967; Robb 1954; Scharf 1996; Vaksberg 1994.

General Bibliography

Archive Material: List of Archives

A.C.E.A. = Archive, Centre d'Études Acadiennes, Université de Moncton
A.U.L. = Archive Université Laval
B.B.C WA C .= B.B.C. Written Archives, Caversham
B.Y.U.F.A. = Brigham Young University Folklore Archive
C.C.N.S. = Collection of the Center for Newfoundland Studies, Memorial University of Newfoundland
FIFE = Fife Folklore Archive, Utah State University, Logan
F.A.Y.O. = Folklore Archive York University, Canada
M.U.N.F.L.A. = Memorial University of Newfoundland Folklore Archive
S.F.G.B. = Scottish File House of Humor and Laughter, Gabrovo Bulgaria
U.C.B.F.A. = University of California, Berkeley Folklore Archive

C.C.N.S. Archive Material

C.C.N.S. = Collection of the Center for Newfoundland Studies, Memorial University of Newfoundland includes:
Mercer, Paul. n.d. "The Newfoundland Joke." Newfoundland School Broadcasts.
Miller, Elizabeth. 1982. "Ted Russell, Newfoundland's Contribution to the World of Humor." Paper presented to the International Conference on Humor at Arizona State University, April 1982.
The Record. 1957. Magazine of Bishop Abraham Memorial School and Saint Peter's School, Upper Island Cove.

Unpublished Theses and Dissertations

Katz, Michael. 1979. "The Study of Ethnic Jokes." Diss., Institute of Folklore, University of Indiana, Bloomington.
Kimmel, Tom. 1977. "An Analysis of the Black Joke." Diss., Institute of Folklore, University of Indiana, Bloomington.
Roth, Julia Ann. 1970. The Multi-Nationality Joke, a Study of Blason Populaire. M.A. thesis, University of California, Berkeley.

Published Sources

Aberdeen and Temair, Marquess of. 1929. *Jokes Cracked by Lord Aberdeen*. Dundee, Scotland, Valentine.

Adams, Phillip, and Patrice Newell. 1994. *The Penguin Book of Australian Jokes*. Ringwood Victoria, Penguin.

af Klintberg, Bengt. 1983. "Negervitsar." *Tradisjon*, Vol. 13, pp. 23-45.

After Dinner Scraps Number 2. 1924. Bloomfield Iowa, Bloomfield.

Aitchison, J., and T. Chan. 1995. *Revenge of the Sarong Party Girl*. Singapore, Angsana.

Aitchison, J., and T. Chan. 1996. *The SPG Rides Again*. Singapore, Angsana.

Aitkin, John. n.d. *The Humors of Ayrshire; or Travels with a Bookstall*. Kilmarnock, D. Brown.

Allard, Louis-Paul. 1976. *Le Coin du Newfie*, Vol. I. Montréal, Héritage.

———. 1978. *Le Coin du Newfie, No 2*. Montréal, Héritage.

Allen, Irving Lewis. 1983. *The Language of Ethnic Conflict: Social Organisation and Lexical Culture*. New York, Columbia University Press.

Allen, John. 1984. *The Humour of Barry Humphries*. Sydney, Currency.

Alperin, Mimi. 1988. "Jap Jokes, Hateful Humor." *Humor: International Journal of Humor Research* 2(4): 412-416.

Andreski, Stanislav Leonard. 1973. *The Prospect of a Revolution in the USA*. London, Tom Stacey.

Arendt, Hannah. 1946. "From the Dreyfus Affair to France Today" in Koppel S. Pinson (ed.), *Essays on Anti-Semitism*. New York, Conference on Jewish Relations.

Aristotle. *The Poetics* (trans. Margoliouth D.S., 1911). London, Hodder and Stoughton.

Ausubel, Nathan. 1951. *A Treasury of Jewish Humor*. Garden City, Doubleday & Co.

Baechler, Jean. 1979. *Suicides*. Oxford, Basil Blackwell.

Bales, Robert. 1962. "Attitudes towards Drinking in the Irish Culture." pp. 157-187 in David J. Pittman and Charles R. Snyder (eds.), *Society, Culture and Drinking Patterns*. New York, John Wiley & Sons.

Barkas, Janet. 1975. *The Vegetable Passion*. London, Routledge Kegan Paul.

Baron, Salo W. 1946. Foreword in Koppel S. Pinson (ed.), *Essays on Anti-Semitism*.

Barr, Ann, and Peter York. 1982. *The Official Sloane Ranger Handbook*. London, Ebury.

Barron, John, and Paul Anthony. 1977. *Murder of a Gentle Land, the Untold Story of Communist Genocide in Cambodia*. New York, Readers' Digest.

Bartley, John Oliver. 1954. *Teague, Shenkin and Sawney*. Cork, Cork University Press.

Bason, Lilian. 1977. *Those Foolish Molboes*. New York, Coward, McCann and Geoghegan.

Bates, David. 1989. William the Conqueror. London, George Philip.

Baxter, Stanley. 1985. *Suburban Shocker*. Leith, Waterfront.

Bayor, Ronald H. 1978. *Neighbors in Conflict. The Irish, Germans, Jews and Italians of New York City 1919-41*. Baltimore, MD, Johns Hopkins University Press.

Beattie, James. 1778. *Essays on Poetry and Music as They Effect the Mind; On Laughter, and Ludicrous Composition; On the Utility of Classical Learning*. Edinburgh, W. Creech.

Bell, Daniel. 1979. *The Cultural Contradictions of Capitalism*. London, Heinemann.

Bell, John Joy. 1929. *Hoots*. Dundee, Scotland, Valentine.

Ben Amos, Dan. 1973. "The Myth of Jewish Humor." *Western Folklore* 32(2): 112-131.

Berger, Arthur Asa. 1993. *An Anatomy of Humor*. New Brunswick, NJ, Transaction Publishers.

Berger, Peter L. 1997. *Redeeming Laughter, The Comic Dimension of Human Experience* Berlin, Walter de Gruyter.

Bergson, Henri. 1911. *Laughter, An Essay on the Meaning of the Comic*. London, Macmillan.

Bermant, Chaim. 1986. *What's the Joke? A Study of Jewish Humour Through the Ages.* London, Weidenfeld and Nicholson.

Besley, Rupert. 1990. *Scotland for Beginners.* Glasgow, Neil Wilson.

Bethel, Nicholas. 1976. *The War Hitler Won.* London, Futura.

Bible, The (King James Authorized Version, 1611).

Bier, Jesse. 1988. "The Problem of the Polish Joke in Derogatory American Humor." *Humor, International Journal of Humor Research* 1-2: 135-141.

Birnbaum, Pierre. 1992. *Anti-Semitism in France.* Oxford, Blackwell.

Blackman, J. 1991. *Don't Come the Raw Prawn the Aussie Phrase Book.* Sydney, Sun.

Blanchard, Claude. 1986. *Les Histoires Drôles de Claude Blanchard.* Montréal, Editions de l'Époque.

Blue, Lionel 1985, *Rabbi Lionel Blue's Thoughts for the Day.* London, BBC.

_____. 1986. *Bolts from the Blue.* London, Hodder and Stoughton.

Blyth, R. H. 1959. *Oriental Humor.* Tokyo, Hokuseido.

_____. 1963 *Japanese Humor.* Tokyo, Japan Travel Bureau.

Bodnar, John. 1976. "Immigration and Modernization, the Case of Slavic Peasants in Industrial America." *Journal of Social History* Vol. 10, No 1, Fall: 44-72.

Bowles, Colin. 1984. *The Wit's Dictionary.* Sydney, Angus and Robertson.

_____. 1986. *G'Day! Teach Yourself Australian.* North Ryde, New South Wales, Angus and Robertson.

Bramieri, Gino. 1980. *Il Grande Libro delle barzellette.* Milan, De Vecchi.

Brandon, Ruth, and Christie Davies. 1975. *Wrongful Imprisonment: Mistaken Imprisonment and Its Consequences.* London, Allen and Unwin.

Brewer, Daniel Chauncey. 1926. *The Conquest of New England by the Immigrant.* New York, G. P. Putnam's Sons.

Brill, A. A. 1935. Introduction, in S. Felix Mendelsohn, *The Jew Laughs, Humorous Stories and Anecdotes.* Chicago, L. M. Stein.

Brissenden, R. F. 1981. Introduction, in Barry Humphries, *A Nice Night's Entertainment.* Sydney, Currency.

Bukowczyk, John J. 1987. *And My Children Did Not Know Me: A History of Polish-Americans.* Bloomington, Indiana University Press.

Buksbazen, Victor. 1984. *The Gospel in the Feasts of Israel.* Fort Washington, Christian Literature Crusade.

Burke, Joseph Chesley. 1981. *A Treasury of Newfoundland Humour and Wit.* Halifax Nova Scotia, Kingfisher.

Burns, Stan, and Mel Weinstein. 1978. *The Book of Jewish World Records.* Los Angeles, Pinnacle.

Button Busters, Jolly Jokes No. 49. 1915. Baltimore, MD, L. and M. Ottenheim.

Buzo, Alex. 1994. *Kiwese.* Port Melbourne, Mandarin.

Cagney, Peter. 1979. *The Official Aussie Joke Book.* London, Futura.

Canuck, Jack (pseud.). 1967. *Dictionary of Canadianisms.* Toronto, W. J. Gage.

Carmichael, Joel. 1992. *The Satanizing of the Jews.* New York, Fromm.

Carswell, Donald. 1927. *Brother Scots,* London, Constable.

Chadwick, St. John. 1967. *Newfoundland, Island into Province.* London, Cambridge University Press.

Chanfrault, Bernard. 1992. The Stereotypes of Deep France in the *Almanac Vermot, Humor, International Journal of Humor Research,* 7-31.

Charteris, A. H. 1932. *When the Scot Smiles.* London, Maclehose.

Chetkin, Len. 1985. *Guess Who's Jewish?* Norfolk/Virginia Beach, VA, Donning.

Chia, Corinne, K. K. Seet, and Pat M. Wong. 1985. *Made in Singapore.* Singapore, Times Books International.

Clements, William M. 1973. "The Types of the Polish Joke." *Folklore Forum*, Bibliographic and Special Series 3.

Climent-Galant, Jackie. 1979. *Les Meillures de Lui*. Paris, Filipacchi.

Cohn, Norman. 1970. *Warrant for Genocide, the Myth of the Jewish World Conspiracy and the Protocols of the Elders of Zion*. Harmondsworth, Penguin.

Cohn-Sherbok, Dan and Lavinia. 1995. *The American Jew, Voices from an American Jewish Community*. Grand Rapids, MI, Eerdmans.

Coish, Calvin E. 1979. *Season of the Seal*. St. John's Newfoundland, Breakwater.

Coleman, Peter. 1991. *The Real Barry Humphries*. London, Coronet.

Conway, Ronald. 1974. *The Great Australian Stupor, An Interpretation of the Australian Way of Life*. Melbourne, Sun.

Coser, Ruth L. 1959. "Some Social Functions of Laughter: A Study of Humor in a Hospital Setting." *Human Relations*, Vol. 12, pp. 171-82.

Courtois, Stéphane, Nicholas Werth, Jean-Louis Panné, Andrzej Paczkowski, Karel Bartosek, Jean-Louis Margolin. 1999. *The Black Book of Communism, Crimes, Terror Repression*. Cambridge, MA, Harvard University Press.

Craigie, William Alexander. 1898. "Evald Tang Kristensen a Danish folklorist." *Folklore*, Vol. 9, No. 3, p.220.

Crooked Mick of the Speewa (pseud. Richard Beckett). 1986. *The Dinkum Aussie Dictionary*. French's Forest, New South Wales, Australia.

Crosland, Thomas William Hodgson. 1922. *The Fine Old Hebrew Gentleman*. London, T. Werner.

Crowl, Philip A. 1986. *The Intelligent Travellers' Guide to Historic Scotland*. London, Sidgewick and Jackson.

Daily Mail. 2000. "Car Firebomb Terror, Extremists Hit at Staff of Animal Test Centre." August 29: 25.

Davies, Christie. 1972. "Asians of East Africa." *Quest* 77, 33-9.

_____. 1982. "Ethnic Jokes, Moral Values and Social Boundaries." *British Journal of Sociology* 33, No. 3, 383-403.

_____. 1982A. "Sexual Taboos and Social Boundaries." *American Journal of Sociology* 87, No. 5, 1032-1063.

_____. 1985. "Ethnic Jokes and Social Change: The Case of the Welsh." *Immigrants and Minorities*, Vol. 4, No. 1 (March): 46-63.

_____. 1986. "Jewish Jokes, Hebredonian Jokes and Anti-Semitic Jokes," in Avner Ziv (ed.), *Jewish Humor*. Tel-Aviv, Papyrus/Tel-Aviv University.

_____. 1988, "Stupidity and Rationality: Jokes from the Iron Cage," in Chris Powell and George E. C. Paton (eds.), *Humour in Society, Resistance and Control*, London, Macmillan.

_____. 1988A. "The Irish Joke as a Social Phenomenon," in John Durrant and Jonathan Miller (eds.), *Laughing Matters, a Serious Look at Humour*. Harlow, Longman.

_____. 1989. "Humor for the Future and a Future for Humor," in Alexander Shtromas and Morton Kaplan (eds.), *The Soviet Union and the Challenge of the Future*, Vol. 3 *Ideology, Culture and Nationalism*. New York, Paragon.

_____. 1990. *Ethnic Humor Around the World: A Comparative Analysis*. Bloomington, Indiana University Press.

_____. 1990A. "Nasty Legends, 'Sick' Humour and Ethnic Jokes about Stupidity," in Gillian Bennett and Paul Smith (eds.), *A Nest of Vipers*. Sheffield, Sheffield Academic Press.

_____. 1991. Fooltowns: Traditional and Modern, Local Regional and Ethnic Jokes about Stupidity," in Gillian Bennett (ed.), *Spoken in Jest*. Folklore Society Mistletoe Series 21, Sheffield, Sheffield Academic Press.

_____. 1992. "Religion, Identity and the Enforcement of Morality," in Bryan R. Wilson (ed.) *Religion: Contemporary Issues*. London, Bellew.

_____. 1992A. "The Protestant Ethic and the Comic Spirit of Capitalism." *British Journal of Sociology*, Vol. 43, No. 3, (September): 421-432.

_____. 1992B. Review of Gloria Kaufman (ed.). "In Stitches." *Humor, the International Journal of Humor Research* 5, 4: 431-5.

_____. 1994. "Crime and the Rise and Decline of a Relational Society," in J. Burnside and N. Baker (eds.), *Relational Justice*. Winchester, Waterside.

_____. 1994A. "Does Religion Prevent Crime? The Long Term Inverse Relationship between Crime and Religion in Britain." *Informationes Theologiae Europae*, pp 76-93.

_____. 1995. "Denying Dirt, Decay and Death in Britain and America," in Glennys Howarth and Peter Jupp (eds.), *Contemporary Issues in the Sociology of Death, Dying and Disposal*. Basingstoke, Macmillan.

_____. 1998. *Jokes and Their Relation to Society*. Berlin and New York, Mouton de Gruyter.

_____. 1998A. "The Dog That Didn't Bark in the Night: A New Sociological Approach to the Cross Cultural Study of Humor," in Willibald Ruch (ed.), *The Sense of Humor*. Berlin and New York, Mouton de Gruyter.

_____. 1999. "Jokes on the Death of Diana," in Tony Walter (ed.), *The Mourning for Diana*. Oxford, Berg.

_____. 1999A. "Change and Continuity in One of Europe's Oldest Ethnic Scripts." *Humor: The International Journal of Humor Research* 12-1: 1-32.

_____. 1999B. "The Fragmentation of the Religious Tradition of the Creation, After-life and Morality: Modernity not Post-Modernity." *Journal of Contemporary Religion* 12, 1: 1-32.

_____. 2000. "Brave New Olympics." *Spectator*, September 14:5.

Davies, Christie, and Mark Neal. 2000. "Durkheim's Altruistic and Fatalistic Suicide," in W. S. F. Pickering and Geoffrey Walford (eds.), *Durkheim's Suicide: A Century of Research and Debate*. London, Routledge.

Davis, Hyram, and Peter Crofts. 1988. "Humor in Australia," in Avner Ziv (ed.).

Davis, A. F., and S. Encel (eds.). 1965. *Australian Society*. London, Pall Mall.

Debate. 1997. "Humor and Political Correctness." *Humor, the International Journal of Humor Research* 10-4: 453-513.

De Colleville, Vicomte, and de Zepelin, Fritz. 1896. *Contes grotesques du Danemark*, Paris, Chamuel.

Deriaben, Peter, and Frank Gibney. 1960. *The Secret War*. London, Arthur Baker.

DesRuisseaux, Pierre. 1973. *Croyances et Pratiques Populaires au Canada Francais*. Montréal, Editions du Jour.

_____. 1979. *Le Livre des Expressions Québecoises*. Ville LaSalle, Quebec, Hurtubise.

de Witt, Hugh. 1970. *Bawdy Barrack-Room Ballads*. London, Universal.

Dhavan, Rajeev, and Christie Davies. 1978. *Censorship and Obscenity*. London, Martin Robertson.

Dicks, Kathie. 1994. "Bologna or Bologney? Maple Leaf Big Stick a Delicious Alternative." *The Newfoundland Herald*, August 27: 2.

Dictionary of National Biography. 1897. Vol. XLIX (ed. Sidney Lee). London, Smith Elder.

Diesendruck, Z. 1946. "Anti-Semitism and Ourselves," in Koppel S. Pinson (ed.), *Essays on Anti-Semitism*. New York, Conference on Jewish Relations.

Dolot, Miron. 1985. *Execution by Hunger*. New York, W.W. Norton & Co.

Douglas, Mary. 1970. *Natural Symbols*. London, Barrie and Rockliff.

Douglas, David C. 1964. *William the Conqueror, the Norman Impact upon England*. London, Eyre and Spottiswode.

Downey, James. 1986. *The Great Canadian Joke: Towards a Sociology of Ethnic Joke-Telling in Canada.* [1986 John Porter Memorial Lecture]. Ottawa, Carleton University.

Doyle, David Noel, and Owen Dudley Edwards (eds.). 1980. *America and Ireland 1776-1976, The American Identity and the Irish Connection.* Westport, CT, Greenwood.

Draitser, Emil. 1994. "Sociological Aspects of the Russian Jewish Jokes of the Exodus." *Humor, International Journal of Humor Research* 7-3: 245-267.

_____. 1998. *Taking Penguins to the Movies Ethnic Humor in Russia.* Detroit, Wayne State University Press.

Dundes, Alan. 1971. "A Study of Ethnic Slurs: The Jew and the Polack in the United States." *Journal of American Folklore* 84(332): 186-203.

_____. 1975. "Slurs International: Folk Comparisons of Ethnicity and National Character." *Southern Folklore Quarterly*, Vol. 39, pp. 15-38.

_____. 1979. "Polish Pope Jokes." *Journal of American Folklore*, Vol. 92, pp. 219-222.

_____. 1984. *Life is Like a Chicken Coop Ladder, A Portrait of German Culture through Folklore.* New York, Columbia University Press.

_____. 1987. *Cracking Jokes: Studies of Sick Humor Cycles and Stereotypes.* Berkeley, CA, Ten Speed Press.

_____ (ed). 1991. *The Blood Libel Legend, A Casebook of Anti-Semitic Folklore.* Madison, University of Wisconsin Press.

_____. 1997. *From Game to War.* Lexington, University Press of Kentucky.

_____. 1997A. *Two Tales of Crow and Sparrow.* Oxford, Rowman and Littlefield.

_____. 1999. *Holy Writ as Oral Lit, The Bible as Folklore.* Lanham, Rowman and Littlefield.

Dunne, Finley Peter. 1942. *Mr. Dooley at His Best.* New York, Charles Scribner's Sons.

_____. 1963 (first pub. 1898-1906). *Mr. Dooley on Ivrything and Ivrybody.* New York, Dover.

Dupont, Jean-Claude, and Jacques Mathieu. 1986. *Héritage de la Francophonie Canadienne: Traditions Orales.* Sainte-Foy, Quebec, Presses de l'Université Laval.

Durkheim, Emile. 1970. *Suicide: A Study in Sociology.* London, Routledge Kegan Paul.

Earle, George H. 1987. *Old Foolishness or Folklore.* St. John's, Newfoundland, Harry Cuff.

Eban, Abba. 1976. "Israel, Anti-Semitism and the United Nations." *The Jerusalem Quarterly*, No. 1, Fall: 110-120.

Eco, Umberto. 1983. *The Name of the Rose.* New York, Harcourt Brace Jovanovich.

Elias, Norbet. 1982. *The Civilizing Process.* Oxford, Basil Blackwell.

Eliezer, Ben. 1984. *The World's Best Jewish Jokes.* North Ryde, Australia, Angus and Robertson.

Ellis, Bill. 2001. A Model for Collecting and Interpreting World Trade Center Disaster Jokes, *New Directions in Folklore*, http://www.temple.edu/isllc/newfolk/wtchumor.html, 5 October: 1-12.

England, George Allan. 1969 (1924). *The Greatest Hunt in the World.* Montreal, Tundra.

Eysenck, H. J. 1985. *Decline and Fall of the Freudian Empire.* Harmondsworth, Viking.

Fahey, M. G. 1993. *Jokes from the Rock.* Scarborough Ontario, M. G. Fahey.

Fanning, Charles. 1980. "Mr. Dooley in Chicago: Finley, Peter Dunne as Historian of the Irish in America," in David Noel Doyle and Owen Dudley Edwards (eds.), *America and Ireland 1776-1976, the American Identity and the Irish Connection.* Westport, CT, Greenwood.

Fasti Ecclesiae Scoticana. 1928. Vol. 2 (ed. W. S. Crockett and Francis Grant). Edinburgh, Oliver and Boyd.

Feinburg, Leonard. 1978. *The Secret of Humor.* Amsterdam, Rodopi.

Feldman, David M. 1974. *Marital Relations, Birth Control and Abortion in Jewish Law.* New York, Schocken.

Ferguson, Euan. 2001. "Yes, I Have Heard the One About...A Long Time Ago." *The Guardian*, 20 October, http://www.observer.co.uk.

Ferguson, James. 1933. *The Table in a Roar*. London, Methuen.

Fieldhouse, Paul. 1986. *Food, Nutrition, Customs and Culture*. London, Croom Helm.

Finnigan (Peter Stoney and Jim Flynn). 1981. *Newfie Jokes from the Scripts of Atlantic Canada's Top Musical Comedy Act*. Dartmouth Nova Scotia, Mackenzie.

Fish, Lydia. 1980. "Is the Pope Polish? Some Notes on the Polish Joke in Transition." *Journal of American Folklore* 93: 450-454.

Fisk, Robert. 1985. *In Time of War*. London, Paladin.

Fitzgibbon, Louis. 1971. *Katyn, A Crime without Parallel*. London, Tom Stacey.

Foggo, Daniel. 2000. "Neo-Nazis Join Animal Rights Group. *Sunday Telegraph* September 3: 5.

Ford, Robert. 1891. *Thistledown*. Paisley, Scotland, Alexander Gardner.

Ford, "Senator" Ed, Harry Hershfield, Joe Laurie, Jr. 1947. *Cream of the Crop*. New York, Grosset and Dunlap.

Fowkes, Edith. 1982. *Folktales of French Canada*. Toronto, N.C. Press.

Freud, Sigmund. 1960 (1905). *Jokes and Their Relation to the Unconscious* (Vol. 8 of *Complete Psychological Works*). London, Hogarth.

Friedländer, Saul. 1976. "The Historical Significance of the Holocaust." *The Jerusalem Quarterly*, No. 1 Fall: 36-59.

Frondorf, Shirley. 1990. *Death of a Jewish American Princess*. New York, Berkley.

Fuchs, Esther. 1986. Humor and Sexism the Case of the Jewish Joke pp. 111-122 in Ziv (ed).

Gaidoz, Henri, and Sébillot, Paul. 1884. *Blason populaire de la France*. Paris, Leopold Cerf.

Gans, Herbert. 1974. Introduction, in Neil C. Sandberg, *Ethnic Identity and Assimilation: The Polish-American Community, A Case Study of Metropolitan*. Los Angeles, New York, Praeger.

Garrett, Stephen A. 1996. *Conscience and Power*. New York, St. Martin's Press.

Geiger, Raymond. 1923. *Histoires Juives*. Paris, Nouvelle Revue Francaise.

_____. 1925. *Nouvelles Histoires Juives*. Paris, Gallimard.

Geikie, Sir Archibald. 1904. *Scottish Reminiscences*. Glasgow, James Maclehose.

Gesta Normannorum Ducum, of William of Jumièges, Orderic Vitalis and Robert of Norigni. Vol. 2 (edited by Elisabeth van Houts). Oxford, Clarendon.

Gillespie, John. 1904. *The Humours of Scottish Life*. Edinburgh, Blackwood,

Ginger, Ray. 1974. *Ray Ginger's Jokebook about American History*. New York, New Viewpoints.

Glad, Donald Davison. 1947. "Attitudes and Experiences of American-Jewish and American-Irish Male Youth as Related to Differences in Adult Rates of Inebriety." *Quarterly Journal of Studies on Alcohol*, Vol. 8, No. 3, December.

Glatt, M. M. 1973. "Alcoholism and Drug Dependence amongst Jews," in Ailan Shiloh and Ida Cohen Selavon (eds.), *Ethnic Groups of America, Their Morbidity, Morallity, and Behavior Disorders*, Vol. 1 *The Jews*. Springfield, IL, Charles Thomas.

Glazer, Nathan. 1960. "Social Characteristics of American Jews," in Louis Finkelstein (ed.), *The Jews, Their History, Culture and Religion*, Vol. 2. London, Peter Owen.

Glazer, Nathan, and Daniel P. Moynihan. (eds.). 1975. *Ethnicity, Theory and Experience*. Cambridge, MA, Harvard University Press.

Goebbels, Josef. 1948. *The Goebbels Diaries* (ed. and trans. Louis P. Lochner). London, Hamish Hamilton.

Goebbels, Josef. 1982. *The Goebbels Diaries 1939-41* (ed. Fred Taylor). London, Sphere.

Golden, Harry. 1965. Introduction, in Immanuel Olsvanger, *Röyte Pomerantsen*. New York, Schocken.

Goldhagen, Daniel Jonah. 1996. *Hitler's Willing Executioners*. London, Little Brown & Co.

Gould, Allen. 1992. *The Big Book of Canadian Humour*. Toronto, Macmillan.

Greeley, Andrew M. 1972. *The Denominational Society*. Glenview, IL, Scott Foresman.

Greenburg, Andrea. 1972. "The Ethnic Joke: Form and Function." *Keystone Folklore Quarterly* 17(4), Winter: 144-56.

Greenough, William Parker. 1897. *Canadian Folk-life and Folklore*. New York, George H. Richmond.

Grotjahn, Martin. 1970. "Jewish Jokes and Their Relation to Masochism," in Werner M. Mendel (ed.). *A Celebration of Laughter*. Los Angeles, Mara.

Gruner, Charles R. 1997. *The Game of Humor, A Comprehensive Theory of Why We Laugh*. New Brunswick, NJ, Transaction Publishers.

Guillois, Mina, and Guillois, André. 1979. *Les meilleures Histoires Ecossaises, Anglaises Irlandaises, Galloises*. Paris, Mengès.

Guinness, Michele. 1985. *Child of the Covenant*. London, Hodder and Stoughton.

Gurian, Waldeman. 1946. "Anti-Semitism in Modern Germany," in Koppel S. Pinson (ed.), *Essays on Anti-Semitism*. New York, Conference on Jewish Relations.

Hall, J. Mortimer. 1934. *Anecdota Americana Second Series*. Boston, Humphrey Adams.

Hallpike, C. R. 1976. "Is There a Primitive Mentality?" *Man*, Vol. II, No. 2: 253-270.

_____. 1979. *The Foundations of Primitive Thought*. Oxford, Clarendon.

Hamilton, Ian. 1990. *The Erosion of Calvinist Orthodoxy, Seceders and Subscription in Scottish Presbyterianism*. Edinburgh, Rutherford House.

Harris, David A., and Israil Rabinovich. 1986. *'On a Lighter Note?' Soviet Jewish Humor*. New York, American Jewish Committee.

_____. 1988. *The Jokes of Oppression. The Humor of Soviet Jews*. Northvale, NJ, Jason Aronson.

Harvey, William. 1904. *Irish Life and Humour*. Stirling, Scotland, Eneas Mackay.

Hašek Jaroslav. 1974 (1921-3). *The Good Soldier Švejk and His Fortunes in the World War* (trans. Sir Cecil Parrott). Harmondsworth, Penguin.

Hayman, Robert. 1628. *Quodlibets Lately Come over from New Britaniola, Old New-foundland*. London, Roger Michel.

Heffer, Simon. 2000. A Cricketing Legend Leaves the Field. *Sunday Telegraph*, January 23.

Helmreich, William B. 1982. *The Things They Say behind Your Back*. New York, Doubleday & Co.

Himmelfarb, Gertrude. 1995. *The De-Moralization of Society*. London, IEA Health and Welfare Unit.

Hiscock, Philip. 1990A. "No Joking Matter: Where Humor Reveals a Cruel Side." *Northumberland Signal*, February 18-24.

_____. 1990B. "Torbay 'Jokes' Evidence of Something Unfunny." *The Sunday Express*, Newfoundland, December 2: 37.

Hitler, Adolf. 1974. *Mein Kampf*. London: Hutchinson.

Hobbes, Thomas. 1840 (1650). Human Nature or the Fundamental Elements of Policie, in *The English Works of Thomas Hobbes* (1840). London, Bohn.

Hodes, Max. 1978. *The Official Scottish Joke Book*. London, Futura.

Hoff, Trygve, J. B. 1949 (1939). *Economic Calculation in the Socialist Society*. London, William Hodge.

Holbek, Bengt. 1975. "The Ethnic Joke in Denmark," in W. van Nespen (ed.), *Miscellanea Prof Em. Dr. K.C. Peeters, Door Vrienden en Collega hem aangeboden ter gelegenheid van zyn emeritaat*. Antwerp, Govaerts.

Holmes, Colin. 1979. *Anti-Semitism in British Society 1876-1939*. London, Edward Arnold.

Hope, A. D. 1979. "Full as a Boot," from *The Drifting Continent,* cited in Bill Wannan, *Great Aussie Insults.* Ringwood Australia, Penguin, 1995.

Horecký, Michal. 1985. *Humor do Vrecka alebo vtipy na každý den,* Košice, Vychodoslovenské Vydavatel'stvo.

Hornby, Peter. 1978. *The Official Irish Jokebook No. 3. No. 2 to follow.* London, Futura.

Horowitz, Irving Louis. 1977. *Genocide, State Power and Mass Murder.* New Brunswick, NJ, Transaction Publishers.

Houts, Elizabeth van (see *Gesta Normannorum*).

Howcraft, Wilbur G. 1977. *Black with White Cockatoos or Mopokes and Mallee Roots.* Melbourne, Hawthorn.

Hudson, Bob, and Larry Pickering. 1987. *The First Australian Dictionary of Vulgarities and Obscenities.* Newton Abbot, Devon, England David and Charles.

Humphries, Barry. 1981. *A Nice Night's Entertainment.* Sydney, Currency.

_____. 1993. *More Please.* Ringwood Australia, Penguin.

Humphries, Barry, and Nicholas Garland. 1968. *The Wonderful World of Barry McKenzie.* London, Macdonald.

_____. 1972. *Bazza Pulls It Off, More Adventures of Barry McKenzie.* London Private Eye/Andre Deutsch.

_____. 1988. *The Complete Barry McKenzie.* London, Methuen.

Ingrams, Richard. 1971. *The Life and Times of Private Eye* Harmondsworth Penguin.

Innes, Cosmo. 1874 (first edition 1858). "A Memoir of Dean Ramsay," in Dean Edward Bannerman Ramsay, *Reminiscences of Scottish Life and Character.* Edinburgh, Gall and Inglis, 22nd edition.

Instad, Helge. 1966. *Land Under the Pole Star.* London, Jonathan Cape.

Jackson, W. Turrentine. 1968. *The Enterprising Scot.* Edinburgh, Edinburgh University Press.

Jacobson, Howard. 1993. *Roots Schmoots, Journeys among Jews.* Harmondworth, Penguin.

Jagendorff, M. 1938. *Tyll Ulenspiegel's Merry Pranks.* New York, Vanguard.

_____. 1957. *Noodlehead Stories from Around the World.* New York, Vanguard.

Jellinek, E. M. 1962. "Cultural Differences in the Meaning of Alcoholism," in David J. Pittman and Charles R. Snyder (eds.), *Society, Culture and Drinking Patterns.* New York, John Wiley & Sons.

Jerdan, Charles. 1920. *Scottish Clerical Stories and Reminiscences.* Edinburgh, Oliphants.

Johansen, Lenie "Midge." 1988. *The Penguin Book of Australian Slang,* Ringwood Victoria, Penguin.

Johnston, Charles. 1912. *Why the World Laughs.* New York, Harper.

Johnstone, T. B. 1897. *The Land of Cakes and Brither Scots.* Paisley, Scotland, Alexander Gardner.

Jones, Dorothy. 1997. "Setting Limits: Humor and Australian National Identity." *Australian Journal of Comedy* 3(1): 33-42.

Jones, Frederick. 1990. "The Antis Gain the Day," Newfoundland and Confederation in 1869 in Ged Martin (ed), *The Causes of Canadian Confederation.* Fredericton, Canada, Acadiensis.

Jones, Maldwynn Allen. 1960. *American Immigration.* Chicago: University of Chicago Press.

Jones, R.V. 1990. *Reflections on Intelligence.* London, Mandarin.

Junior, Allan. 1925. *Canny Tales fae Aberdeen.* Dundee, Scotland, Valentine.

_____. 1927. *The Aberdeen Jew,.* Dundee, Scotland, Valentine.

_____. 1928. *Aberdeen Again.* Dundee, Scotland, Valentine.

Kant, Immanuel. 1951. *Critique of Judgement* (trans J. H. Bernard). New York, Hafner.

Karbusický, Vladimir. 1998. *Jewish Anecdotes from Prague*. Prague, V. Raji,.

Kelly, Sean, and Ted Mann. 1978. *National Lampoon, Slightly Higher in Canada*. New York, National Lampoon.

Kerr, John. 1903. *Memories Grave and Gay*. Edinburgh, William Blackwood.

_____. 1904. *Other Memories, Old and New*. Edinburgh, William Blackwood.

Kington, Miles (ed.). 1977. *Punch on Scotland*. London, Robson.

Klymasz, Robert B. 1970. "The Ethnic Joke in Canada Today." *Kentucky Folklore Quarterly*, Vol. 25, pp. 167-73.

Knott, Blanche. 1982. *Truly Tasteless Jokes*. New York, Ballantine.

Koestler, Arthur. 1964. *The Act of Creation*. London, Hutchinson.

Kowalski, Mike. 1974. *The Polish Joke-Book*. New York, Belmont Tower.

Kravitz, Seth. 1977. "London Jokes and Ethnic Stereotypes." *Western Folklore* 36(4): 275-301.

Kuipers, Giselinde. 2000. The Difference between a Surinamese and a Turk: Ethnic Jokes and the Position of Ethnic Minorities in the Netherlands. *Humor, the Internatioanl Journal of Humor Research* 13, 2: 141-75.

Kuipers, Giselinde Maniouschka Marije. 2001. *Goede humor, slechte smaak*. Amsterdam, University of Amsterdam.

Kumove, Shirley. 1986. *Words Like Arrows, A Treasury of Yiddish Folk Sayings*. New York, Warner.

Kusielewicz, Eugene. 1973 (1969). Reflections on the Cultural Condition of the Polish-American Community, in Frank Renkiewicz (ed.), *The Poles in America, 1608-1972*. New York, Oceana.

Laba, Martin. 1977. "The Bayman's Food Market is in the Townie Dump: Identity and the Townie Newfoundlander." *Culture and Tradition*, Vol. 3:7-16.

Labelle, Ronald. 1984. *Inventaire des Sources en Folklore Acadien*. Moncton, Canada, Centre d'Études Acadiennes Université Moncton.

Lahr, John. 1992. *Dame Edna Everage and the Rise of Western Civilization, Backstage with Barry Humphries*. New York, Farrar, Strauss, & Giroux.

Lamb, John A. 1930. *Fasti of the United Free Church of Scotland 1900-1929*. Edinburgh,

Lamson, Cynthia. 1979. *Bloody Decks and a Bumper Crop: The Rhetoric of Sealing Counter-Protest*. St. Johns, Newfoundland.

Lauder, Afferbeck. 1965. Australian for Alphabetical Order, pseudonym of Alistair Morrison. *Let Stalk Strine*. Sydney, Ure Smith.

_____. 1969. *Fraffly Strine Everything*. Sydney, Ure Smith.

Lauder, Sir Harry. 1929. *My Best Scotch Stories*. Dundee, Valentine.

Leavey, James (ed). 1996. *The Forest Smoker's Guide to Scotland*. London, Quiller.

Lee, C. P. 1998. "Yeah and I Used to be a Hunchback," in Stephen Wagg (ed.), *Because I Tell a Joke or Two*. London, Routledge..

Lefaivre, Daniel. 1991. *Les plus folles histoires de peche du Québec*. Montréal, Edimag.

Legaré, Clément. 1982. *Pierre la Fève et autres contes de la Mauricie*. Montréal, Les Quinze.

Legman, Gershon. 1968. (Vol. 1), 1975 (Vol. 2). *No Laughing Matter, An Analysis of Sexual Humor*. Bloomington, Indiana University Press.

Lenski, Gerhard. 1961. *The Religious Factor*. Garden City, NY, Doubleday.

Lepage, Gaston. 1983. *L'Humour en Folie*. Pointe-Claire Quebec, Robinet.

Levin, Bernard. 1979. *Taking Sides*. London: Jonathan Cape.

Lewis, Paul. 1997. "The Killing Jokes of the American Eighties." *Humor, International Journal of Humor Research* 10-3: 251-283.

Littell, Robert (ed). 1969. *The Czech Black Book* (prepared by the Institute of History of the Czechoslovak Academy of Sciences). London, Pall Mall.

Littlewood, Jane, and Michael Pickering. 1998. "Heard the One about the White Middle-

Class Heterosexual Father-in-Law?" in Stephen Wagg (ed.), *Because I Tell a Joke or Two*. London, Routledge.

Litvinoff, Emmanuel. 1974. *Soviet Anti-Semitism: The Paris Trial*. London, Wildwood House.

Lopata Helen Znaniecka. 1976. *Polish-Americans, Status Competition in an Ethnic Community*. Englewood Cliffs, NJ, Prentice Hall.

Low, David. 1949. *Years of Wrath, a Cartoon History 1932-1945*. London, Gollancz.

Luik, John C. 1994. *Pandora's Box, The Dangers of Politically Corrupted Science for Democratic Public Policy*. Boston, University of Boston.

Lussier, Doris. 1982. *Viens Faire l'Humour*. Montréal, Québecor.

Lynn, Richard. 1979. "The Social Ecology of Intelligence in the British Isles." *British Journal of Social and Clinical Psychology*, Vol. 18, pp. 1-12.

_____. 1979A. "The Social Ecology of Intelligence in the British Isles, France and Spain," in M. P. Morton, et al., *Intelligence and Learning*. New York, Plenum.

MacDonald, W. H. 1915. *Yarns, Ancient and Modern*. Edinburgh: Hodge.

MacHale, Des. 1984. *More of the World's Best Irish Jokes*. London, Angus Robertson.

_____. 1987. *The World's Best Mother-in-Law Jokes*. North Ryde Australia, Angus Robertson.

_____. 1988. *The World's Best Scottish Jokes*. North Ryde Australia, Angus and Robertson.

Macinnes, John. 1951. *The Evangelical Movement in the Highlands of Scotland 1668-1800*. Aberdeen, Scotland, Aberdeen University Press.

Mackay, Charles. 1882. *The Poetry and Humour of the Scottish Language*, Paisley, Scotland, Alexander Gardner.

Mackenzie, Alice Mure. 1941. *Scotland in Modern Times 1720-1939*. London, Chambers.

Macklin, Pat, and Manny Erdman. 1976. *Polish Jokes*. New York, Patman.

Macrae, David. 1896. *A Pennyworth of Highland Humour*. Glasgow, Morison.

_____. 1904. *National Humour*. Paisley, Alexander Gardner.

Mahler, Raphael. 1946. "Anti-Semitism in Poland," in Koppel S. Pinson (ed.), *Essays on Anti-Semitism*. New York, Conference on Jewish Relations.

Malong, Rawbone (Robin Malan). 1972. *Ah Big Yaws? A Guard to Sow Theffricun Innglish*. Cape Town, David Philip.

Mann, Bill. 1977. *The Retarded Giant*. Montreal, Tundra.

Marshall, Gordon. 1980. *Presbyteries and Profits; Calvinism and the Development of Capitalism in Scotland 1560-1707*. Oxford, Clarendon.

Mason, Jackie. 1987. *The World According to Me*. New York, Simon and Schuster.

Massicotte, Leo Arsène (Rev. Frère Ladislas), and L'Abbé, J.C. Massicotte. 1951. *30,000 Milles en Avion*. Montmagny Québec, Edition Marquis.

Matthews, William. 1893. *Wit and Humor, Their Use and Abuse*. Chicago, S. C. Griggs.

May, Phil. 1914. *Humorous Masterpieces*. Glasgow, Gowans and Gray.

McCaffrey, Lawrence J. 1976. *The Irish Diaspora in America*, Bloomington, Indiana University Press.

McCallum, John. 1998. "Cringe and Strut Comedy and National Identity in Post-War Australia," in Stephen Wagg (ed.), *Because I Tell a Joke or Two*. London, Routledge.

McCosh, Sandra. 1976. *Children's Humor*. London, Grenada.

McNaught, Kenneth William Kirkpatrick. 1969. *The Pelican History of Canada*. Harmondsworth, Penguin.

Mencken, H .L. 1964 (1936). *The American Language* (4th edition). New York, Alfred A. Knopf.

_____. 1977 *The American Language Supplement One*. New York, Alfred A. Knopf.

Mendel, Werner M. (ed.). 1970. *A Celebration of Laughter*. Los Angeles, Mara.

Mendelsohn, S. Felix. 1935. *The Jew Laughs, Humorous Stories and Anecdotes*. Chicago, L. M. Stein.

Middleton, Russell. 1959. Negro and White Reactions to Racial Humor. *Sociometry*, Vol. 22, pp. 175-183.

Middleton, Russell, and J. Moland. 1959. Humor in Negro and White Subcultures: A Study of Jokes among University Students." *American Sociological Review*, Vol. 24, pp. 61-9.

Mikes, George. 1980. *English Humour for Beginners.* London, Unwin.

Mintz, Larry. 1986. "The Rabbi versus the Priest and Other Jewish Stories," pp. 125-131 in Avner Ziv (ed.).

Mises von, Ludwig. 1974. *Socialism, an Economic and Sociological Analysis.* London, Jonathan Cape.

Mitchell, Alanna. 1994. Canadians Swarming to West Coast. *The Globe and Mail,* August 5: A4.

Moffat, Graham. 1928. *The Pawky Scot.* Dundee, Scotland, Valentine.

Moon, Penderel. 1961. *Divide and Quit.* London, Chatto and Windus.

Morawska, Eva T. 1977. *The Maintenance of Ethnicity: A Case Study of the Polish-American Community in Greater Boston.* San Francisco, R. and E. Research.

Morgan, Edwin (ed). 1970. *Scottish Satirical Verse.* Manchester, Carcanet.

Mr. Punch in Scotland. 1933. *New Punch Library* Vol. 10. London, Educational.

Mr. Punch's Scottish Humor. 1908. London, Educational Book Company.

Mulkay, Michael. 1987. "Humour and Social Structure," in W. Oathwaite and M. Mulkay (eds.) *Social Theory and Social Criticism.* Oxford, Blackwell.

Naiman, Arthur. 1981. *Every Goy's Guide to Common Jewish Expressions.* New York, Ballantine.

Narváez Peter. 1983. "Joseph R Smallwood, 'The Barrelman,' the Broadcaster as Folklorist." *Canadian Folklore Canadien* 5, 1-2:60-78.

_____. 1991. Newfoundland Berry Pickers and the Fairies: Maintaining Apatical, Temporal and Moral Boundaries through Legendry, in Peter Narváez (ed.), *The Good People: New Fairylore Essays.* New York, Garland.

_____. 1994. Newfie an Insider Term of Endearment. *Evening Telegram,* April 3.

Neal, Mark, and Christie Davies. 1998. *The Corporation under Siege...Exposing the Devices Used by Activists and Regulators in the Non-Risk Society.* London, SAU.

Nevo, Ofra. 1986. "Do Jews in Israel Still Laugh at Themselves," pp. 191-200 in Ziv (ed).

_____. 1991. "What's in a Jewish Joke?" *Humor, International Journal of Humor Research* 4-2: 251-60.

Newbine, Jos. 1984. *Newfies: 300 Nouvelles Histoires.* Montréal, Editions Québecor.

Newby, Eric I. 1975. *Love and War in Apennines.* Harmondsworth, Penguin.

New Yorker War Album, The. 1973. London, Hamish Hamilton.

Nilsen, Alleen Pace, and Don L. F Nilsen. 2000. *Encyclopaedia of American Humor,* Phoenix, Oryx.

Noel, Sidney John Roderick. 1971. *Politics in Newfoundland.* Toronto, University of Toronto Press.

Norden, E. 1991. "Counting the Jews." *Commentary* 92(4): 36-43.

Novak, Michael. 1973. *The Rise of the Unmeltable Ethnics.* New York, Macmillan.

Novak, William, and Moshe Waldoks. 1981. *The Big Book of Jewish Humor.* New York, Harper and Row.

Obrdlik, Antonin J. 1942. "Gallows Humor—A Sociological Phenomenon." *American Sociological Review* Vol. 47: 709-716.

Ocker, A. N. (pseud.). 1986. *The World's Best Aussie Jokes.* North Ryde, Angus and Robertson.

O'Grady, John. 1965. *Aussie English.* Sydney, Ure Smith.

_____. 1971. *Aussie Etiket.* Sydney, Ure Smith.

Oldenburg, Carl. 1975. *Frog Croaks, Haiku Tongue in Cheek.* New York, Crown Publishers.
Olson, James M., Gregory R. Maio, Karen L. Hobden. 1999. "The (Null) Effects of Exposure to Disparagement Humor on Stereotypes and Attitudes." *Humor, International Journal of Humor Research* 12-2: 195-219.
Olsvanger, Immanuel. 1965. *Röyte Pomerantsen,* New York, Schocken.
Oring, Elliott. 1981. *Israeli Humor, the Content and Structure of the Chizbat of the Palmakh.* Albany, State University of New York Press.
_____. 1984. *The Jokes of Sigmund Freud: A Study in Humor and Jewish Identity.* Philadelphia, University of Pennsylvania Press.
_____. 1992. *Jokes and Their Relations.* Lexington, University Press of Kentucky.
Orso, Ethelyn G. 1979. *Modern Greek Humor, a Collection of Jokes and Ribald Tales.* Bloomington, Indiana University Press.
Oshima, Kimi. 2000. "Ethnic Jokes and Social Function in Hawaii." *Humor, International Journal of Humor Research* 13-1: 41-57.
Oxley, H.. G. 1978. *Mateship in Local Organisation.* St. Lucia, University of Queensland Press.
Pahl, Raymond Edward. 1984. *Divisions of Labour.* Oxford: Blackwell.
Palmer Alasdair. 2000. "The Evil in the Animal Lovers." *Sunday Telegraph,* September 3: 35.
Paros, Lawrence. 1984. *The Erotic Tongue.* Seattle, Madrona.
Partington, Geoffrey. 1994. *The Australian Nation, Its British and Irish Roots.* Melbourne, Australian Scholarly.
Patey, Francis. 1990. *A Battle Lost.* Grand Falls. Newfoundland Canada, Robinson Blackmore.
_____. 1992. *The Jolly Poker.* St. John's, Harry Cuff.
Patten, William. 1909. *Among the Humorists and After-dinner Speakers.* New York: Collier.
Patterson, Dr. Sir Leslie Colin. 1986. *The Traveller's Tool.* London, Hodder.
Pattison, Ian. 1990. *Rab C. Nesbitt, The Scripts.* London, BBC.
Phillips, Pearson. 1984. *YAPs, the Complete Guide to Young Aspiring Professionals.* London, Arrow.
Pinson, Koppel S. (ed). 1946. *Essays on Anti-Semitism.* New York, Conference on Jewish Relations.
Pittman, David J., and Charles R. Snyder (eds.). 1962. *Society, Culture and Drinking Patterns.* New York, John Wiley and Sons.
Pocius, Gerald. 1994. "Folklore and National Identity: Canadian Perspectives." *Australian Folklore* 9, pp. 36-43.
Podhoretz, Norman. 1986. "The Hate That Dare Not Speak Its Name." *Commentary* 82(5): 21-32.
Pumphrey, Ron. 1973. *Newfie Tales of Ron Pumphrey.* St. John's, Newfoundland, Pumphrey.
_____. 1975. *The Latest Hilarious Rib-Tickling Newfie Jokes.* St. John's, Newfoundland, Pumphrey.
Ralph, Gord, Leo Finney, Teresa Kield, and Don McDonald. 1990. *Pork, Cabbage and Other Stuff.* Grand Falls Windsor, Newfoundland, Robinson Blackmore.
Ramsay, Dean Edward Bannerman. 1874 (first edition 1858). *Reminiscences of Scottish Life and Character,* 22nd edition. Edinburgh, Gall and Inglis
Raskin, Richard. 1993. "The Origins and Evolution of a Classic Jewish Joke," in Avner Ziv and Anat Zajdman (eds.), *Semites and Stereotypes.* Westport, CT, Greenwood.
_____. 1993A. *Life is Like a Glass of Tea: Studies of Classic Jewish Jokes.* Aarhus, Denmark, Aarhus, U.P.
Raskin, Victor. 1985. *Semantic Mechanisms of Humor.* Dordrecht, Reidel.
Raverat, Gwen. 1960. *Period Piece a Cambridge Childhood.* London, Faber.

Reader, H. J. 1967. *Newfoundland Wit, Humor and Folklore*. Corner Brook, Newfoundland, H. J. Reader.

Reid, J. M. 1960. *Kirk and Nation*. London, Skeffington.

Reitlinger, Gerald. 1967. *The Final Solution*. London, Valentine Mitchell.

Renkiewicz, Frank (ed.). 1973 (1969). *The Poles in America, 1608-1972*. New York, Oceana.

Richman, Marsha, and Kate O'Donnell. 1978. *The Shikse's Guide to Jewish Men*. New York, Bantam.

Rinder, I. R. 1973. "Mental Health of American Jewish Urbanites: A Review of Literature and Predictions in A. Shiloh and I. C. Selavon (eds.), *Ethnic Groups of America: Their Morbidity, Mortality and Behaviour Disorders,* Vol. I *The Jews*. Springfield, Charles C Thomas.

Ripley, LaVern J. 1985. *The Immigrant Experience in Wisconsin*. Boston, Twayne.

Roazen, Paul. 1976. *Freud and His Followers*. London, Allen Lane.

Roback, Abraham Aaron. 1944. *A Dictionary of International Slurs*. Cambridge MA, Sci-Art.

Robb, James J. 1954. *Working Class Anti-Semite*. London, Tavistock.

Robey, George. 1920. *After-Dinner Stories*. London, Grant Richards.

Rockwell, Joan. 1981. *Evald Tang Kristensen, A Lifelong Adventure in Folklore*. Aalborg, Aalborg University Press.

Roethlisberger, Fritz Jules, and William J. Dickson. 1942. *Management and the Worker*. Cambridge MA, Harvard University Press.

Rogers, Charles. 1867. *Traits and Stories of the Scottish People*. London, Houlston.

Rosemarine, B. 1962. *Haimische Laffs and Chaffs*. Altringham, UK, John Sherratt.

Rosenberg, Bernard, and Gilbert Schapiro. 1958. "Marginality and Jewish Humor." *Midstream* 4.70-80.

Rosten, Leo Calvin. 1970. *The Joys of Yiddish*. London, W. H. Allen.

_____. 1983. *Hooray for Yiddish! A Book about English*. London, Elm Tree.

Roth, Philip. 1969. *Portnoy's Complaint*. London, Jonathan Cape.

Rubinstein, Aryeh (ed.). 1975. *Hasidism*. Jerusalem, Keter.

Rushton, Dorgan. 1983. *Brush Up Your Pidgin*. London, Willow.

Russell, Ted. 1984. *The Best of Ted Russell Number 1 and Stories from Uncle Mose*, St. John's, Newfoundland, Harry Cuff.

Sahl, Mort. 1976. *Heartland*. New York, Harcourt, Brace, Jovanovich.

Sandberg, Neil C. 1974. *Ethnic Identity and Assimilation: The Polish-American Community, A Case Study of Metropolitan Los Angeles*. New York, Praeger.

Saper, Bernard. 1991. "A Cognitve and Behavioral Formulation of the Relation between the Jewish Joke and Anti-Semitism." *Humor, the International Journal of Humor Research*, 4-2: 223-239.

_____. 1993. "Since When is Jewish Humor Not Anti-Semitic?" in Avner Ziv and Anat Zajdman (eds.), *Semites and Stereotypes*. Westport CT, Greenwood.

_____. 1995. "Joking in the Context of Political Correctness." *Humor, the International Journal of Humor Research*, 8-1: 65-76.

Sargent, Margaret. 1979. *Drinking and Alcoholism in Australia*. Melbourne, Longman Cheshire.

Saunders, Peter. 1996. *Unequal But Fair? A Study of Class Barriers in Britain*. London, IEA Health and Welfare Unit.

Scharf, Rafael F. 1996. *Co Mnie I Tobie Polsko...Eseje bez uprzedzen/Poland What Have I to Do with Thee...Essays without Prejudice*. Kraków, Fundacja Judaica.

Schmitz, Nancy. 1991. *Irish for a Day. St. Patrick's Day Celebrations in Québec City 1765-1990*. Sainte-Foy, Quebec, Carraig.

Schoeck, Helmut. 1969. Envy: A *Theory of Social Behavior*. London, Secker and Warburg.

Schostak, Rabbi Zev. 1983. *A Guide to Jewish Family Laws*. Spring Valley, NY, Philip Feldheim.

Schutz, Alfred. 1962. *Collected Papers* Vol. I, *The Problem of Social Reality*. The Hague, Martinus Nijhoff.

Schutz, Charles E. 1989. "The Sociability of Ethnic Jokes." *Humor, International Journal of Humor Research* 2-2: 165-177.

Schwartz, Alvin. 1973. *Witcracks; Jokes and Jests from American Folklore*. Philadelphia, Lippincott.

Scott, W. W. 1931. *Breaks*. London, Jonathan Cape.

Sebag-Montefiore, Hugh. 2001. *Enigma, The Battle for the Code*. London, Phoenix.

Selitz, "Commodore" Bruce, Helen "Speed" Merkin, "Sir Edmund Nachus," "Mitch" Conroy, and "Doctor" Seldom. 1987. *The Jewish Adventurers' Club*. New York, Dell.

Sequoia, Anna (née Schneider). 1982. *The Official J.A.P. Handbook*. New York, New American Library.

Sharot, Stephen. 1998. Judaism and Jewish Ethnicity: Changing Interrelationships and Differentiations in the Diaspora and Israel, in Ernest Krausz and Gitta Tulea (eds.), *Jewish Survival, The Identity Problem at the Close of the Twentieth Century*. New Brunswick, NJ, Transaction Publishers.

Shelley, Robert. *The Great Canadian Jokebook*. Don Mills Ontario, Paperjacks, General Publishing.

Sheppard, Robert, and Edwin Noftle. 1979. *Newfie Laffs*. Lewisporte Newfoundland, B and B.

Shiloh, Ailan, and Ida Cohen Selavon (eds.). 1973. *Ethnic Groups of America Their Morbidity, Mortality, and Behavior Disorders* Vol. 1 *The Jews*. Springfield. IL, Charles Thomas.

Sinha, Surajit. 1975. "Religion in an Affluent Society," in James P. Spradley and Michael A. Rynkiewich (eds.), *The Nacirema Readings in American Culture* Boston, Little Brown & Co.

Sjölinder, Rolf. 1964. *Presbyterian Reunion in Scotland 1907-1921*. Edinburgh, T and T. Clark.

Smith, Rev. Sydney. 1839. *The Works of the Reverend Sydney Smith*, Vol. 1. London, Longman Orne.

Smout, Thomas Christopher. 1972. *A History of the Scottish People 1530-1830*. London, Collins.

_____. 1986. *A Century of the Scottish People*. London, Collins.

Snyder, Charles R. 1962. "Culture and Jewish Sobriety, the In-Group and Out-Group Factor," in David J. Pittman and Charles R. Snyder (eds.), *Society, Culture and Drinking Patterns*. New York, John Wiley & Sons.

Somerville, Edith Oenone, and Martin Ross (pseud. Violet Florence Martin). 1899. *Some Experiences of an Irish R. M.* London, Longman.

_____. 1908. *Further Experiences of an Irish R. M.* London, Longman.

Sowell, Thomas. 1981. *Ethnic America, A History*. New York, Basic Books.

Spalding, Henry D. 1969. *Encyclopaedia of Jewish Humor*. New York, Jonathan David.

_____. 1976. *A Treasure Trove of American Jewish Humor*. New York, Jonathan David.

Standish, James T. 1984. *The Funniest Book in Newfoundland*. St. John's, Newfoundland, Jester.

Stelchin, Stan. 1997. *Abandoned*. London, Marshall Pickering.

Stenton, Sir Frank Merry. 1908. *William the Conqueror, the Rule of the Normans*. New York, G. P. Putnam's Sons.

Stern, Jane, and Michael Stern. 1990. *Encyclopaedia of Bad Taste* New York, Harper.

Still, Bayrd. 1965 (1948). *Milwaukee: The History of a City*. Madison, State Historical Society of Wisconsin.

Stivers, Richard. 1976A. *Hair of the Dog, Irish Drinking and American Stereotype.* University Park, Pennsylvania University Press.

Stoney, Peter, and Jim Flynn (Finnigan). 1981. *Newfy Jokes.* Dartmouth Nova Scotia, Mackenzie.

Storey, G. M., W. J. Kirwin, and J. D. A. Widdowson. 1990. *Dictionary of Newfoundland English.* Toronto, University of Toronto Press.

Sword, Keith. 1996. *Identity in Flux: The Polish Community in Britain.* London, School of Slavonic and East European Studies.

Szarota, Tomasz. 1978. "Poland and Poles in German Eyes during World War II." *Polish Western Affairs* No. 2, pp. 229-254.

Taggart, Sir James. 1927. *Stories Told by Sir James Taggart.* Dundee, Scotland, Valentine.

Telushkin, Rabbi Joseph. 1992. *Jewish Humor: What the Best Jewish Jokes Say about the Jews.* New York, William Morrow & Co.

Theroux, Paul. 1967. Hating the Asians. *Transition* 7(ii)(33): 46-51.

Thomas, Gerald. 1976. "Newfie Jokes," in Edith Fowkes (ed.) *Folklore of Canada.* Toronto, McClelland and Stewart.

_____. 1976A. "Some Examples of Blason Populaire from the French Tradition of Western Newfoundland." *Regional Language Studies, Newfoundland,* No. 7, June: 29-33.

_____. 1979. "The Folktale and Folktale Style in the Tradition of French Newfoundlanders." *Canadian Folklore Canadien,* Vol. 1, Nos. 1-2, pp. 71-78.

_____. 1980. "Other Worlds: Folktale in Soap Opera in Newfoundland's French Tradition," in Kenneth S. Goldstein and Neil V. Rosenberg (eds.), *Folklore Studies in Honour of Herbert Halpert, A Festschrift.* St. John's Memorial University of Newfoundland.

_____. 1982. "Public and Private Storytelling Situations in Franco-Newfoundland Tradition." *Arv Scandinavian Yearbook of Folklore,* Vol. 36, pp. 175-181 Uppsala, Sweden, Royal Gustavus Adolphus Academy.

_____. 1987. "Albert Ding-Dong Simon: A Tall Tale Teller from Newfoundland's French Tradition." *Newfoundland Studies* 3, 2: 227-250.

_____. 1991. "Modernity in Contemporary Märchen: Some Newfoundland Examples." *Lore and Language* 10/1: 59-66.

Thomas, William I., and Florian Znaniecki. 1958. *The Polish Peasant in Europe and America.* New York, Dover.

Tolstoy Nikolai. 1982. *Stalin's Secret War.* London, Pan.

Toynbee, Arnold J. 1915. *Armenian Atrocities, The Murder of a Nation.* London, Hodder and Stoughton.

Triverton, Sanford. 1981. *Complete Book of Ethnic Jokes.* New York, Galahad.

Tulk, Bob. 1971. *Newfie Jokes.* Corner Brook, Newfoundland.

_____. 1972. *Newfie Jokes.* Corner Brook, Newfoundland.

_____. 1973. *Bob Tulk's Newfie Jokes.* Corner Brook, Newfoundland.

_____. 1974. *Even Funnier Newfie Jokes.* Mount Pearl, Newfoundland.

Tulks, The. n.d.. *Newfie Jokes,* Vols. 1-8. Corner Brook, Newfoundland.

Tünnes und Schäll Witze. 1976. Frankfurt, Fischer.

Utley, Francis Lee. 1971-3. "The Urban and Rural Jest." *Béaloideas,* Nos. 39-41. pp. 344-357.

Vaksberg, Arkady. 1994. *Stalin Against the Jews.* New York, Alfred A. Knopf.

Wagg, Stephen (ed.). 1998. *Because I Tell a Joke or Two.* London, Routledge.

Walker, Caroline, and Geoffrey Cannon. 1985. *The Food Scandal.* London, Century.

Wannan, Bill. 1995. *Great Aussie Insults.* Ringwood Australia, Penguin.

Warren, W. L. 1973. *Henry II.* London, Eyre Methuen.

Weber, Max. 1930. *The Protestant Ethic and the Spirit of Capitalism.* London, Unwin.

Wechsler, H., H. W. Demone Jr., D. Thurn, and E. H. Kasey. 1973. "Religious-Ethnic

Difference in Alcohol Consumption," in A. Shiloh and I. C. Selavon (eds.) *Ethnic Groups of America, Their Morbidity, Morality, and Behavior Disorders,* Vol. 1, *The Jews.* Springfield, IL, Charles Thomas.

Weise, R. E. 1996. "Partisan Perceptions of Political Humor." *Humor, International Journal of Humor Research* 9-2: 199-207.

Welsch, Roger L. 1967. American Numskull Tales: The Polack Joke. *Western Folklore* 26, 183-186.

Whatley, Chris. 2000. *Scottish Society 1700–1830, Beyond Jacobiteism Towards Industrialization.* Manchester, Manchester University Press.

Wildavsky, Aaron. 1995. *But is it True? A Citizen's Guide to Environmental Health and Safety Issues.* Cambridge, MA, Harvard University Press.

Wilde, Larry. 1973. *The Official Polish/Italian Jokebook.* Los Angeles, Pinnacle.

———. 1974. *The Official Jewish/Irish Jokebook.* Los Angeles, Pinnacle.

———. 1975. *More, the Official Polish/Italian Jokebook.* Los Angeles, Pinnacle.

———. 1975A. *The Official White Folks/Black Folks Jokebook.* New York, Pinnacle.

———. 1977. *The Last Official Polish Joke-Book.* Los Angeles, Pinnacle.

———. 1978. *The Complete Book of Ethnic Humor.* Los Angeles, Corwin.

———. 1978A. *The Last Official Italian Jokebook.* Los Angeles, Pinnacle.

———. 1979. *More the Official Jewish/Irish Jokebook.* Los Angeles, Pinnacle.

———. 1980. *The Last Official Jewish Jokebook.* New York, Bantam.

———. 1983. *The Absolutely Last Official Polish Joke Book.* New York Bantam.

———. 1983A. *The Last Official Irish Joke Book.* New York, Bantam.

———. 1986. *The Ultimate Jewish Joke Book.* New York, Bantam.

Wilson, Christopher P. 1979. *Jokes; Form, Content, Use and Function.* London, Academic Press.

Wilson, Kevin Bloody. 1994. *Blackout from the Outback* (audio cassette). Northampton UK.

Wilson. Paul. 1980. "Drinking Habits in the United Kingdom." *Population Trends* 22, (winter): 14-28.

Wise Willy. 1991. *Wise Willy's Newf Dictionary.* St. John's New Brunswick, East Coast Publishing.

Wolff, H. A., C. E. Smith, and H. A. Murray. 1934. "The Psychology of Humor, A Study of Responses to Race-Disparagement Jokes." *Journal of Abnormal and Social Psychology* 28(4), January-March: 341-65.

Wrobel, Paul. 1979. *Our Way, Family and Neighborhood in a Polish-American Community.* South Bend IN, University of Notre Dame Press.

Wynn Jones, Michael. 1971. *The Cartoon History of Britain.* London, Tom Stacey.

Wytrwal, Joseph A. 1977. *Behold the Polish-Americans.* Detroit, Endurance.

Yao, George (ed.). 1946. Chinese Wit and Humor. New York, Coward-McCann.

Zajdman, Anat. 1991. "Contextualization of Canned Jokes in Discourse." *Humor, International Journal of Humor Research* 4-1: 23-40.

Zenner, Walter P. 1970. "Joking and Ethnic Stereotyping." *Anthropological Quarterly* 43, 93-113.

Zewbskewiecz, E. D., Jerome Kuligowski, and Harvey Krulka. 1965. *It's Fun to be a Polack.* Glendale CA, Collectors.

Ziegler, P. Thomas. 1956. *The Meat We Eat.* Danville, IL, Interstate.

Ziv, Avner. 1984. *Personality and Sense of Humor.* New York, Springer.

Ziv, Avner. 1986. *Jewish Humor.* Tel-Aviv, Papyrus/Tel-Aviv University.

Ziv Avner. 1986A. Psycho-Social Aspects of Jewish Humor in Israel and in the Diaspora, in Avner. Ziv (ed.), *Jewish Humor.* Tel-Aviv: Papyrus/Tel-Aviv University.

Ziv, Avner. 1988. *National Styles of Humor.* New York, Greenwood.

Ziv Avner. 1986A. Humor in Israel, in Avner Ziv (ed), *National Styles of Humor*. New York, Greenwood.

Ziv, Avner, and Anat Zajdman. 1993. *Semites and Stereotypes, Characteristics of Jewish Humor*. Westport, CT, Greenwood.

Zurawski, Joseph W. 1975. *Polish American History and Culture, a Classified Bibliography*. Chicago, Polish Museum of America.

Index